BEFORE THEY CHANGED THE WORLD

Brimming with creative inspiration, how-to projects, and useful information to enrich your everyday life, Quarto Knows is a favorite destination for those pursuing their interests and passions. Visit our site and dig deeper with our books into your area of interest: Quarto Creates, Quarto Cooks, Quarto Homes, Quarto Lives, Quarto Drives, Quarto Explores, Quarto Gifts, or Quarto Kids.

For Sally (1937–2007)
Who Also Changed the World

Text © 2009 by Edwin Kiester

This edition published in 2018 by Crestline, an imprint of The Quarto Group,
142 West 36th Street, 4th Floor, New York, NY 10018, USA
T (212) 779-4972 **F** (212) 779-6058
www.QuartoKnows.com

First published in the USA in 2009 by Fair Winds Press, an imprint of The Quarto Group,
100 Cummings Center, Suite 265D, Beverly, MA 01915-6101
www.fairwindspress.com

Crestline titles are also available at discount for retail, wholesale, promotional, and bulk purchase. For details, contact the Special Sales Manager by email at specialsales@quarto.com or by mail at The Quarto Group, Attn: Special Sales Manager, 401 Second Avenue North, Suite 310, Minneapolis, MN 55401, USA.

10 9 8 7 6 5 4 3 2 1

ISBN: 978-0-7858-3667-4

Cover design: Keira McGuinness
Book design & layout: Sheila Hart
Cover image credits (from left to right):
Albert Einstein, 1879-1955, Photographer: Orren Jack Turner;
Napoleon Bonaparte;
Joan of Arc;
Prime Minister Winston Churchill of Great Britain
Library of Congress Prints and Photographs Division Washington, D.C.

Printed in China

BEFORE THEY CHANGED THE WORLD

*Pivotal Moments That Changed
the Lives of Great Leaders Before
They Became Famous*

EDWIN KIESTER JR.

CRESTLINE

CONTENTS

Introduction .6

CHAPTER 1:   Hannibal of Carthage, 247–190 BCE:

The Avenging Son Who Pitted Himself Against Rome 8

CHAPTER 2:   Joan of Arc, 1412–1431: The Voices that Led to a Revolution . . 22

CHAPTER 3:   Queen Elizabeth I, 1533–1603: Henry VIII's Embattled

Daughter's Rite of Passage into Adulthood. 36

CHAPTER 4:   Samuel de Champlain, 1567–1635: A Horrifying and

Unforgettable Encounter with New World Indians 48

CHAPTER 5:   George Washington, 1732–1799:

Learning to Lead the Hard Way 60

CHAPTER 6:   Horatio Nelson, 1758–1805:

Becoming a Hero by Breaking the Rules 72

CHAPTER 7:   Napoleon Bonaparte, 1769–1821:

His Proving Ground at the Siege of Toulon 86

CHAPTER 8:   Simón Bolívar, 1783–1830:

A Youth's Oath to Free a Country 98

CHAPTER 9:   Giuseppe Garibaldi, 1807–1882:

The Political Awakening of a Patriot 110

CHAPTER 10:   Abraham Lincoln, 1809–1865:

The Legacy of a Slave Market Encounter 120

CHAPTER 11:   Ulysses S. Grant, 1822–1885: How Persistence in the

Face of Grinding Poverty Shaped a Leader 130

CHAPTER 12:   Theodore Roosevelt, 1858–1919:

"The Four-Eyed Dude from New York" 142

CHAPTER 13: Edith Cowan, 1861–1932: A Child of Tragedy

Becomes a Champion for All Children 154

CHAPTER 14: Mohandas Gandhi, 1869–1948: The Transformation of

a Shy Barrister into a Human Rights Leader 164

CHAPTER 15: Winston Churchill, 1874–1965:

Learning Early about the Horror of War. 174

CHAPTER 16: Albert Einstein, 1879–1955:

A Compass Points the Way for a Young Genius 190

CHAPTER 17: Kemal Atatürk, 1881–1938: A Young Turk Grows Up 200

CHAPTER 18: Ho Chi Minh, 1890–1969:

A Kitchen Hand Leads a Revolution. 214

CHAPTER 19: Charles De Gaulle, 1890–1970:

A POW's Five Escape Attempts. 226

CHAPTER 20: Rosa Parks, 1913–2005:

The Bus Ride that Changed History 238

CHAPTER 21: John F. Kennedy, 1917–1963:

"Everybody into the Water!" 248

CHAPTER 22: Mikhail Gorbachev, 1931– :

A Brush with Stalinism Creates a Bold Reformer 262

Resources 272

Acknowledgments 279

About the Author 280

Index 281

INTRODUCTION

J ust after I began work on this book, I was sitting in a California coffee shop sipping a latte and reading a book whose jacket proclaimed *Hannibal* in large letters. A fellow customer noted the book, caught my eye, and brought his coffee to my table. "Hannibal!" he exclaimed. "Hannibal of Carthage! He must have been quite a guy!"

I nodded and asked whether he was a history buff or teacher, since he was acquainted with such a long-ago figure. He shook his head. "No, but I've been fascinated with him ever since school. He took elephants over the Alps! And in winter, too! The Romans couldn't believe it." He handed the book back. "Quite a guy!" he repeated. "He really shook things up, didn't he?"

Across the vast sweep of history, in every culture and every century, there have been men and women who "shook things up," leaving a lasting impact on their surroundings, their contemporaries, and history itself. They inherited one world and changed it into another. Not all of these earth-shakers were military geniuses who became political leaders like Hannibal or Napoleon Bonaparte. Mohandas Gandhi, after all, was a pacifist, and his deeds and his teachings still resound around the world. Nor were they all wealthy, educated, or titled. Winston Churchill, to be sure, was born in a palace given to an heroic ancestor by the English king, but Abraham Lincoln was born in a log cabin and taught himself to read. Some of these heroes were unsung in their lifetimes, their influence only felt later. Some burst on the scene unheralded—think Joan of Arc—minus popular appreciation or support, yet departed wreathed in glory.

Historians, psychologists, and others have endlessly debated whether such figures were born to greatness or simply had greatness thrust on them by a cascade of events. Or, indeed, whether they perhaps carried some special gene that was expressed only by circumstance.

What they all seemed to possess is that at some point in their formative years, some incident, some happening, some tragedy, sometimes something trivial and transitory, transformed them and inspired them to perform memorable feats both powerful and enduring. Their names and their stories, like Hannibal's, ring through history.

A single racial slur in South Africa, for instance, transformed Gandhi from an aspiring English barrister into an eloquent protestor in spectacles and loin-cloth whose message upended the British Empire and swept the world. An angry eight-year-old went to school in Salonica one embarrassing day in ballooning white trousers and insisted on a transfer to a military school, which launched a military career that made Kemal Ataturk architect of the modern Turkey. Jack Kennedy had a simple, self-deprecatory explanation for how he became a hero in the Solomon Islands at the age of twenty-three, and eventually president of the United States: "They sank my boat." He neglected to mention that he engineered the rescue of eleven fellow crew members and plunged into South Pacific waters after his Patrol Torpedo boat was run over by a Japanese destroyer.

This book recounts the narratives of twenty-two of these legendary figures whose deeds changed the world and of the formative events that shaped them and whose names still echo and provoke spirited conversations in coffee shops.

HANNIBAL OF CARTHAGE, 247–190 BCE: THE AVENGING SON WHO PITTED HIMSELF AGAINST ROME

Although Hannibal was born into a warrior caste, it was his father's bitter experience with the Romans that determined the direction young Hannibal's life would take.

The eight-year-old boy begged and pleaded, but his father would not relent. Hamilcar Barca, the anointed leader of Carthage, was about to embark on an audacious mission in the nation's struggle against Rome. For days and weeks, Hamilcar's young son had listened to the tramp of marching feet, the clank of armor, and the rattling of swords as the Carthaginian armies trudged out of their stronghold on Mount Eryx overlooking the Mediterranean Sea. He had watched as teams of workers threw up triple walls to protect the bustling city and its vital ports. Hamilcar Barca was girding the nation for war. It would be a daring stroke against Rome, which had humiliated Carthage during the First Punic War of 264–241 BCE. At this historic moment, his hero-worshipping son wanted to be at his father's side.

Hamilcar Barca—the Barca name translates to "Thunderbolt"—expected his son to follow in his warrior footsteps. The rival Barca and Hanno clans had dominated the Carthage military for years. Young Hannibal Barca was being brought up in a military atmosphere, almost an armed camp. He was exposed daily to soldiers and soldiering.

As the moment approached for Hamilcar's departure, the Carthaginian leader summoned Carthage's nobles and military officers to accompany him

With one hand on the sacrificial lamb, eight-year-old Hannibal pledged to "ever remain an enemy of Rome." Hannibal swearing eternal enmity to Rome (oil on canvas), Amigoni, Jacopo (1675–1752) / Private Collection © Agnew's, London, UK / The Bridgeman Art Library

to the Meliart shrine of Baal, the sun-god, atop Mount Byrsa. The men entered the sanctuary, and young Hannibal followed. Inside he watched his father slit the throat of a sacrificial lamb and lay the sacrifice on the altar. Chanting prayers, Hamilcar raised a goblet and asked the sun god's blessing on the coming endeavor.

Then, waving the others back, Hamilcar beckoned to Hannibal standing at the side of the altar. He asked the boy whether he still wished to accompany him on the expedition. Hannibal nodded eagerly. His father took him by the hand and led him to the altar. There he placed the boy's hand on the sacrificial lamb. He asked Hannibal to bow his head and take an oath. He must swear that he would ever be an enemy to Rome, the determined foe of Carthage.

Two decades later, Hannibal, twenty-nine, would carry out that pledge in ways that would change the world and earn him an indelible place in the history books.

DELENDA EST CARTAGO ("CARTHAGE MUST BE DESTROYED")

Carthage and Rome had been rivals in the Mediterranean for more than two centuries. The Carthaginians were actually a Middle Eastern people; Carthage had been founded by seagoing merchants from Phoenicia (now the country of Lebanon). On the Mediterranean south shore, at the present site of Tunis, the Phoenicians had found a harbor that was ideal for shipping goods from the rich African hinterland to Italy, Greece, and Egypt. The Phoenician colony of Carthage soon became an independent city-state that dominated North Africa and the Mediterranean trade routes.

Sicily, at the toe of Italy, commanded the central Mediterranean and was a stepping stone to the markets of Europe. The colonizing Carthaginians establish their fiefdom on it. Sardinia and Corsica, islands closer to the European mainland, also became Carthaginian colonies. Other peoples around the inland sea also fell into line, either as allies or because they were conquered by the Carthaginians' burgeoning armies.

Beginning in the fourth century BCE, an upstart nation arose on the Italian peninsula. Rome began to build an empire based on military power and territorial takeovers, rivaling Carthage itself. The Roman Empire was to expand into the entire Italian boot and the Germanic lands to the north, then spread eastward to Greece and across the Adriatic, then westward toward Spain. Because Carthage

247 BCE
Hannibal, son of Hamilcar Barca, leader of Carthage, is born.

241 BCE
Roman battle fleet defeats Carthage off Sicily. Carthage is forced to give up the islands of Sicily, Sardinia, and Corsica and pay indemnity.

239 BCE
Hamilcar Barca leaves Carthage to found a colony in Spain.

239 BCE
Hannibal takes an oath to be a lifelong enemy of Rome.

228 BCE
Hamilcar Barca is killed. His son-in-law Hasdrubal succeeds him as the leader of Carthage.

226 BCE
Hasdrubal agrees to partition Spain into Carthaginian and Roman spheres of influence at Ebro River.

225 BCE
"New Carthage" is founded on the Spanish Mediterranean coast.

221 BCE
Hasdrubal assassinated. Hannibal, twenty-six, succeeds him.

219 BCE
Hannibal attacks Roman ally Saguntum. Second Punic War is declared

September 218 BCE
Hannibal leads an invasion toward Rome, crossing the Pyrenees and Alps with forty elephants and 40,000 troops.

November 218 BCE
Crossing is completed. Offensive into Italy begins.

April 217 BCE
Hannibal scores a decisive victory over the Romans at Lake Trasimeno and moves toward Rome.

August 216 BCE
Hannibal destroys the Roman army at Cannae with innovative double-envelopment strategy. Rome loses 70,000 men, Hannibal 2,000.

June 215 BCE
Undefeated, Hannibal reaches the walls of Rome but is unable to storm or siege.

209 BCE
Roman general Scipio Africanus invades Spain and captures New Carthage.

202 BCE
Scipio lands troops in Africa and captures Carthage. Hannibal is called home for defense and suffers first defeat in the Battle of Zuma. Carthage sues for peace and must yield overseas colonies and give up its army and navy.

195 BCE
Hannibal is forced into exile in Syria.

183 BCE
Hannibal commits suicide by taking poison. He is sixty-four.

had long since established colonies and trading posts along the Mediterranean north shore, it was inevitable that the two colonizing powers would clash.

The First Punic War—Phoenicians were *Poeni* in Latin—humiliated Carthage. After a surprising Roman naval victory off Sicily, the Roman consul Regulus dictated harsh terms to the humbled Carthaginians. To save the city from Roman occupation, Carthage was forced to yield Sardinia, drop all claims to Corsica, withdraw from Sicily, and agree to abstain from starting new colonies for five years. Carthage also had to pay a stiff indemnity to compensate for Roman war costs, repatriate all Roman prisoners, and dismantle its battle fleet. It could not declare war or take other action without Roman consent.

Hamilcar Barca passed on to his son Hannibal his lingering hatred of the Romans, who had caused him disgrace.

Just as Carthage was about to agree, a sudden violent storm wiped out the entire Roman fleet. Robbed of naval support, the stranded Roman legions were attacked by Carthaginian ships and land forces. Half of the men were taken prisoner, including Regulus. Exhausted, the two sides agreed to a cease-fire. Carthage would retain its sovereignty but would continue to pay an indemnity, and Rome would retain control of Sicily and Sardinia. Hamilcar debated three days before bitterly accepting surrender. He passed on to his son his lingering hatred of the Romans, who had caused him disgrace.

Hamilcar first sought to outflank the Romans. He brought his war party and invasion fleet, with Hannibal as a passenger, past the Strait of Gibraltar and into the Atlantic Ocean. Just beyond the Rock of Gibraltar, he established an outpost colony on the ruins of an old seaport, Gades (now known as Cádiz). The new location would give Carthage a window on the Atlantic and new mercantile opportunities, even opening the Celtic settlements on the British Isles to trade. They would also be within a few days' sail of their other Mediterranean outposts. Hamilcar quickly built the new city, and there on Spanish soil Hannibal grew to manhood. He would not see Carthage again for thirty-six years.

TRAINING FOR LEADERSHIP

Hamilcar was determined that his son and heir-apparent should be a learned man as well as a soldier. He brought a Greek tutor to Gades for the boy. He especially wanted his son to learn Greek, which was the language of the educated classes. Hannibal became fluent in written and spoken Greek, and he also mastered several languages spoken by the men of Carthage's fighting forces.

Unlike Rome, Carthage did not maintain a standing army. When troops were needed, the Carthaginians recruited or conscripted them from subjugated peoples. The men who fought under Hannibal's banner came from all parts of Europe and Africa; they included Celtiberians, Libyans, Ligurians, Greeks, and Spaniards. The Carthaginian army's elite unit was its Numidian cavalry, skilled horsemen from the deserts of Libya who rode without saddle, stirrups, or reins. The Carthaginian army's chief offensive weapons were three types of missile-throwing slings wielded by men from the Balearic Islands.

Hannibal's linguistic skills were also an asset in diplomacy. Many of his later triumphs came not through force or arms, but through convincing speeches persuading tribal leaders to rally to his cause.

When Hannibal grew older, he accompanied his father on a mission to enlarge the Carthaginian economic stake in Spain. Hamilcar imported engineers and builders to develop the plains. He sowed wheat where only grass had grown, opened mines to exploit the salt beds, harvested the oak forests for construction timber, and set up sluice beds in the rushing streams to separate gold from gravel. Then Hamilcar Barca was killed.

Legend says Hamilcar, Hannibal, and a younger son were lured into an ambush by tribesmen who had requested treaty. The three escaped the trap, but the tribesmen followed. At a fork in the trail, Hamilcar sent the boys one way, while he took the other fork. His pursuers caught him at a river and killed him.

The Carthaginian officers conferred to choose Hamilcar's successor. Hannibal was deemed too young, so the choice fell to Hasdrubal, husband of Hamilcar's oldest daughter and a known Hamilcar favorite whom he was also grooming for leadership. Then the Carthaginians mustered their terrifying elephants, stormed and destroyed the assailants' villages, and enslaved the survivors.

Hannibal thus tasted his first experience of war. Thereafter he rode at Hasdrubal's side, gradually assumed command of one wing of the army, and became the acknowledged second-in-command. Hannibal and Hasdrubal expanded on Hamilcar's vision of Carthaginian rule across the Iberian peninsula. They exploited silver deposits in the Sierra Morena and set up smelters. Commerce thrived. Boat traffic tripled on the rivers as wheat and precious metals were shipped for export.

Hasdrubal and Hannibal were more natural diplomats than the sometimes blustery Hamilcar. They won over local chieftains by soft words and gifts rather than threats and conquest. As a crowning touch, they shifted headquarters from Gades on the ocean to a fine natural bay on the Mediterranean. There they constructed a new seaport and city two miles (3.2 km) in diameter, complete with shipyards, religious temples, palaces, and even a mint to stamp out coins. They called it New Carthage.

Hannibal was twenty-six, a daring young man who swam rivers ahead of his troops, lived simply and without the trappings of rank, spoke quickly, laughed easily, and led from the front of his forces.

Then Hasdrubal, too, was killed, apparently by a disgruntled Celt from northern Spain. The next day, the officers caucused again to select a leader. Not surprisingly, they chose Hannibal, the popular leader-in-waiting who was qualified both by lineage and experience. Hannibal was twenty-six, a daring young man who swam rivers ahead of his troops, lived simply and without the trappings of rank, spoke quickly, laughed easily, and led from the front of his forces. And he had promises to keep.

THE FOLDS OF WAR

One piece of Hasdrubal's diplomacy with which Hannibal strongly disagreed was a covenant he had reached with the Romans in 226 BCE. As New Carthage was being built, merchants in Massiolotes (now Marseille) watched with trepidation. Soon, they were sure, Carthaginian ships would be launched from the new seaport and threaten their markets around the Mediterranean basin. And they could visualize powerful Carthaginian armies marching up the coast to colonize new territory. Massiolotes considered itself a protectorate of Rome, and it appealed to Rome for aid. Rome sent a delegation to Hasdrubal, seeking a pledge that Carthaginians would not cross the Ebro River "with weapons in their hands." The Ebro flowed into the Mediterranean at Tartossa, several miles south of the present site of Barcelona.

Hasdrubal apparently felt that he had enough turf to protect. After mild negotiation, he acceded to the pledge, setting up opposing Roman and Carthaginian spheres of influence. Young Hannibal was already showing a grasp of geomilitary strategy. He recognized it was a mistake to allow Rome to advance beyond the rugged Pyrenees, which were a natural and seemingly impregnable barrier to invasion. The Romans were clearly creeping toward the Carthaginian holdings, and challenging Carthaginian supremacy across the peninsula. Hannibal debated whether the time might have come to act on his oath of so many years ago. Then the Romans made the decision for him.

Saguntum (now Sagunto) was a fortress on the Gulf of Valencia midway between New Carthage and the Ebro River. It housed a colony of Greek merchants who were loyal to Rome, along with supporters of Carthage. In the spring of 219, a two-man Roman delegation visited Hannibal in New Carthage. They told Hannibal that Saguntians had killed local tribesmen affiliated with Carthage and had appealed to Rome for protection. Hannibal, a studious reader of maps, noted that Saguntum was well within the Carthaginian sphere of influence as spelled out in Hasdrubal's covenant of 226. Rome had no authority south of the Ebro. Moreover, Hannibal added, the Saguntians had oppressed the Tartessian tribe. "It is the hereditary custom of Carthage to aid an oppressed people," he declared.

The envoys went over Hannibal's head to the governing council in Carthage. They demanded that Saguntum be neutralized and Hannibal punished, along with his chief lieutenants. The council declined. It stood by Hannibal; he and the other officers had simply been upholding the covenant of 226. The meeting broke up without agreement.

When summer came, the young commander laid siege to Saguntum. A second Roman delegation then called on Carthage. The five legates were headed by Fabius Maximus, who was a veteran senator with a flair for the melodramatic. Again, the Romans asked for the surrender of Hannibal and his chief lieutenants. Again, they were refused. Fabius asked: Would Carthage disavow Hannibal's attack

The Battle of Sagunto in 219 BCE opened a new chapter in the ongoing war between Carthage and Rome and launched Hannibal's military career. The Final Day of Sagunto in 219BC, 1869 (oil on canvas), Domingo Marques, Francisco (1824–1920) / Museo de Bellas Artes, Valencia, Spain / The Bridgeman Art Library

on Saguntum? A spirited and legalistic argument broke out. Did or did not the Romans accept the covenant? If they did not, what were their objections?

Finally, Fabius rose to his feet, gathering his toga around him. "These phrases weary me," he intoned. He clasped his hands in front of the toga. "I hold within this fold of my toga war or peace? Carthaginians, choose which you will have." The *shofet*, Carthage's royal magistrate, took his councilors into conference. When they returned, the answer was neither peace nor war. "Choose for yourself," the

shofet said. Fabius ostentatiously opened his toga. "Then it will be war," he said. "We accept!" the councilors shouted.

Couriers quickly took the news to Hannibal in Spain. Remembering his oath, he quickly began his preparations for war.

A FEW STEPS AHEAD OF ROME

The Roman legions were busy fighting a rebellion in southern Italy. Rome's consuls, the senior executives, assumed that the war would be fought in Spain and leisurely made ready to transfer the legions when the rebellion was squelched. Rome itself and Italy felt safe from attack. After the naval debacle at Messina, Rome had rebuilt its battle fleet and now had more warships than Carthage. A seaborne invasion seemed out of the question. The only land route was from the north, where the towering Alps stood in the way. No army, wise heads agreed, could mount an invasion from that direction.

Hannibal, of course, felt otherwise. Rome's very smugness, its confidence that it was fully protected against an invasion from the north, tempted him. Of course, he would have the alpine winter snows to contend with, and it was already late summer. Speed was of the essence. Hannibal began to build an invasion army of mercenaries and tribesmen. It soon numbered more than 60,000 ground troops plus his elite Numidians. He enlisted more slingers from the Balearic Islands, Libyans, Celtiberians. Many troops were African tribesmen with little combat experience. More than half the force were Spaniards.

Not least, Hannibal brought in forty elephants. He planned to use the huge beasts like tanks would later be used in the twentieth century, encasing them in leather to fend off spears and arrows. Lumbering ahead of the infantry, the elephants would destroy formations, and smash and trample fortifications, buildings, and entrenched positions. Above all, they would strike fear into the hearts of enemies.

Hannibal's initial battle plan did not envision invading Italy over the Alps. He expected to meet the Romans in the open country around Marseille, and then perhaps push up the Mediterranean coast. Then alarming intelligence came from Carthage. The Romans were amassing an invasion fleet in the Mediterranean, and they were apparently planning a landing in Africa that would threaten Carthage itself. Hannibal's troops might be called back to defend the mother city. Hannibal conceived an alternate plan. He would launch a diversionary attack over the Alps into Italy, and the Romans would be forced to repatriate their legions to protect the imperial capital.

Hannibal's analysis was right on target. The legions reversed course and headed for Europe. In a series of forced marches, Hannibal reached the turbulent Rhone River above Marseille and turned toward Italy. Roman commander Publius Cornelius Scipio was told Hannibal was on the Rhone. "You mean the Ebro," he corrected. No, he was told, the Rhone, 300 miles (480 km) closer to Italy. Publius couldn't believe troops could move that swiftly. He dispatched his legions to intercept and confront them, but Hannibal always seemed to be a few steps ahead.

Instead of crossing the Rhone near its mouth, Hannibal took his polyglot force upstream. Inspired by their leader, who plunged into the icy waters himself, the troops forded the rushing Rhone and coaxed the elephants across. (The imaginative Hannibal sent a female elephant into the river first, and the larger males followed her scent.) After difficult battles against tribal Gauls, he reached the foothills of the Alps. Undaunted by the challenging terrain, he summoned the elephants and a full baggage train.

OVER THE TOP

It took Hannibal's army fifteen days to cross the rugged range, even with the help of local guides. Historians disagree about which route he followed; but even the lower passes were well above 10,000 feet (3 km), followed narrow trails that were little more than rocky footpaths, with steep drops of more than 1,000 feet (305 m) on either side, and rarified air that left men and animals gasping for oxygen.

Tribesmen used to the high altitude harried the supply trains to loot them of goods. Wagons and screaming horses skidded and plunged into the valleys below. Some of the elephants toppled with them. Blowing and drifting snow lashed the men's faces, piled up on the trail, and rendered footing precarious.

Hannibal kept his men slogging forward with inspirational speeches and promises of booty. Then late on the ninth day, a cry went up from the front of the line and cheering spread through the ranks. The footpath went no farther; the vanguard had reached the summit. Nothing was beyond but lower ground.

The black line in this early map traces Hannibal's flanking-attack route through Gaul and over the Alps to Italy. A Map of the Route Hannibal took through Gaul and over the Alps into Italy (engraving), English School / Private Collection, Ken Welsh / The Bridgeman Art Library

Hannibal gave the weary troops two days' rest and began a difficult descent. It was now nearly November, storm clouds were growing, and Rome was still 400 miles (650 km) away. He had lost all but 23,000 of the 60,000 who had reached the Rhone and most of the elephants. Hannibal rode one of the last survivors. But he had achieved one of the epic events of military history. And he had lived up to his oath.

Hannibal was rewarded by months of success. In the valley of the Po that spread before him, a Roman army awaited. Hannibal's fast-moving Numidians decimated their ranks. Northern Italian Gallic tribes subjugated by Rome switched sides and joined Hannibal, doubling his army. The frantic Roman Senate chose a new consul and military leader, Quintus Fabius Maximus. The new man's strategy was to avoid battle, play for time, and wait Hannibal out. Romans angrily called him "the Delayer." After several large skirmishes and some shifts in Roman command, Hannibal ambushed the main Roman army at Lake Trasimeno and routed it. The Senate replaced "the Delayer" with two more aggressive leaders. With 80,000 men to Hannibal's 50,000, they confidently confronted him at Cannae (now Canosa) in the level plains of Campania.

Positioning his force in two formidable wings, Hannibal originated his now-famous double-envelopment strategy, which became the model for the German Schlieffen Plan against France in 1914 and is still taught in military schools. The center of the Carthaginian line fell back, luring the Romans forward. Then the Carthaginian wings swept around the Romans from both directions, pinned them down from behind, and cut them to pieces. It was the worst defeat in Roman history. Rome lost 70,000 killed, wounded, or captured; Hannibal 2,000.

Hannibal then advanced to the very walls of Rome. But he didn't have enough troops to storm the city, nor enough equipment or supplies for a protracted siege. The hard-

Hannibal's father, Hamilcar Barca, as he appeared on this Punic coin of 230 BCE.
Punic coin bearing the head of Hamilcar Barca (c. 270-228 BCE) minted at Carthage, c. 230 BCE / Private Collection, / The Bridgeman Art Library

Atop his personal Asian elephant, Hannibal led his forces over the 10,000-foot (3 km) passes, as visualized in this oil painting from the 1400s. Hannibal Crossing the Alps (fresco), Ripanda, Jacopo (fl.1490–1530) / Pinacoteca Capitolina, Palazzo Conservatori, Rome, Italy / The Bridgeman Art Library

pressed Carthage government offered little support. Then a young Roman general, Scipio, ignoring Hannibal but learning from him, launched a diversionary attack on Carthaginian Spain, Hannibal's base of supply. Scipio conquered Spain and divided it into two provinces. Next, Scipio invaded Africa and took Carthage itself. The council sued for peace, leaving Hannibal high and dry. One condition demanded by Scipio was that Hannibal leave Italy and not be resupplied. The great young general complied. His military career was basically finished, along with Carthage's cause. He had won every battle but had lost the war.

When Hannibal had reached the walls of Rome and realized he could neither besiege nor storm it, he seized a javelin from one of his cavalrymen and hurled it with all his strength over the Roman wall. That was his declaration that he was living up to the oath he had taken as an eight year old.

CHAPTER TWO

JOAN OF ARC, 1412–1431: THE VOICES THAT LED TO A REVOLUTION

A French peasant girl's claims that voices from heaven urged her to drive the English out of her homeland changed the course of history for her country.

The soft call of the "Angelus" floated across the Meuse River Valley in northeastern France, reminding the faithful of the hour for evening prayer. In a flowered meadow overlooking the tiny village of Domrémy, a twelve-year-old shepherdess dutifully dropped to her knees among the cowslips and buttercups, crossed herself, bowed her head, and began to recite: "*Ave Maria, Mater Dei...*", repeating the traditional prayer to the Blessed Virgin three times, as the ritual required. The prayer finished, she crossed herself again and began to rise, staff in hand, to drive a herd of grazing sheep and cattle back to the village below.

In the French village custom known as *le paturage*, all the local livestock were brought together each morning and taken to the upland pasture for the day. Families took turns furnishing a member as the herder, usually a preteen daughter. It was her job to tend the flock, watch for strays, lead the animals to water, and redistribute them to their owners at the end of the day. Most youngsters heartily disliked the chore and tried to avoid it. Being isolated in a far-off field, away from friends, and with only sheep and cows for company was not a medieval child's notion of amusement.

Jeanne d'Arc was different. She liked being a shepherd and actually looked forward to the assignment. She enjoyed the outdoors, the grass, the trees, and the smell of the flowers. The high setting and the surroundings made her feel closer

Joan of Arc has been pictured many times in paintings and films, but was never portrayed in her lifetime. This fanciful oil painting from 1879 shows a slim, attractive young woman listening to her "voices" in her garden. In fact, Joan described herself as short and "swart" (dark). Joan of Arc (c1412–1431). French national heroine. Oil on canvas, 1879, by Jules Bastien-Lepage/The Granger Collection, New York.

to God. The ringing of the bells punctuated her feeling of devotion. The chimes in the belfry of Domrémy's little church ordered the villagers' day. Their notes summoned the village to mass and notified them of matins, vespers, and curfew. Jeanne responded to all of them. She was a pious girl, praying as often as five times a day and "bending the knee," as her father said, at each summons of the bell.

On this particular summer evening in 1424, as the Angelus told her to gather her flock for the homeward trip, she heard something odd. In the clangor of the bells, she seemed to detect the sound of voices. Unearthly voices. A bright glow appeared in the heavens. A male voice spoke directly to her. "Jeanne, Jeanne," the voice said, using her baptismal name, "Joan," in English. "Jeanne, do not be afraid." Now she could distinguish dimly two other voices—female voices—also calling her by name.

Not surprisingly, Jeanne was badly frightened by the voices speaking to her from the heavens, as she was to repeat many times in describing the incident. "You are a good girl," the male voice assured her. "God loves you." The voices praised her piety and her religious devotions. They promised her that a loving God heard her prayers and was pleased by them. She must continue to pray and ask for His guidance. The voices identified themselves as Saint Michael the Archangel and Saints Margaret and Catherine. They would help her and watch over her and tell her of God's bidding. Then the great light faded, and the voices died away.

By now Jeanne had recovered from her initial fright. She was convinced that she had, indeed, conversed with saints. Such unearthly visitations were much reported in medieval France. Two centuries before, a young boy declared that his dead brother had appeared and announced that God had directed that a heretical sect in another part of France must be forcefully stamped out. The result was the bloody, twenty-year Albigensian Crusade. And Jeanne had frequently prayed to saints, asking them to intercede with God to grant her prayers. It was not too much of an intellectual reach for her to believe that the saints were now responding and that she must obey their instructions. Their messages were to lead Jeanne in paths that would drastically upend her simple rural life, change the destiny of medieval France, and leave an impact on the world that still resounds.

THE VILLAGE GOOD GIRL

Jeanne d'Arc (now known worldwide as Saint Joan) was born in Domrémy on January 6, 1412, the feast of the Epiphany, or Twelfth Night, to Jacques d'Arc and his wife, Isabelle Romée. Jeanne was the third of six children and the

January 6, 1412
Joan of Arc is born in Domrémy village, in the Meuse River Valley, northeastern France, bordering the province of Lorraine. She is the daughter of peasants Jacques d'Arc and Isabelle Romée, and the third of six children (one of whom died in infancy).

Midsummer 1424
Hears voices said to be those of saints while tending sheep above the village.

May 1428
Voices instruct the lowly peasant girl to visit Charles, "Le Dauphin," presumed king of France, raise an army, drive the English out of France, and install Charles on the French throne.

January–February 1429
Leaves home to ask for relative's help for an audience with the king. Does not return home.

February 23, 1429
Gets a horse and her first suit of armor and sets off for the Chinon palace in the Loire Valley, a trek of more than 250 miles (400 km), to see the king.

March 6, 1429
Arrives at the palace in Chinon.

March 9, 1429
Received by the king. He accepts her tale of heavenly voices' commands and subsequently makes her commander in chief *(chef de guerre)* of the army, with the mission to raise the English siege of Orléans.

April 28, 1429
Arrives with her army at Orléans.

April 29–May 10, 1429
Battles at Orléans, after which the English and Burgundians withdraw.

July 16, 1429
After a series of victories en route, Joan arrives at Reims for the coronation of "Le Dauphin" as Charles VII.

July 19, 1429
Charles is anointed and crowned king in the great Cathedral of Reims with Joan, in white armor, looking on.

September 8, 1429
Joan attacks Paris and is wounded.

May 23, 1430
After the assault on Compiègne, where she is wounded again, Joan is taken prisoner.

May 25, 1430–May 30, 1431
Held prisoner in a tower of a castle in Rouen.

January 3, 1431
The English turn Joan over to the Inquisition and Church for trial.

January 9, 1431
Trial for heresy begins.

May 24, 1431
Joan recants her story of voices.

May 29, 1431
Joan withdraws her recantation.

May 30, 1431
Burned at the stake as a "lapsed heretic" in the public square at Rouen.

July 1456
Pope Calixtus III overturns the verdict and revokes Joan's sentence.

January 1904
Pope Pius X gives Joan the title "Venerable," a step toward canonization.

April 18, 1909
Joan is beatified.

May 16, 1920
Joan is canonized as Saint Joan by Pope Benedict XV.

A CENTURY OF WARFARE

In 1428, the English and French had been at each other's throats for more than ninety years. But the Hundred Years' War was not a continuous all-out struggle with marked battlefronts, known enemies, and stated objectives, like World War I or World War II. The Hundred Years' War had no definite beginning or final surrender; fighting was spasmodic and irregular, with truces and ceasefires and pauses that sometimes went on for years. Allies came and went, armies fought and were dispersed, and leaders battled and were succeeded by other leaders. The warfare politely paused for weddings. After Henry V's famous victory at Agincourt in 1415, glamorized in the Shakespeare play, Henry V of England married Catherine, daughter of the king of France, and the two countries were temporarily united under one crown until Henry V and Charles VI of France both died in 1422 and the fighting resumed.

The war was actually a family squabble. Since the Norman conquest of England in 1066, blood relatives, distant cousins, occupied thrones on both sides of the English

Mad King Charles VI, nominal father of Joan's "Dauphin," insisted he was made of glass. The Genealogy of Charles V and Charles VI, detail of Charles VI (1368-1422) (vellum), French School, (15th century)

only surviving daughter. The family owned a few acres of land and was highly respected for their probity and piety.

Hard-working, fair-minded Jacques, known as "Jacquot," had even been named a *doyen*, or elder, the third in rank in the village hierarchy. He had early been chosen to referee a longstanding dispute between the village and a landowner over a business contract and disagreements were thereafter brought to him for judgment. The d'Arcs were virtuous and faithful in their religious obligations. Jacquot insisted that Romée, as his wife was known, school their daughter in the *Ave Maria* and the *Paternoster*.

Joan, as English readers know her, was admired in Domrémy, too, as an obedient, respectful, and helpful child, praised for her skills in spinning and weaving.

Channel. Chunks of traditional France came under English rule. When the French king Philip IV died, Edward III of England claimed the French crown on grounds that he was Philip's grandson, and the son of Philip's daughter, and the next male in line. The French Count Philip of Valois, the son of Philip's younger brother, counterclaimed that the crown should be his because it could not be inherited through the female line. In 1337, Philip of Valois took over the duchy of Gascony, where the English had planted their flag. Other dukedoms and regimes chose sides.

It was a desultory war. In 1346, the English won a decisive victory at Crécy and another ten years later at Poitiers, consolidating their hold on French territory. The French king John died in English captivity in 1364. His able son, Charles V, took the throne only to be succeeded in 1380 by his mad son, Charles VI, who was paranoid and so deluded that he was convinced he was made of glass. His wife, Princess Isabeau of Bavaria, was scarcely better, afflicted with phobias about disease and crowds, and known for her serial infidelities. In 1420, she signed the Treaty of Troyes, naming Henry V of England regent of France and heir to the throne. The treaty specifically disinherited Isabeau's own son, implying that he was the illegitimate product of one of her numerous liaisons.

France divided into Armagnacs and Burgundians, the Armagnacs supporting the claims of the descendants of Charles V, and the Burgundians lined up behind Henry V's infant son, Henry VI, and his uncle the Duke of Bedford. Domrémy, situated on the east bank of the Meuse, straddled the border between the province of Lorraine and the duchy of Bar, and it was loyal to France. Burgundy was next door. Raids by underpaid, underfed English and Burgundian soldiers on the Domrémy farms and flocks were common, once forcing the villagers to flee en masse. Joan grew up hating Burgundians and "goddams," as the marauding English infantry were known. Her father, as a village official, was loyal to the French crown.

She had many close friends among the young, and enjoyed playing and dancing with them on the village green, although she considered their belief in fairies and their "fairy dance" silly.

Although Joan was close to her mother, she never told her mother nor her father about the voices or the strange incident that occurred in that high pasture that afternoon. Nor did Joan confide in her friends or her confessor, the local priest. But the next day in her father's garden, Joan heard the voices again. They became regular visitors and soon she could visualize as well as hear them, and, when she felt the need for guidance, she could summon them at will.

Gradually, while the voices continued to commend Joan's faith and devotion, they began to speak of more secular matters and to assign her specific duties to carry out. In 1428, just after Joan's sixteenth birthday, she was told that she must personally come to the defense of beleaguered France and its rightful king. The French had been fighting English and England's ally Burgundy since 1337, tearing France apart in what historians were to call the Hundred Years' War.

The faithful, illiterate peasant girl who had never rode a horse, never traveled more than five miles (8 km) from home, and who had no knowledge of spears or shields or weapons must take command of the French army, she was told, and expel the English and Burgundians from French soil. She must see that *Le Dauphin*, (the title given to the heir to the throne of France) who had been denied the throne, was properly and rightfully crowned as the king of France. And to do all this, Joan must first achieve a seemingly impossible task. She must travel to the palace of Le Dauphin at Chinon, some 250 miles away (400 km) in the Loire Valley, inform him of her holy mission, lay her plans before him, and persuade him to turn over his army to a sixteen-year-old girl.

THE RELUCTANT KING

Le Dauphin, the Armagnac candidate, had very little to recommend him. He had, after all, been disowned by his own mother. He was not an impressive figure, either. He was skinny and knock-kneed, with a bulbous nose and small, deep-set eyes. He was indecisive, played favorites, and was so self-indulgent and extravagant that he had to borrow money from his cook to keep his palace operating.

Basically he only wanted to be left alone to wallow in the corrupt life of his court at Chinon, far from the governmental problems and intrigues of Paris. But his wife, Marie d'Anjou, came from an anti-Burgundian house, and by bloodlines she was called upon to oppose the English. Le Dauphin seemed unlikely to welcome a visit from a peasant girl from Lorraine, even if she did claim to be sent by God.

If Joan was to carry out her voices' instructions, she must find a way to convince the dauphin, which was a daunting task for a sixteen-year-old who had never learned to read or write and spoke the patois of rural France. Steeled by her voices, though, she was determined to find a way. She had an "uncle," Durand Lassois—actually an older cousin—with connections. On the pretext of going to help Lassois's wife with a new baby, Joan went to visit Lassois and laid her plans before him. He was at first taken aback: Most young girls with a religious vocation would choose a convent, not the military. But something in Joan's passion and piety convinced him.

After a few days of Joan's pleas, Lassois introduced her to Robert de Baudri-court, the ranking military authority in the district. A gruff, battle-hardened career solider, de Baudricourt was at first bemused by Joan's insistence on command of an army and an audience with the king. But in time de Baudricourt, too, was won over. A realist, however, he recognized that a teenaged girl, even one supposedly sent by God, would be a mighty temptation to soldiers traveling with her. De Baudricourt dressed Joan as a common soldier, outfitted her in a suit of armor, gave her a horse, and agreed to accompany her on the proposed nine-day journey to Chinon. More than that, he mustered a force of 4,000 men, including a cavalry troop, and sent a messenger ahead to announce that France's savior was on her way.

Charles VII was indecisive, played favorites, and was so self-indulgent and extravagant that he had to borrow money from his cook to keep his palace operating.

The strange procession set out on the first Sunday of Lent in 1429. Joan did not even say goodbye to her parents. She was, after all, following God's com-mand. Her reputation preceded her. Whole villages turned out for a glimpse of the girl who said she communicated with saints and promised to deliver the countryside from the marauding invaders. She led them in prayer and deliv-ered passionate roadside speeches balancing patriotic and religious themes; hundreds of villagers now joined her procession. Not surprisingly, word of the oncoming hordes reached Charles's palace at Chinon. He reacted in trademark fashion: He hid.

Charles VII's retinue argued that he could hardly ignore this outpouring of humanity, so the retinue pulled him out of hiding, and he agreed to greet her. But he craftily devised another stratagem. He dressed a courtier in the royal robes while he pretended to be a lower-level hanger-on. Joan was not fooled. Admitted to the court, she marched directly up to Charles. She curtsied awkwardly in her boy's suit and heavy armor.

"*Non, non,*" Charles protested and pointed to the impostor. "It is he." Joan curtsied again. "*Non,* Your Majesty. You. You are the king." Charles led her aside, and the two began to whisper. According to Joan's testimony at her trial later, she asked Charles about three things he had asked God in his All Saints' Day prayers—prayers only he and God would have heard. She recited them. He acknowledged that her version was true and that her knowledge was a miracle. He then summoned his military leadership and introduced their new leader.

STRIKING THE ENGLISH HEAD-ON

Obediently the leadership took Joan into their council, but they treated her more as a mascot than a comrade in arms, and certainly not a military leader. A mere teenager? A female? Sure, her passionate sense of mission and her religious fervor might inspire the troops. But she had no combat experience and no grasp of military strategy. She obviously could not be trusted to lead an army in the field.

One who disagreed was the Comte de Dunois, known as the Bastard of Orléans, the sobriquet recognizing that he was the illegitimate son of Charles VI. The Bastard, which in 1429 was not a derogatory title, but one that signified his royal roots, held military command of besieged Orléans. He explained the French position to Joan. Orléans was the key city on the Loire River, and French commerce was strangled by an English siege.

The English surrounded the walled city on three sides. A small French garrison held the city itself. Only one gate remained open, so that the garrison could be meagerly supplied. Dunois's suggested plan was to push a large force through the gate so that the garrison could be supplied and reinforced. Then he took Joan to the opposite shore of the Loire River where French troops had been massed. The French could either be taken upstream in boats to take the enemy in the rear, or a pontoon bridge could be built to directly cross the river.

Joan was furious. "I have not traveled all this way to sit on one side of the river and gaze at the English across the water," she said. They must strike the English head-on. That was what her voices had told her. After a considerable argument, the novice commander was persuaded to land the troops just above the city walls, out of range of English archers, and then attack the besieging army.

But at the appointed hour for the assault next morning, a stiff wind was blowing downstream, hampering the efforts to board and launch the boats. Dunois was in despair. Joan laid a consoling hand on his arm. "Do not worry," she said. "The wind will turn in five minutes." Sure enough, the wind died away to a gentle upstream breeze. Her prediction may only have been a country girl's familiarity with the fickleness of weather, but Dunois was now convinced that she had indeed been ordained by God, and he became her most loyal lieutenant. Dunois suggested she and he enter Orléans together.

"FOLLOW MY BANNER!"

Joan had designed a personal banner that she planned to carry at the head of her troops. Flowing white satin, it was fringed with green and splashed with the fleur-de-lis. Now an accomplished horsewoman, Joan insisted that she ride in the forward position on a white horse where all the men could see her. Before a force of 400, she and Dunois entered the city, greeted by a jubilant population and the celebratory clangor of church bells. The siege

Charles VII (center) disguised a courtier as the king when Joan arrived for an audience. She recognized him anyway. Ms 1151 f.1 Charles VII (1403-61) Surrounded by his Court and Joan of Arc (1412-31) (vellum), French School, (15th century) / Bibliotheque Municipale, Rouen, France, Lauros / Giraudon / The Bridgeman Art Library

was not yet lifted. Five days passed while Joan gathered and exhorted an army estimated between 3,500 and 9,000. Then in bloody fighting, she and her army overwhelmed the most formidable of English strongpoints around the city. She followed up by picking off other forts until finally the last English stronghold was conquered. The English surrendered, and their commander was taken prisoner.

Joan herself was wounded by a spear just above the left breast, but she is said to have pulled the spear out and continued fighting. Although Joan was armed and now skilled with a lance, she did not claim any victims, but in the thick of the fighting she is said to have dismounted, knelt by a wounded English soldier, cra-

In 1429 England had besieged the city of Orleans on three sides. In bloody fighting, Joan lifted the siege, as depicted in this 15th century artwork. Ms Fr 5054 fol.54v The Siege of Orleans, from the Vigils of Charles VII, c.1484 (vellum) (b/w photo), Martial de Paris (known as Auvergne) (fl.15th century) / Bibliotheque Nationale, Paris, France, Giraudon / The Bridgeman Art Library

dled him in her arms, and treated his wound. Cheering men carried her off the field in triumph, loudly praising the leader who called herself simply "La Pucelle" ("The Maid"). Then Joan ordered all of the men to a Mass of thanksgiving.

Joan's voices were not yet finished, however. The second part of her mission must still be fulfilled: The Dauphin must be crowned with full ceremony as king of France. And the coronation must take place in the great cathedral of Reims, 60 miles (100 km) northwest of Paris and very much in English hands. Reims had been the traditional venue for French coronations since the fifth-century investiture of Clovis. According to legend, a dove carrying the sacred coronation oil in its beak had flown over Clovis's coronation procession as it approached the cathedral and dropped the oil, thus anointing him the new French monarch. The tradition had been observed ever since, and it certainly must be observed now.

As Joan held her banner aloft and spurred her horse, after a series of battles she led her burgeoning army to the gates of Reims. The English quickly evacuated the city with only minor fighting. A coronation was hastily arranged. It lacked many of the traditional props. Charles was reluctant. Although he had waited nearly seven years for the crown, he now wanted to postpone it further. He wanted an elaborate coronation with full pomp and ceremony, with himself attired in glorious monarchical robes. Joan squelched the idea.

Joan's voices had told her to see that he was restored to the French throne, and she wanted no delay or interference. On July 19, 1429, Joan stood at Charles's side, holding her banner and wearing a suit of white armor, and looked on approvingly as the archbishop of Reims pressed the venerable crown of France on the brow of the trembling Dauphin, now Charles VII. He wore the crown until 1461, eight years after the Hundred Years' War petered out.

A triumphant Joan had now fulfilled her mission. Just past seventeen, she might now have returned to her home village; the voices had not asked for more. She had been called to oust the English from Orléans and to restore the crown to its rightful owner, and she had accomplished it. But the English still besieged Paris. Joan regalvanized her army for an offensive on the capital. But now Charles, safe again on his throne, turned his back on the young woman whose visions had re-established French sovereignty. The spendthrift king withheld supplies and troops necessary for victory. With a dwindling army, Joan fought several inconclusive battles until the English withdrew.

Joan now set out to lift the siege of Compiègne, another vital city and gateway to Paris. Here she was wounded and captured. While an ungrateful Charles ignored her plight, her Burgundian captors sold her to the English for ransom money so that she could be prosecuted as a witch. The English turned her over to an ecclesiastical court presided over by a rabid English partisan, Bishop Pierre Cauchon, Bishop of Beauvais.

The trial went on for five months and has been immortalized in theater and cinema, most notably in George Bernard Shaw's *Saint Joan*. The illiterate peasant girl (who finally learned to write her name in prison) parried and confounded the learned clerics who were her judges. In one famous exchange, she was asked the damned-if-you-do-damned-if-you-don't-question: "Are you in a state of grace?" If Joan said yes, she was guilty of heresy; only God could

say who was in a state of grace. If Joan said no, then she was clearly a sinner and a heretic. Joan neatly sidestepped: "If I am, may God keep me there. If I am not, may He place me there."

One of the most serious charges in the eyes of the medieval church was that Joan wore men's clothes, which was incontrovertible evidence of heresy. Twelve of the charges against her dealt with cross-dressing. After a lengthy trial, Joan was found guilty of heresy, on grounds that she heretically stated that she obeyed only the voices of God, when instruction in the faith came only through the church hierarchy. Joan had a great fear of fire. ("I would rather be beheaded seven times than burned," she said.) Told that she would be sentenced to death, she now renounced her voices and denied their existence. Instead, she was told she would be imprisoned for life. The girl who had loved the pasturage and the outdoors at Domrémy was horrified.

"Lock me up like a rat in a hole? Shut me off from the trees and the flowers? Then bring on your fire!" She was burned at the stake May 30, 1431 in the public square at Rouen. As the flames leaped up, an English soldier offered Joan two sticks, which she formed into a cross and famously held toward heaven. "God forgive us," the English soldier said. "We have burned a saint."

The soldier's prophecy was fulfilled five centuries later. Twenty years after Joan's execution, pressed by the outcries of the French population, the obsequious Charles agreed to a tribunal that revoked her sentence. Joan's trial, however, remained controversial for centuries. Then in 1909, Pope Pius X beatified her, the final step toward sainthood, and in 1920 the little shepherd girl who heard voices was officially proclaimed a saint.

Wounded and captured in fighting at Compiègne, Joan was imprisoned as a heretic and harassed and taunted by her jailers, as depicted in this painting. After a five-month trial, she was burned at the stake in 1430. Joan of Arc (1412-31) Insulted in Prison, 1866 (oil on canvas), Patrois, Isidore (1811–84) / Musee des Beaux-Arts, Angers, France, Giraudon / The Bridgeman Art Library

QUEEN ELIZABETH I, 1533–1603: HENRY VII'S EMBATTLED DAUGHTER'S RITE OF PASSAGE INTO ADULTHOOD

Accused of conspiring with her reputed lover to seize the throne from her half-brother King Edward VI, fifteen-year-old Elizabeth Tudor must rely on her wits and will to survive. Despite the overwhelming odds, she navigates her way to freedom—and eventually the throne.

In January 1549, Sir Robert Tyrwhit was assigned by the Royal Privy Council to investigate an alleged plot to seize the royal throne from young King Edward VI. The suspects included Lord Admiral Thomas Seymour; the king's half sister, Elizabeth Tudor; Elizabeth's governess, Kat Ashley; and cofferer Tom Parry, who oversaw the Royal Household. Seymour, Ashley, and Parry were arrested and imprisoned in the dreaded Tower of London. Tyrwhit and his wife assumed guardianship of Elizabeth, moving into her manor at Hatfield in the south of England. While spared the indignity of being held in the Tower, Elizabeth was a virtual prisoner in her own home. Tyrwhit approached his duties with much determination. A sharp, respected man, and accomplished courtier, Tyrwhit had assumed he would be able to get Elizabeth to confess at once. He was not prepared for what awaited him.

Accustomed to dealing with diplomats and heads of state, Tyrwhit grossly underestimated his suspect. Elizabeth was alternately haughty, forlorn, argumentative, angry, and contrite. She averred her innocence with a conviction that surprised her interrogator. The accusations were false, she insisted. She and her

Born a princess, Elizabeth Tudor's childhood was marked by turmoil. The resilient daughter of Henry VIII went on to become one of England's most beloved monarchs. Elizabeth I, Armada portrait, c.1588 (oil on panel), English School, (16th century) / Private Collection / The Bridgeman Art Library International

attendants were being unfairly charged. She demanded that Ashley and Parry be released and reinstated in her employ.

Although only fifteen years old, Elizabeth possessed the steely determination and quick wit of her father, the late King Henry VIII. The gravity of the situation was not lost on the girl. A treason conviction could result in a date with the executioner. Frightened and surrounded by adults who believed she was guilty, she dug her heels in and stood firm. Had she not succeeded, the history of England would be far different.

Elizabeth was first and foremost a survivor. During his lifetime, King Henry married six times. Elizabeth's fortunes, title, and living arrangements were in constant flux because of her father's moods and romantic entanglements. Her childhood had been marked by a series of horrors and tragedies, beginning at age three when her mother, Anne Boleyn, was beheaded. Boleyn had usurped the king's first wife, the Spanish-born Catherine of Aragon, who had been unable to produce a male heir. One of the queen's ladies, Boleyn surprised the king by refusing his romantic advances. A sensual, sloe-eyed woman, Anne was not considered a great beauty, but her disinterest in the king served to ignite his passion.

Henry plotted to divorce Catherine so that he could marry Anne, whom he was certain would produce the healthy son he longed for. England fell under the authority of the Roman Catholic Church, which forbade divorce. Catherine had been previously married to Henry's brother, whose death made her a widow. Henry, ingenious and determined, found a passage in the Bible that decreed "if a man shall take his brother's wife, it is an unclean thing." Henry used the biblical passage to support a charge of incest, and he demanded that the union be annulled. Catherine, however, did not go quietly, making a strong case against annulment, which would not only dethrone her but also make the couple's daughter, Mary, a bastard. Despite opposition from Catherine and the Church, Henry would not back down. In the end, he severed ties with the Roman Catholic Church and married Boleyn.

Eventually Henry grew bored with Boleyn, and when she did not bear him a son he lodged charges of adultery and treason against her and ordered her execution. Just weeks after Boleyn's death, the king married his third wife, Jane Seymour. Elizabeth, like her half sister Mary before her, was now declared a royal bastard. Perplexed by her new name change, a precocious three-year old Elizabeth inquired, "How haps it, governor, yesterday my Lady Princess, today

September 7, 1533
Elizabeth Tudor is born in Greenwich, England,
to King Henry VIII and Anne Boleyn.

May 19, 1536
Boleyn is executed.
May 30, 1536
The king marries his third wife, Jane Seymour.
October 12, 1537
Edward, Elizabeth's half brother, is born to Henry and Seymour. Elizabeth is
stripped of her title and made illegitimate. Seymour dies shortly after childbirth.

January 6, 1539
Henry marries Anne of Cleves. The union is quickly annulled.
July 28, 1540
The king marries Catherine Howard, Elizabeth's cousin on her mother's side.
February 13, 1542
Howard is executed for adultery.
July 12, 1543
Catherine Parr becomes the king's sixth and last wife.

January 1547
King Henry dies. Nine-year old Edward Tudor becomes king.
Spring 1547
Parr marries Admiral Thomas Seymour, brother of the late Jane Seymour.
Elizabeth shares a house in Chelsea with Parr and her new stepfather.
1548
Suspecting Seymour's interest in Elizabeth is less than innocent,
Parr asks her stepdaughter to move out. Elizabeth relocates
to a family manor in Hatfield, England.
January–March 1549
Elizabeth and two members of her staff are implicated, but later
exonerated, in a plot to overthrow the king. Thomas Seymour, the architect
of the conspiracy, is convicted of treason and executed.

July 6, 1553
King Edward VI dies from tuberculosis at the age of fifteen. His elder half
sister Mary assumes the throne.
1554
Elizabeth is accused of conspiring to unseat Queen Mary and
imprisoned in the Tower of London for two months.
Upon her release, she regains Mary's favor.
November 17, 1558
Mary dies, and Elizabeth becomes queen of England.
1565
Elizabeth's cousin Mary Queen of Scots conspires
to overthrow Elizabeth and seize the English throne.

1568
Mary Queen of Scots is arrested and confined to house arrest.
February 8, 1587
Elizabeth succumbs to pressure from the Privy Council and has Mary
executed for conspiracy.
August 8, 1588
England wins its greatest victory with the defeat of Spanish Armada.

March 24, 1603
Queen Elizabeth I dies at the age of seventy, allegedly of blood poisoning.
Her cousin James I is crowned king of England.

SIR THOS SEYMOUR

LORD SUDLEY

The politically ambitious Admiral Thomas Seymour set in motion a chain of events that ultimately cost him his life. Portrait of Thomas Seymour (1508-49) 1st Baron of Sudeley from 'Memoirs of the court of Queen Elizabeth', published in 1825 (w/c and gouache on paper), Essex, Sarah Countess of (d.1838) / Private Collection / The Stapleton Collection / The Bridgeman Art Library International

but my Lady Elizabeth?" Several years later, Henry reinstated Elizabeth's title as well as her right of inheritance and claim to the throne.

Seymour died after giving birth to Edward VI, the male heir the king had longed for. Henry married three more times before his death in 1547. With each marriage, young Elizabeth was shuffled from household to household, falling in and out of favor with her mercurial father. Elizabeth grew close to her fifth stepmother, Catherine Howard, a woman who doted on the child and relished her parental role. The security Elizabeth felt was shattered when Howard was accused of adultery, dragged to the Tower, and beheaded. Elizabeth was eight years old and already learning to equate marriage with defamation and death.

The next queen of England, Catherine Parr, outlived the king. Like Howard, Parr was fond of Elizabeth and continued on as her guardian after the king's death. However, Parr inadvertently played a part in Elizabeth's first adult ordeal and scandal by introducing the scurrilous Admiral Thomas Seymour into her life. Shortly after King Henry died, Parr married Seymour, a dashing, politically ambitious womanizer with designs on the throne.

Seymour was inappropriately attentive to his new stepdaughter, paying surprise visits to her bedchamber, where, still dressed in his nightclothes, he would proceed to tickle the girl and slap her backside. Such horseplay scandalized Elizabeth's governess, Kat Ashley. She took the matter up with Parr, who thereafter accompanied her husband on his morning visits. In one particularly bizarre incident, Parr held Elizabeth down in the garden while her husband cut the dress the girl was wearing into a dozen little pieces. Parr's participation in the frequent romps dropped off when she became pregnant. Deeply in love with her husband, she convinced herself his attention to Elizabeth was innocent and harmless. Her attitude changed when she spied him embracing her teenaged stepdaughter. Elizabeth was sent away. Like many women of that time, Parr died after childbirth of puerperal sepsis. Widower Thomas Seymour wasted little time in pursuing Princess Elizabeth.

SCANDALS AND DANGEROUS SCHEMES

An unmarried princess was a great asset to a country. Royal marriages were arranged for political reasons, and a successful match could increase England's power base and finances. According to King Henry's will, Elizabeth would be disinherited and lose any future claim to the throne should she marry without the express permission of the Privy Council. Still, that did not dissuade Thomas Seymour. Elizabeth was clearly taken with her former stepfather, but she was keenly aware that such a marriage was impossible. Additionally, she may have had serious misgivings about marriage in general. When she was eight years old, she told a friend she never wanted to get married.

Seymour had long resented his brother Edward's higher position in the court. Appointed Protector and Duke of Somerset, Edward Seymour was responsible for the welfare of young King Edward, a job Thomas Seymour believed should be shared jointly between the brothers. At ten years old, Edward Tudor was little more than a puppet king. The men in charge of his care wielded the real power. Thomas Seymour ingratiated himself with the child king, fawning over him and giving him the pocket money his frugal brother withheld from the boy. He hoped the boy would intervene in his favor with the Privy Council and have him appointed as the king's new guardian.

Thomas Seymour spoke to Elizabeth's governess, Ashley, and Parry, her cofferer, about marrying the teenager. The Privy Council would never have approved such a union because Seymour lacked the rank and status to marry a princess. He also had a reputation as a schemer. Soon he was suspected of conspiring to marry Elizabeth, overthrow young King Edward, dispose of Mary, who was next in line, and secure the throne for himself. When the Privy Council learned of Seymour's seditious plans, he was promptly arrested. Ashley and Parry, who had done little more than indulge Seymour's fantasies of royal marriage, were implicated in the plot along with his alleged lover and former stepdaughter, Princess Elizabeth.

Elizabeth was adamant that nothing untoward had occurred between her and Seymour. She chastised Tyrwhit for believing such scurrilous gossip. The investigator did not think the princess was guilty of treason, but he did believe that she and her staff actively encouraged Seymour's romantic advances. Elizabeth was fiercely loyal to her staff and refused to implicate them. Not only was she innocent, but so were Ashley and Parry, she insisted. Tyrwhit reported to the council: "I do believe that there hath been some secret promise between my Lady, Mistress Ashley, and the cofferer, never to confess till death; and if it be so, it will never be gotten of her, but either by the King's Majesty or else by your Grace."

Tyrwhit was not above using tricks in an effort to elicit a confession from the princess. He spoke of letters and evidence that proved her guilt. Elizabeth called his bluff. She knew no such evidence existed. Tyrwhit told her England was abuzz with news that she was locked up in the tower and pregnant with Seymour's bastard child. Instead of throwing her off balance, Tyrwhit merely succeeded in evoking righteous outrage in the girl. She demanded permission to appear before the Privy Council to show them that she was most certainly not with child. Permission was denied.

Elizabeth continued to ask Tyrwhit to bring her before the council. Exasperated, he agreed to allow her to write to the council. In her letter, she reminded them that she was the king's sister and insisted that the council quell the vicious rumors Tyrwhit spoke of. The council agreed to prosecute any gossipmongers she identified. Unmollified, Elizabeth explained that it was not her duty, but theirs to ferret out the guilty parties. For her to do so, would be "but breeding of an evil name of me that I am glad to punish them and so get the evil of the people, which thing I would be loathe to have."

The questioning went on for nearly two months. A few times, Tyrwhit thought he caught a glimpse of the blood rushing to Elizabeth's cheeks, but it was his vanity playing tricks on him. "I do see it in her face that she is guilty," he wrote to the council. The pale-skinned, red-headed young girl remained composed, her unblemished face a smooth, even blank slate. There was no blushing, no wringing of the hands, no twirling of the hair, no tapping of the feet that could be taken as signs of guilt. Instead, Elizabeth met his eyes with a look of defiance. At times, the accused became indignant, turning the tables on her accuser and demanding an apology for his mistreatment of her. Losing patience, but unwilling to admit defeat, Tyrwhit resorted to espionage in the form of a young woman who was introduced into the household for the sole purpose of eliciting information from the princess. Elizabeth was cordial to the mole but did not confide in her.

CONFESSIONS AND CONTRITION

Confined in the cold, dank tower and subjected to intense interrogations, Tom Parry broke down and confessed that Seymour was attempting to woo the princess and secure her hand in marriage. Parry also admitted that the admiral had made inquires about the princess's finances. He said that the governess Kat Ashley had encouraged Seymour in his pursuit. When confronted, the governess accused Parry of being a "false wench," and reminded him that he had promised her he would "never confess it to death."

The situation proved too much for Ashley, and she confessed everything she knew about Seymour's intentions toward Elizabeth. Ashley was protective of Elizabeth, but not immune to Seymour's charms. When he assured her that the Privy Council would approve of the marriage, she foolishly believed him.

Armed with Ashley and Parry's confessions, Tyrwhit confronted the princess. Her face grew hot as Tyrwhit spoke of the frolicking and romping that went on between Elizabeth and her former stepfather. When Tyrwhit told her that Parry had betrayed Ashley by revealing the details she confided to him, Elizabeth remarked, "It was a great matter for him to promise such a promise, and to break it." As for Kat Ashley, she had recounted everything—the unseemly morning visits to Elizabeth's bedchamber, the peculiar incident in the garden, and Seymour's plans to wed the teenager. For Elizabeth, this information was proof not of guilt but of her own foolish girlhood behavior. She had been flattered by Seymour's attentions but would never deign to defy the wishes of her late father or the Privy Council.

"She was much abased and half breathless," Tyrwhit reported to Protector Edward Seymour. When Elizabeth regained her composure, she avowed that there was nothing so much in their confessions as to implicate her in any secret plot to marry Seymour. She insisted that she would never consent to marry without the express permission and blessing of the Privy Council. Nor would her servants encourage her to do so.

Tyrwhit informed the princess that his wife was replacing Kat Ashley as her governess. Elizabeth burst into angry tears, explaining that she had done nothing to warrant such punishment. To replace Ashley was to tell the country she had been found guilty of bad behavior. When Elizabeth's tears had dried, she agreed

Elizabeth steadfastly declared her innocence when accused of plotting to unseat both her predecessors to the throne.
Princess Elizabeth (1533–1603) at the Tower (oil on canvas), Hillingford, Robert Alexander (1825-1904) / Private Collection / Photo © Bonhams, London, UK / The Bridgeman Art Library International

to write out a confession. Tyrwhit, who was eager to be discharged from his position, breathed a sigh of relief. He had been flummoxed by the tactics and tantrums of his charge. However, Tyrwhit was crestfallen when he read the so-called confession. Elizabeth admitted she was aware of the gossip about her relationship with Seymour, and that her attendants had informed her of his interest in marrying her. She also noted that on one occasion Seymour told her he would like to

visit her. The "confession" was nothing more than a detailed accounting of flirtation and gossip.

"[W]hen doth any more things happen in my mind which I have forgotten I assure your Grace I will declare them most willingly," Elizabeth wrote, "for I would not (as I trust you have not) so evil a opinion of me that I would conceal anything that I knew, for it were no purpose; and surely forgetfulness may well cause me to hide things, but undoubtedly else I will declare all that I know."

Reluctantly, Tyrwhit acknowledged he had met his match, writing of Elizabeth, "She hath a very good wit and nothing is gotten of her but by great policy." Elizabeth was cleared of charges. Her servants Ashley and Parry were exonerated and reinstated in her employ. Admiral Seymour was not so lucky. Found guilty of treason, he was executed on the Tower Green. Upon hearing of his death, Elizabeth is said to have remarked, "This day died a man with much wit and very little judgement."

The Seymour affair, as it has come to be known, was Elizabeth's rite of passage into adulthood.

THE PRINCESS BECOMES A QUEEN

Elizabeth Tudor ascended the throne on November 17, 1558. She was twenty-six years old and had outlived her half siblings Edward and Mary, both of whom died during their reign. Elizabeth was exceptionally popular with the English people. Hordes of commoners filled the streets to greet her as she passed by in her litter, presenting her with nosegays and home-baked treats and shouting, "God save Queen Elizabeth!"

Elizabeth was gracious, receiving their wishes and presents with great and genuine gratitude. She credited much of her success to the people. "Though God hath raised me high, yet this I count the glory of my crown: that I have reigned with your loves," declared the new queen. "And though you have had, and may have, many mightier and wiser princes sitting in this seat; yet you never had, nor shall have any that will love you better."

Early on, Elizabeth adopted a policy of moderation. A court advisor counseled the young queen to be noncommittal in matters of state so that "neither the old nor new should know what you mean." Elizabeth took this advice to heart. Throughout her reign, she frustrated the Privy Council with what it perceived as womanly indecisiveness. In fact, Elizabeth turned hesitancy into an art form and a powerful political policy. She often commented, "I see, and say nothing." This policy allowed her to successfully navigate her way through potential political minefields. By taking not taking sides, she was able to remain in good standing with all of the council members.

Known as the "Virgin Queen," Elizabeth never married. She is believed to have enjoyed several dalliances and to have viewed her moniker in symbolic, rather than literal terms. The queen used her matrimonial status to her advantage, accepting suitors and hinting that she was genuinely considering marriage to several royal candidates. It is likely that Elizabeth had no intention of marrying. She was strong and independent and enjoyed her position as England's sole monarch. To marry would have reduced her power, her status, and her independence.

The England that Elizabeth inherited was on the brink of bankruptcy. Her half siblings King Edward and later Queen Mary had involved the country in several unsuccessful military campaigns. Elizabeth kept a tight lid of the country's coffers, appointed brilliant strategists and economists to the council, and signed off on fewer military campaigns. England's greatest victory occurred during her reign, when in 1588 the country defeated the formidable Spanish Armada.

The arts flourished under Elizabeth, a well-read woman who spoke several languages and supported the English theater. William Shakespeare and Christopher Marlowe made their mark during what has come to be known as the Elizabethan Age. By the time Elizabeth died in March 1603, England had been transformed into a rich world power. The fifth and last of the Tudor line, Elizabeth was succeeded by her cousin, James I.

CHAPTER FOUR

SAMUEL DE CHAMPLAIN, 1567–1635: A HORRIFYING AND UNFORGETTABLE ENCOUNTER WITH NEW WORLD INDIANS

During an expedition to Mexico, Samuel de Champlain saw how the Spanish brutalized the Indians. That experience made a lasting impression. Three years later, when the king of France sent de Champlain to Canada to establish a French colony, de Champlain treated the Indian tribes he encountered as friends and allies.

On a Sunday morning in 1599, Samuel de Champlain walked to the church in a Mexican village to hear Mass. Inside he joined a congregation of Spanish colonists and Indians. The Spanish stood in the front, closest to the altar, while the Indians stood behind them. At the appointed time, the priest, accompanied by two altar boys, entered the sanctuary and genuflected before the altar. But instead of beginning the familiar ritual, the priest drew a sheet of paper from beneath his vestments and began to read a list of names. One by one the Indians in the congregation raised their hands as they heard their names. But to a few names there was no response; in those cases the priest made a mark on his list. Once the priest had finished, he replaced the paper inside his pocket and began the prayers of the Mass.

The moment the liturgy was over, de Champlain noticed an official of the parish—known as the fiscal—hurrying out of church. He was followed by the congregation, most of whom lingered in the churchyard. In a few minutes, the parish priest joined them.

In a short time, the fiscal returned with a few Indians—the ones who had not come to church that morning. The priest asked each one why he or she had been

In Mexico de Champlain saw church officials beat Indians who failed to attend Mass. In New France de Champlain took a different approach, treating the Indians as friends, allies, and mentors. The Granger Collection, New York

Etched by M.M.

absent. Those who had a good reason he excused, but there were a few whose answers did not satisfy him. At the priest's order, the fiscal took a stick and beat the truants across their backs, giving each thirty or forty blows. Before the church door. In front of all their neighbors and friends.

"This is the system that is maintained to keep them in religion," de Champlain wrote in his journal, "in which they remain, partly from fear of being beaten."

The incident that Sunday morning in a Mexican village made a deep impression on de Champlain. At this point, of course, he had no vision of himself as an empire-builder in New France. He had come to the Spanish colonies seeking any information that his king might find valuable. But the way the priest and the fiscal treated the Indians, and the stories he heard about the severity of the Inquisition, violated de Champlain's sense of justice. He had very limited experience with the Indians of the Americas, but on that Sunday morning he came to the realization that if the Spanish model prevailed, nothing but resentment and animosity would exist between the European colonists and the people of the New World.

The sight of the Indians being beaten for missing Mass affected de Champlain not least because he was a convert to Catholicism himself. De Champlain and his family were Huguenots, French Protestants, but about the year 1593 de Champlain renounced his Protestant faith and asked to be received into the Catholic Church. Conversions of convenience—either to one faith or another— were commonplace in Reformation Europe, but de Champlain was sincere. For the rest of his life, he was an exemplary Catholic who became more and more devout with each passing year. Keeping converts on such a short leash, then, and having them beaten when they failed to come to church seemed to de Champlain more likely to make the Indians resentful than devoted to their new religion.

There was one consolation—at least the Indians were no longer subject to the Inquisition. In his journal, de Champlain recorded, "At the commencement of his conquests [the king of Spain] had established the Inquisition amongst them." The Inquisition treated the Indians as unrepentant heretics, burning many at the stake. Meanwhile countless more Indians were killed outright by the Spanish, were so cruelly mistreated that they died of the abuse, or were made slaves. To escape these horrors, some Indians fled into the mountains; any Spanish troops who pursued them the Indians killed, then cooked and ate in a ritual meal.

Realizing at last that such mistreatment of the Indians was counter-productive, the king of Spain withdrew the Inquisition and ordered the colonial government

c. 1567–1570
Samuel de Champlain is born in Brouage, France.

1587
Joins French army in its war against Spain and the Catholic League.
1598
After peace is declared, sails with his uncle to return Spanish prisoners from Blavet, France, to Cádiz, Spain.
1599–1602
Joins a Spanish fleet sailing to the New World. Visits the Caribbean, Mexico, and Panama.

1602
Returns to France. Inherits his uncle's estate. Henry IV names de Champlain geographer to the king.
1603
Travels with Indian guides up the Saguenay River in what is now Quebec, and follows the Saint Lawrence River to the Lachine Rapids near the present-day city of Montreal.
1604–1607
Maps the coastline of Acadia and identifies possible locations for settlements.
1605
Is one of the founders of Port Royal on the Bay of Fundy, the first permanent European settlement in North America.

1608
Founds Quebec City and forms alliances with the Hurons, Algonquin, and Montagnais tribes.
July 30, 1609
Joins his Indian allies in a battle against their enemies, the Iroquois. De Champlain shoots and kills two Iroquois chiefs and an Iroquois warrior, thereby making the Iroquois the enemies of the French in North America.
1610
Back in France, marries Hélène Boullé, age twelve; de Champlain is about forty years old. Hélène's parents insist the couple must wait two years before living together.
1611
Returns to Canada and founds Montreal.

1613
Follows and maps the Ottawa River, hoping it will be the Northwest Passage to the Pacific Ocean.
1615
Explores Lake Huron and Lake Ontario. Wounded in an attack on an Iroquois village.
1616
Recuperates in a Huron village where he records the life and customs of the tribe.
1617–1620
Makes several journeys to France to recruit colonists. In 1620, Hélène visits Quebec.

1628
In war between England and France, de Champlain compelled to surrender Quebec to the English.
1630
Peace treaty restores Quebec to France.
1633
Returns to Quebec as governor.
December 25, 1635
Dies in his house in Quebec City.

1640
The chapel built over de Champlain's tomb burns to the ground; the grave is lost and never found.

By the late 16th century, the king of Spain had come to the conclusion that subjecting American Indians to the rigors of the Inquisition was counter-productive. He issued an edict curtailing the Inquisiton's authority in the New World.

The Inquisition in Spain (w/c on paper), Champlain, Samuel de (1567–1635) / Brown University Library, Providence, Rhode Island, USA / The Bridgeman Art Library

in Mexico to allow the Indians "personal liberty, granting them a more mild and tolerable rule of life, to bring them to the knowledge of God and the belief of the Holy Church. For if they had continued still to chastise them according to the rigor of the said Inquisition," de Champlain wrote, "they would have caused them all to die by fire."

When de Champlain established a colony in New France, laying the foundation for present-day Canada, there was no wholesale slaughter of the Indians, nor were they enslaved, nor were they marched to the baptismal font at swordpoint. De Champlain and his fellow French colonists lived peaceably with the tribes (the exception being the Iroquois). French Jesuit missionary priests worked tirelessly to present the Catholic faith in a way the Indians would understand, but they never compelled any Indian to convert. And if an Indian convert lost his religious fervor, or returned to the traditional religion of his tribe, he wasn't hauled before a priest to be beaten.

A FRENCH SPY IN NEW SPAIN

In 1598, when de Champlain was about twenty-eight years old (the exact date of his birth is a subject for debate), he became fascinated by the quest for the passage across the Americas that would lead to the Pacific Ocean and onward to the riches of Asia. French explorer Jacques Cartier and English explorer Martin Frobisher had searched for the Northwest Passage in North America and returned home disappointed. De Champlain thought that he might have better luck if he searched for a Southwest Passage in South America.

This would be a risky venture. The lands that de Champlain planned to explore were in the hands of the Spanish, who did not welcome foreigners. In fact, Spanish colonial officials tended to regard non-Spanish visitors to South America as spies, and the penalties for spying included hanging, life imprisonment, or a life sentence chained to an oar as a galley slave. If de Champlain were to travel around the Spanish colonies, he would need a plausible excuse to be there.

A recently concluded war between France and Spain gave de Champlain the necessary pretext. One of the articles of the peace treaty required an exchange of prisoners, but there were so many Spanish prisoners in the town of Blavet in Brittany that the government in Madrid found it expedient to charter French ships to bring the Spanish troops home. One of the chartered ships, the *Saint-Julien*, was captained by a renowned seaman named Guillaume Allene, who was de Champlain's uncle.

It was a big ship of 500 tons (454,000 kg) that had been used most recently as a fishing boat, bringing barrels of salted cod from the waters off the coast of Newfoundland to France. It must have smelled awful, but de Champlain was willing to overlook the stench if the ship would get him to Spain. He signed on with his uncle. Although de Champlain had training as a sailor (de Champlain's father had been a sea captain, too), it appears that he had no real job aboard the *Saint-Julien*. He was just tagging along until he could find a way to get to the New World.

Uncle Guillaume unloaded his cargo of Spanish soldiers at Cádiz, a city on Spain's southwest coast and one of the country's primary ports of call for ships traveling to and from the Spanish colonies in the Americas. De Champlain and his uncle's timing was excellent. The English Earl of Cumberland had just seized Puerto Rico, an island that lay directly in the path of the trade and treasure route between the Americas and Spain. The Spanish were eager to recapture their colony, but they were short on ships. Building and outfitting an armada would take too long, so they extended the charter agreement with the French captains.

Allene had other commitments that prevented him from sailing to Puerto Rico, but he was content to permit a Spanish captain to take command of the *Saint-Julien*, on the condition that his nephew, de Champlain, remain aboard to keep an eye on his uncle's interests. The commander of the rescue mission, Don Francisco Coloma, agreed, and so at last Champlain the Frenchman had his excuse for visiting the Spanish colonies.

THE FIRST ENCOUNTER

De Champlain first set foot in the New World on the island of Guadeloupe, where he rowed ashore with a boat full of Spanish sailors to gather fruit and replenish the ship's water casks. "As we landed," he wrote in his journal, "we saw more than 300 savages." De Champlain waded through the surf toward the Indians, eager to talk with them, but at his approach they "fled into the mountains, without our being able to overtake a single one of them, they being more nimble in running."

This was de Champlain's first experience with the native people of the Americas, and they would fascinate him for the rest of his life. Years later in Canada, de Champlain would regard the Indians as people who could reveal to the French the marvels of the New World, just as the French had marvels from the Old World that they could share with the Indians.

Unlike many of de Champlain's contemporaries, he did not regard the Indians as subhuman. Many Europeans used that notion as an excuse for mistreating and enslaving the Indians, Africans, and other non-Europeans. It was a convenient point of view that slave traders and slave owners would cling to for another 300 years, until the abolition of slavery in the nineteenth century.

But de Champlain's point of view was not unique to him. Others in the Americas and in Europe recognized that the Indians were as human as they were. One of these was Pope Paul III, who in 1537 published a decree, *Sublimis Deus*, in which he declared, "the Indians themselves indeed are true men [who]… should not be deprived of their liberty or of their possessions." Paul III hoped his decree would put an end to the slave trade in the Americas. It proved instead to be a well-intentioned but futile gesture. No papal document could compel the colonists to give up their slaves.

Readers of de Champlain's journals will notice that he refers to the Indians as "savages," but he uses the term in a descriptive rather than a disparaging sense. Relativism, the idea that one school of thought or one way of life is as good as any other, was virtually unknown in the sixteenth and seventeenth centuries. De Champlain found a great deal to admire in the Indians, but he would never have agreed that their way of life was comparable to how Europeans lived, or that the religion of the Indians was just as good as Christianity. When de Champlain called the Indians "savages," he wasn't being insulting. He was just making a precise distinction between Indians and Europeans. Once de Champlain reached Canada and came in contact with the Huron, Algonquin, and Iroquois, he discovered to his surprise (and perhaps his amusement) that these northern tribes considered the French to be inferior.

Samuel de Champlain made his first visit to the Americas when he was about 28 years old. Instantly he was astonished by the possibilities of the New World and fascinated by the culture of the Native Americans. Time & Life Pictures/Getty Images

IMAGINING A PATH BETWEEN THE SEAS

Although de Champlain was a member of a Spanish expedition and essentially a guest of Spain's colonial government in the Americas, he never ceased studying any facet of Spanish colonial life that would be useful to France. We know that de Champlain was acquainted with his king, Henry IV, although where and when they met is a mystery. Throughout his life, de Champlain was a loyal servant of the French crown, and in the Spanish colonies he tried to collect information that Henry IV would find useful, particularly if the king planned to establish French colonies in the vast lands north of New Spain.

For example, in Europe at this time there was an enormous market for the magnificent scarlet dye known as cochineal. Everyone knew it came only from Central America, but the Spanish guarded the source of cochineal as a state secret. During de Champlain's visit to Mexico, he believed that he had learned the secret: Cochineal was derived from a tropical plant! He was wrong. Cochineal is derived from an insect, in fact a parasite, which infests Opuntia cacti. This

may be a case of de Champlain getting his facts wrong, but it is also possible that he was deliberately misled by some Spaniard.

De Champlain missed the mark again when he confused cacao, another product of the Americas much coveted in Europe as the source of cocoa and chocolate, with agave, a plant used to make tequila.

But de Champlain the spy was not a complete failure. He made an excursion to Panama, to Portobello, a fortified harbor town he described as "the most evil and unhealthy residence in the world." Half of the troops sent to garrison the two forts that guarded the entrance to Portobello died, which was a statistic that de Champlain attributed to the stifling heat, humidity, and heavy rainfall. He would not have known about the swarms of mosquitoes that carried the deadly yellow fever virus.

De Champlain wished to explore Panama, but his Spanish hosts refused him permission. Nonetheless, sitting at Portobello, he discovered that this unhealthy place was the outlet for the treasure of Peru and Bolivia. Spanish treasure ships sailed their cargo of gold and silver along South America's Pacific coast up to Panama where the bullion was loaded onto mules and carried overland to Portobello. De Champlain observed, "If an enemy of the king of Spain held the said Portobello, he could prevent anything from leaving Peru."

And de Champlain noticed something else: If a canal were dug across the narrowest part of the Isthmus of Panama, ships could sail to the Pacific Ocean and Asia much more quickly and safely than making the long, treacherous voyage around South America.

SETTLING NEW FRANCE

The year 1602, when de Champlain returned home to France, brought him both sorrow and great good fortune. Allene died and left his nephew his entire estate. Overnight de Champlain became wealthy. He also went to the court of Henry IV to present the king with his *A Brief Discourse of the Most Remarkable Things that Samuel de Champlain of Brouage Reconnoitered in the West Indies*, a work that is part journal, part travel narrative, and part intelligence report. Henry IV was delighted with de Champlain's work, awarded him a pension that assured de Champlain

France's King Henri IV shared Champlain's belief that France could be revitalized and enriched by the vast resources of what is now Canada and the United States. Portrait of Henri IV (1553–1610) King of France, in a black costume, c.1610 (panel), Pourbus, Frans II (1569–1622) / Louvre, Paris, France / Lauros / Giraudon / The Bridgeman Art Library International

an annual income for the rest of his life, and ordered him to remain at court as geographer to the king.

Blessed with royal favor and a large income, de Champlain was in a position to do as he wished, and by great good luck his interests corresponded with those of his king. Henry IV and de Champlain both believed that France could be revitalized—not to mention enriched—if it founded colonies in New France. The territory was vast: It included modern Canada from the Maritime Provinces to the Rocky Mountains, and a large portion of what is now the United States stretching roughly from the Appalachians to the Rockies and down to the present-day state of Louisiana.

In 1602, there was no French settlement in New France, but French ships sailed there regularly to harvest codfish, furs, and timber. Both Henry IV and de Champlain agreed that there must be more to the resources of New France than this. However, this opinion was not shared by the king's minister of the treasury, the Duc de Sully, who asserted that "great riches are never found above forty degrees [of latitude]."

In addition to wealth, Henry IV hoped to establish an ideal society in New France, where Catholics and Protestants would live peacefully side by side and religious persecution would be unknown, where estates would be granted to nobles and gentlemen based on their merits rather than their rank, where the ordinary citizens would be happy, prosperous, and tolerant. To this de Champlain would have added that in New France the Indians would be treated as the colonists' respected teachers or mentors, they would not be massacred or enslaved, and whether they converted to Catholicism or kept to their own religious tradition, they would be regarded as friends and neighbors. For King Henry IV and de Champlain, New France was a second Eden where mankind would make a fresh start.

And so in 1603, with the encouragement of his king, de Champlain set sail for New France with ambitious, even visionary, plans to create a new, just society in the New World.

On his first exploration of New France in 1603, Champlain relied on Indian guides, who led him deep into the interior of what is now Quebec province via the Saguenay and St. Lawrence rivers. Champlain Exploring the Canadian Wilderness, 1603, from 'The American Continent and its Inhabitants before its Discovery by Columbus', by Anne C. Cady, 1893 (litho) (b&w photo), American School, (19th century) / Library of Congress, Washington D.C., USA / The Bridgeman Art Library International

CHAPTER FIVE

GEORGE WASHINGTON, 1732–1799: LEARNING TO LEAD THE HARD WAY

In the backwoods of Pennsylvania in 1754, a young George Washington surrendered for the only time in his career. That day's painful lessons guided him to Revolutionary War victory and the United States' first presidency.

Using axes and shovels more than musketry, colonial troops under Lieutenant Colonel George Washington were fighting their way through the Pennsylvania wilderness in the spring of 1754. Towering hardwoods and thick undergrowth stood in their way, and progress on their mission was slow. The troops were endeavoring to cut a road that would allow artillery and supply wagons to move through the forest. The farthest Washington's troopers could advance was only a few miles each day. The territory was not called Pennsylvania—"Penn's Woods"—for nothing.

Western Pennsylvania was nominally Indian hunting grounds, mostly those of the Shawnee and Delaware tribes, allied with the Six Nations of the Iroquois Confederacy. But the empire-building French and English had staked their own claims and counterclaims among the oaks and maples. The territory was not unknown; it had been explored and traveled since the 1600s by scouts and pioneers, as well as missionaries, trappers, hunters, and fishermen. One early visitor had been Washington, as an apprentice surveyor inspecting the lands on behalf of Virginia's largest landholder, Lord Thomas Fairfax. He had set aside his transit and level to lead the expedition.

Washington, from a Virginia plantation family, was only twenty-two years old, and just a little over a year before had inherited the family plantation from his brother Lawrence. But at six feet, four inches (193 cm), Washington was an impos-

Young George Washington headed into backwoods Pennsylvania in 1753 to warn the French against building forts in English-claimed territory.

ing figure. With his patrician bearing, strong voice, and air of self-confidence, he seemed a born leader. Now he was commanding a force of 300 militiamen, some of them twice his age. His force was also accompanied by 100 Indians led by an Iroquois chief, Tanacharison, known to the English settlers as the "Half-King."

Washington had no military training, had never heard a shot fired in anger or a war whoop. He had been commissioned only a few months before by Virginia Colonial Governor Robert Dinwiddie. Some of Washington's men were militia veterans trained in military life in the cultivated farmlands of Virginia, but others were attracted by Dinwiddie's promised enlistment bonus of 100 acres of frontier land. They, too, were unfamiliar with wilderness fighting. Some had never seen an Indian nor fired a musket. But the young officer and his detail had been entrusted with an important mission, complying with the wishes of the English king, George II.

Explorers had identified what was christened the "Forks of the Ohio," where two large rivers rushing out of the mountains converged to form a larger river (now called the Ohio). The Ohio then flowed into a giant stream, the Mississippi, called by the local tribes "the Father of Waters," which took a 1,000-mile (1,600 km) course to the sea. The network of rivers drained rich interior lands and opened the heartland of the continent to settlement. Whichever power controlled the "Forks of the Ohio" could then command the whole fertile rivershed. It offered the victorious power untold resources, an outlet for restive populations where colonists could enrich themselves.

Washington's task was to ensure that those lands would be English lands, not French. It was a mission that was to teach him harsh lessons, but eventually lead him to the presidency of the United States.

THE MOUNTAIN BARRIER

In the mid-eighteenth century, English settlements were largely confined to the Atlantic coast. A northeast–southwest barrier of rugged mountains, the Appalachian chain, blocked their westward expansion, not to mention unfriendly Indian tribes. And the French had planted a firm flag in the northern part of the continent, Canada, and at points along the Mississippi. But the English colonial population was growing—rapidly—and expansion seemed vital. And London, with its great sea power, was in an expansionist mood. Thus Washington was now making a second trip into the "Ohio Country."

February 22, 1732
George Washington is born in Westmoreland County, Virginia, to Augustine and Mary Ball Washington.

March 1748
Starts surveying career on behalf of Lord Thomas Fairfax in the Shenandoah Valley, Virginia, frontier.

July 1752
Inherits family Mount Vernon plantation on the death of his brother Lawrence.

November 1753
Travels to a French outpost in Pennsylvania, Fort LeBoeuf, to warn the French they are intruding on English-claimed territory and must withdraw. The message is rejected.

April 18, 1754
As militia lieutenant colonel, leads 300 men in an offensive to drive the French out of the "Ohio Country." Builds "Fort Necessity," but is defeated in battle there and forced to surrender, the only surrender in his career.

June 1755
As aide-de-camp, accompanies English General Edward Braddock and 2,400 "redcoats" in a new effort to push out the French. Braddock refuses Washington's advice and attempts to fight in the stand-up European fashion, and the troops are slaughtered by the French and Indians fighting backwoods style. Braddock is killed.

September 1755
Acclaimed as hero after Braddock's Field, promoted to full colonel at age twenty-three, and named commander in chief of Virginia militia.

June 1758
Commands 700 militia from four colonies as English General John Forbes overwhelms the French in Pennsylvania.

September 1758
Resigns his military command to return to Mount Vernon as a planter. Is elected to the Virginia House of Burgesses.

January 6, 1759
Marries the widow Martha Dandridge Custis.

March 5, 1770
English troops fired on anti-tax protestors in "Boston Massacre." Three are killed and eight wounded, two fatally.

December 16, 1773
"Boston Tea Party" staged to protest colonial taxes by Britain.

September 5, 1774
Chosen Virginia delegate to the First Continental Congress.

April 19, 1775
After Paul Revere's ride to warn the populace, colonial militia and redcoats exchange fire at Lexington and Concord, and the Revolutionary War begins.

May 10, 1775
Is delegate to Second Continental Congress, which names him commander in chief of the colonial army.

July 4, 1776
Congress proclaims the Declaration of Independence.

December 26, 1776
In daring Christmas night attack, Washington and troops cross ice-choked Delaware River to surprise and defeat mercenary Hessian troops at Trenton.

October 17, 1777
British General John Burgoyne, invading from Canada with a large army, surrenders at Saratoga, New York. France now recognizes U.S. independence and offers aid.

December 19, 1777
Takes bedraggled and dispirited army into winter quarters at Valley Forge, Pennsylvania, but holds the army together for later success.

July 11, 1780
French troops arrive to support the United States.

March 2, 1781
Articles of Confederation is signed, formally establishing the U.S. government.

October 19, 1781
Penned into a peninsula at Yorktown, Virginia, by the U.S. and French armies and the French navy, British commander Lord Charles Cornwallis surrenders, effectively ending hostilities.

September 3, 1783
Treaty of Paris officially ends the war.

May 25, 1787
Washington presides over the Constitutional Convention.

September 17, 1787
Constitution is ratified.

April 1, 1789
Washington is sworn in as the first president of the new United States.

September 1793
Reelected to a second term as president.

September 1796
Delivers farewell address, declaring that he will not serve a third term and retires to Mount Vernon.

December 14, 1799
Dies at Mount Vernon at age sixty-seven, apparently of a throat infection followed by bloodletting treatment. The exact cause was controversial.

The year before, in the fall of 1753, Governor Dinwiddie called the young Washington, then only twenty-one, to the colonial capital at Williamsburg. Scouts had reported that the French were constructing a chain of forts from "New France"—Canada—toward the "Forks of the Ohio." They had already established one fort on the southern shore of Lake Erie, Fort Presque Isle, on what the English considered their side of the lake, and had just completed another 30 miles (48 km) farther south, clearly in English-claimed territory, called Fort LeBoeuf (now Waterford, Pennsylvania). They had begun preliminary work on still a third, Fort Machault, at the confluence of French Creek and the Allegheny River (now Franklin, Pennsylvania). The Allegheny was the south-flowing tributary that joined with the north-flowing Monongahela to form the Ohio at the Forks. Fort Machault, deeper into English-claimed territory, would give the French water access to the Forks, the Ohio, and the whole rich interior. England, with its dreams of empire, could not countenance such a threat. Certainly not.

Dinwiddie knew of Washington's surveying on behalf of Lord Fairfax. The young man obviously had experience with the backwoods frontier. That day in 1753, Dinwiddie asked: Would Washington undertake a most important diplomatic mission to warn the French they were trespassing on English soil? Ambitious, impetuous, and eager to make a name for himself, Washington readily assented.

The hardwoods were already turning color, and there was a smell of the forthcoming winter in the air when Washington set out. He was accompanied by Christopher Gist, an experienced frontiersman, scout, and trader who had set up a small farm and trading post and who was familiar with the territory; two others; plus some Native Americans. It was an arduous journey, made more difficult by an early winter. Snow fell and the party continued on snowshoes. They arrived at the site of Fort Machault, where the local French commander declined to accept the warning message; any such high-level communication must go to his superior at Fort LeBoeuf. Washington pressed on for another 30 rugged (48 km) miles, arriving at Fort LeBoeuf in mid-December.

LONG LIVE THE KING!

The LeBoeuf commander, Jacques Lepardeur de Sainte-Pierre, received them graciously. He accepted Dinwiddie's note and invited the travelers to dine with him and sample fine wine from his well-stocked cellar. France and England were friends, their host noted, and a diplomatic mission from a friendly country must be treated courteously and with proper ceremony. Let us have another toast to the English king! But no, he added politely, he could not agree that the French were intruding on English territory and should withdraw.

The area had been claimed by France, it was the property of His Royal Majesty Louis XV, and besides, the French had taken physical possession, and they had no intention of relinquishing their foothold. De Sainte-Pierre shook hands with Washington and thanked him for his visit, then sent him back to the snow and ice, but not before the erstwhile surveyor had taken detailed notes about the fort, which might be valuable in case of future military action.

Because diplomatic niceties hadn't worked, Dinwiddie asked Washington to try again, with a little more of a mailed fist. Scouts had informed Dinwiddie that the eager French had actually reached the Forks and were already constructing a fort there. They had actually evicted a few English who were building their own fort. "Fort Duquesne," named for the governor of New France, would control the vital waterways as well as the Ohio country and the North American interior— an ominous threat to English interests.

Washington was a recent recruit to the Virginia militia. Dinwiddie nonetheless commissioned the young man a field-grade officer with orders to lead a contingent back into the Ohio Country. This time Washington's task was to oust the French from the fort and establish English sovereignty. The Union Jack must fly over the Forks of the Ohio.

Washington first took his men to the English frontier outpost at Wills Creek (now Cumberland, Maryland). This was the jumping-off place for the push over the Pennsylvania mountains, and it was also the headquarters for Washington's nominal superior, an ex-mathematics professor named Major Joshua Fry. (Because Washington was in the militia, but Fry was a British officer, Fry outranked Washington.) Unfortunately, the portly Major Fry had fallen from his horse, was afflicted with gout, and was too injured to travel, so full command of the offensive devolved upon the untried Washington. On April 18, 1754, resplendent in the bright red, full-dress colonial officer's tunic with lace cuffs, a new sword gleaming at his side, Washington set off with his small force to chop his way into Pennsylvania.

The immediate destination was Redstone Creek (now Brownsville, Pennsylvania), where it flowed into the Monongahela River, the Ohio's north-flowing tributary. That would place them 30 miles (48 km) below the fort, with direct water access.

They were still short of Redstone Creek on May 24, when one of the scouts of his Iroquois ally, the Half-King, brought disturbing news. Four hundred pale-faced men carrying muskets, slashing bush, and chopping trees could scarcely go unnoticed in the normally hushed and untrammeled wilderness. Not surprisingly, the French garrison at Fort Duquesne had learned of the English advance and was sending out a welcoming party. Thousands of French soldiers were said to be marching to intercept Washington's little army.

Washington was sure the numbers were overestimated, but he immediately took forty militiamen plus Indian allies under the Half-King on a nighttime maneuver to investigate. At dawn, a wisp of campfire smoke led them to a precipice overlooking a secluded rocky glen traversed by a mountain stream. Washington stationed his men on heights overlooking the glen. Below, a sleepy and half-dressed French patrol was just waking up. One man was shaving. Another was preparing breakfast. Some were still rolled up in blankets, their arms stacked.

A VOLLEY SETS THE WORLD ON FIRE

There are French and English versions of what happened next. The French insisted that the English, unprovoked, fired on defenseless men. Washington believed that a French soldier spotted an officer in his eye-catching uniform, possibly Washington himself. The soldier shouted an alarm, and another soldier fired, after which the firing became general on both sides.

It was a one-sided fight. The English and the Half-King's warriors swooped down into the glen, firing and taking prisoners, including the unit commander, Ensign Joseph Coulon de Jumonville. Washington watched in horror as the Half-King knocked Jumonville to the ground, pinned his arms, cleaved his skull with a tomahawk, and then scalped him. Ten French were killed in the encounter, and twenty-one were taken prisoner. One of Washington's men was killed and several wounded—Washington's first exposure to battle casualties.

"This little skirmish," as Washington was to call it later, was to launch what Americans called the French and Indian War and, after it subsequently leapfrogged to Europe and brought in other nations, the Seven Years' War. Eminent historian Horace Walpole, son of a British prime minister, ringingly declared, "The volley fired by a young Virginian in the backwoods of America set the world on fire."

Washington collected his men and withdrew south with the rest of his force to a grassy, swampy area known as the Great Meadows. In a dispatch back to Governor

Dinwiddie, Washington described the open area of tall grass and small bushes "a charming field for an encounter," and he asked again for reinforcements and supplies. Meanwhile Washington rallied his troops to prepare for the French attack that he was sure was forthcoming.

Washington directed them to cut seventy-five oak trees nine to ten inches (23 to 25 cm) in diameter into ten-foot (3 m) logs, split them lengthwise and axe them to a point at one end. These were driven into the ground upright in a 53-foot (16 m) circle, forming a crude stockade. A 14-foot-square (1.3 m²) log shelter was constructed in the center to store provisions, possessions, ammunition, and barrels of rum; it could also house one company of fifty men. A field was cleared by fire, and a 2½-foot-deep (76 cm) entrenchment dug around the stockade. Mindful of his shortages of men and supplies, Washington, with ironic humor, named it "Fort Necessity." The skeptical Half-King had another name. He derisively called it "that little thing in the meadow," and he advised Washington to retreat to Wills Creek. When Washington declined, the Half-King withdrew his men.

Washington in the scarlet uniform of a Virginia militia colonel. Some say the bright uniform attracted the attention of French snipers, whose firing touched off the French and Indian War. George Washington in the uniform of a Colonel of the Virginia Militia during the French & Indian War (1755–63) (colour litho), Peale, Charles Willson (1741–1827) (after) / Private Collection, Peter Newark American Pictures / The Bridgeman Art Library

But to Washington's immense relief, the long-promised reinforcements arrived—two more companies of Virginians plus two well-trained and well-equipped companies of South Carolina militiamen, numbering 100. They brought with them sixty head of cattle, a supply of powder and shot, and five days' ration of flour.

THE BATTLE IS JOINED

On the morning of July 3, 1754, scouts informed Washington that a "large" force was headed toward the little fort. Washington was perturbed. From the scout's description, Washington concluded that the force numbered at least 700. Reinforcements had increased his own strength to more than 700, but only about 300 were fit for duty, because of illness and injuries sustained during the road-clearing operation. Two companies of regulars from New York were said to be en route, but they were nowhere in sight. Washington was outnumbered nearly two to one. Moreover, ominous thunderheads were building overhead, threatening a huge rainstorm at any minute. But as U.S. Defense Secretary Donald Rumsfeld would say centuries later, "You go to war with the army you have, not the army you wish you had."

At 3 p.m., the first shots were fired. They came, however, not from a visible French army but from the woods abutting the stockade. The Virginians and Carolinians fired back, but their foes were invisible, hidden in brush or behind trees. The well-disciplined South Carolinians had been trained to fire on command, but their officers could not discern targets to shoot at. They had only the flash of musketry to go by. By the time the source could be spotted, the target had moved on. Many of their opponents were skilled Canadian foresters, accustomed to firing from ambush against game or marauding Native Americans. The men in the trenches came under constant fire. Washington himself, surveying the fighting from a parapet, narrowly escaped being hit.

The rains arrived in great downpours. Men in the trenches were soaked to the skin. Worse, their weapons and ammunition were soaked, too, and unable to fire. The trenches began to fill with water. Soon the troops were sloshing in knee-deep water and soft mud. Movement was an exercise in futility. Any organized resistance seemed useless, and casualties were mounting.

"DO YOU WISH TO TALK?"

As darkness arrived, Washington assayed the situation. One-third of his force was killed or wounded, and another one-fourth were ill. He was almost out of ammunition, and what little he had was useless. Then a French voice came out of the darkness: "*Voulez-vous parler?*" ("Do you wish to talk?")

Washington had brought with him a young Dutchman, Captain Jacob van Braam, who had also accompanied him to Fort LeBoeuf and served as his interpreter. Van Braam spoke or understood several languages, including French. The Americans ignored the first shouts, thinking them a ruse. Then Captain van Braam told Washington, "They are asking if you wish to talk terms. They will send an officer to discuss with you." Washington refused; he didn't want the French inside his lines to see his command's plight. When the refusal had been relayed, there came an answering shout. "If you will send an officer, he will be given safe conduct and returned safely," van Braam translated for Washington.

Washington agreed and sent van Braam and another officer. Trudging through the rain and mud, van Braam returned with the offer from the French commander, Captain Louis Coulon de Villiers, who happened to be the older half-brother of Jumonville. The English would be given honorable terms, he said. They would be treated with full military honors, allowed to march out of the fort in formation and with drums beating and bugles playing. They would be permitted to return safely and unmolested to "their own country." They must give up their cannon, ammunition, and *weapons de guerre*. They would not be held as prisoners but must agree not to return to the Ohio Country nor construct any buildings in the territory for one year from the date of surrender.

Washington insisted that the men must be allowed to keep their weapons, else they would be at the mercy of marauding Indians during their retreat. Van Braam dutifully returned to the French position. By the time he came back again to Washington, it was nearly midnight and raining harder than ever. Van Braam was clutching two paper copies of the surrender document written in French, but with the offending "weapons de guerre" lines excised.

The two men and aides stood in the rain while van Braam, his hands trembling, tried to decipher and translate the unfamiliar words by flickering candlelight. Translating from one language not his own to another strange tongue, he stumbled haltingly through the surrender conditions a few words at a time, Washington listening and nodding. Finally van Braam handed the papers to Washington. Unable to read French, Washington simply took them and signed, based on what he had heard.

But the Dutch–French speaker had made a serious and misleading error, which was to redound against Washington in subsequent propaganda. The preamble of the document had stated that the French had not come to trouble the peace between our nations but were merely acting to avenge the "assassination of one of our officers," meaning Jumonville.

Van Braam had apparently never previously encountered the French word "*l'assassin*" or the form in which it was used. Guessing from the context and translating hastily and uncomfortably in the wretched conditions, he had translated the word simply as "death" or "killing." By signing the surrender document, Washington was admitting that he and the English had committed the deliberate murder.

But his signature on the surrender document was not the only mistake the novice commander had made, as he himself and military historians were to concede later. Washington had situated Fort Necessity within easy musket range of the surrounding forest, allowing the skilled Canadian frontiersmen and Native Americans to selectively pick off the fort's entrenched defenders, while remaining well-protected by concealing shrubbery and trees. And Washington had chosen swampy ground, which was relatively dry in early July but quickly flooded in a rainstorm that drained into the trenches and hobbled the defenses.

HIS ONLY SURRENDER

The ignominious surrender was the only time in a historic military career that Washington surrendered. For him it was an important, if costly, learning experience. In June 1755, not quite twelve months later (violating his one-year parole, the French charged), Washington returned to the Ohio Country. The English sent one of their most seasoned commanders, General Edward Braddock, to take Fort Duquesne and drive the French out of the Forks once and for all. Washington, by now a full colonel, went along as Braddock's aide.

Ignoring Washington's advice, Braddock sent his redcoats, 2,400 strong and the largest army ever seen in North America, into battle the European way, in tight formation with drums beating and bugles blowing. But the English had not scouted the nearby woods. The result was a disaster, a virtual carbon copy of the Fort Necessity debacle. Behind every tree and shrub on Braddock's route there seemed to lurk a sharpshooter with a musket. Braddock himself was killed. Washington personally buried him.

But the two experiences formed Washington's character and enhanced his reputation. Governor Dinwiddie acclaimed him a hero and made permanent his promotion to full colonel. Washington, in turn, learned—the hard way—important lessons that would play a key role in his future. He recognized the importance of military organization and administration, as well as strategy, thorough preparation and leadership.

Washington returned once more, in July 1758, commanding four units of colonial militia when General John Forbes marched a formidable army directly across Pennsylvania from Philadelphia, drove the French out of Fort Duquesne, burned it, and replaced it with the British Fort Pitt, raising the Union Jack over the Forks of the Ohio.

When the American Revolution began, the seasoned Washington was the obvious choice for commander in chief of the continental army. He led the army to victory with the British surrender in 1781, then went on to become the first president of the new United States and "First in war, first in peace, and first in the hearts of his countrymen."

English general Edward Braddock was mortally wounded in an ill-starred effort to march on the French Fort Duquesne. Washington, his aide, officiated at his burial.

CHAPTER SIX

HORATIO NELSON, 1758–1805: BECOMING A HERO BY BREAKING THE RULES

The commodore saw a chance for a great victory. So what if the British code of warfare said otherwise?

It certainly wasn't the way things were usually done. On the morning of February 13, 1797, a Spanish fleet of twenty-seven warships, en route to join Napoleon's French fleet at Brest, France, rounded Cape Saint Vincent at the tip of the Iberian Peninsula and headed into the Atlantic. Waiting for the Spaniards, ready to pounce, was the British Mediterranean fleet commanded by Admiral Sir John Jervis. The British fleet consisted of only fifteen vessels against Spain's twenty-seven, which included the four-decker *Santissima Trinidad*, the largest warship in the world. Jervis was not at all intimidated. Soon signal pennants fluttered at the masthead of his flagship *Victory*, instructing the other vessels to form into line of battle and close on the Spanish. Thirteenth in line, third from the end, was the seventy-four-gun *Captain*.

Suddenly the *Captain* wheeled out of line, crossed behind the following vessel and headed directly toward the Spanish fleet. The British navy's permanent fighting instructions of 1744 expressly forbade such freelancing, and it had stiffened them after an admiral had been executed in 1757 for noncompliance. (Of course, the disobedient admiral had also lost the battle.)

Commodore Horatio Nelson of the *Captain* had a reputation for audacity, bravery, and bending the rules. He and Admiral Jervis had little respect for the Spanish, belittling their leadership and the training of their crews. Nelson believed he saw an opportunity here to score an important victory. The Spanish

Disobeying fleet protocol, Horatio Nelson audaciously maneuvered his warship into the French–Spanish battle line, leading to British victory in the battle of Cape St. Vincent. The Battle of Cape St. Vincent, 14th February 1797, Beechey, Richard Bridges (1808–95) / Private Collection, Photo © Bonhams, London, UK / The Bridgeman Art Library

ships were arranged in two lines some distance apart. Standing on deck with his sword drawn and resplendent in full commodore's regalia complete with tricorn hat, Nelson exhorted his cannoneers and took the *Captain* squarely between the two lines, firing from both sides as he came.

Two other ships fell out of line and followed, running a gauntlet of heavy Spanish fire at close range. The *Captain* was severely damaged, losing its mizzenmast and steerageway, with dead and wounded lying across their guns. The British fire crippled two Spanish vessels, the *San Jose* and the *San Nicolas*. As the *San Nicolas* came alongside to aid the *San Jose*, Nelson had another inspiration. Victory at sea in 1797 was achieved not only by long-range shelling but by close-range grappling, boarding, and taking the enemy vessel as a prize. Protocol dictated that a junior officer lead the boarding party. Commodore Nelson aimed to be in the thick of things, not standing aside as a cheerleader. As his crews used grappling irons to attach the two vessels, Nelson, brandishing his sword overhead, leaped from the *Captain* to the poop deck of the *San Jose*. Then, aware that the *San Jose* and *San Nicolas* were secured to each other, he immediately crossed over to the *San Nicolas*. The startled Spanish officers knelt in surrender and offered their swords to Nelson. A veteran crewman tucked the swords under his arm and others hoisted the Union Jack over both ships.

It was the first time in English history that two prizes had been captured at one swoop. The tactic went into the navy manuals as "the Patented Nelson Bridge for Capturing First-Rates [meaning "warships of the line"] as Prizes." It also launched the legend of "Nelson Touch," which would make him England's leading naval hero, his statue atop a towering monument in London's Trafalgar Square.

A SEAFARING PRODIGY

Horace Nelson—he changed his name to Horatio when he was nineteen—joined His Majesty's Navy at a tender age. He was the sixth of fourteen children of "a poor country parson" in Burnham Thorpe in rural Norfolk. Nelson's mother, however, was a grandniece of Sir Robert Walpole, Britain's first prime minister, and a member of the prominent Suckling family. Her uncle, Sir Maurice Suckling, was a ranking naval officer. In 1770, Sir Maurice was given command of the warship *Raisonnable* bound for the West Indies. He offered to sign Nelson on as a midshipman. Nelson was twelve years old.

September 29, 1758
Horace Nelson is born in Burnham Thorpe, Norfolk, England.

January 1, 1771
Appointed to *Raisonnable* as a midshipman.
May 1771–December 1775
Sails to the West Indies, Arctic, East Indies, and India.
March 1776
Stricken with malaria and returned to England.
September 16, 1776
Appointed acting fourth lieutenant on the *Worcester*.
April 9, 1777
Passes the lieutenant's examination.
April 10, 1777
Appointed second lieutenant of the *Lowestoffe*.
September 4, 1777
Appointed first lieutenant of the *Bristol*.

December 8, 1778
Receives his first command, of the brig *Badger*.
June 11, 1779
Appointed post-captain, commanding the *Hinchinbrook*.
May 18, 1784–November 30, 1787
On station in the Caribbean.
March 11, 1787
Marries Frances Nisbet on the island of Nevis.
November 30, 1787
Placed on half pay and sent home to Burnham Thorpe amid navy cutbacks.
1788–1792
On half pay at Burnham Thorpe.

January 6, 1793
Recalled and made commander of the *Agamemnon*.
November 30, 1793
Begins a blockade of the ports in Corsica.
July 12, 1794
During the Siege of Calvi, Corsica, wounded in the right eye
and loses eyesight in his right eye.
1795–1796
On station in the western Mediterranean.
April 9, 1796
Appointed commodore.

February 14, 1797
Battle of Cape Saint Vincent destroys the Spanish fleet.
April 4, 1797
Promoted rear admiral.
July 23, 1797
Leads the first unsuccessful attack on Santa Cruz de Tenerife, Canary Islands
July 25, 1797
Leads the second Santa Cruz attack. Wounded in the right arm,
which is successfully amputated above the elbow on shipboard.
September 27, 1797
Invested Knight of Order of Bath for valor at Cape Saint Vincent.

April 30, 1798
Rejoins the fleet after recovery from the amputation.
June 7, 1798
Begins pursuit of the French fleet in the Mediterranean Sea.
August 1–2, 1798
Battle of the Nile. Captures or destroys eleven warships, stranding
the French invasion force in Egypt.
September 22, 1798
Arrives in Naples to a giant welcome. Meets Sir William and
Lady Emma Hamilton. He and Emma Hamilton become lovers.
November 29, 1798
Transports Neopolitan troops for attack on French-held Rome. Attack defeated.
December 24, 1798
Brings the fleeing royal family and the Hamiltons to refuge in Sicily.

June 5, 1799
Returns the royal family to Naples. They reclaim the throne.
June 29, 1799
Republican leaders arrested and confined on prison ships.
Admiral Francesco Carraciolo tried and hanged for treason.
Ninety-nine Republican leaders executed, others jailed or exiled.
July 17, 1800
Recalled to London. Travels via Trieste, Vienna, Prague, Dresden,
and Hamburg to elaborate welcoming ceremonies.

January 1, 1801
Appointed vice admiral.
April 2, 1801
Battle of Copenhagen with Danish fleet. He rejects the order
to withdraw and wins the battle.
May 15, 1801
Appointed viscount.
October 22, 1801
Moves to Surrey cottage with Emma Hamilton.

April 6, 1803
Sir William Hamilton dies.
May 16, 1803
Named the commander in chief, Mediterranean.
1804
Maintains a blockade of France in the Mediterranean.
May 10, 1805
Learns that the French fleet is heading for the West Indies and takes up pursuit.
September 30–October 20, 1805
Blockades the French/Spanish combined fleet in Cádiz harbor.
October 21, 1805
Battle of Trafalgar is great British victory. Nelson fatally
wounded by a sniper's bullet in the spine.

Britain in 1770 was building a far-flung empire with a massive navy to match. Most of North America, India, and the richest Caribbean islands now flew the British flag. Britain, France, Spain, Portugal, and the Netherlands were vying for other possessions and trade routes across the oceans—rivalries that were to dominate Nelson's later career. Indeed, the destination of Midshipman Nelson's first ship was the Falkland Islands in the South Atlantic.

Horace Nelson—he changed his name to Horatio when he was nineteen—joined His Majesty's Navy at the tender age of twelve.

All of the imperial powers strove to dominate the remote and arid islands, viewing them as a potential resupply stop in traveling around Cape Horn. (The dispute was finally settled in a compromise, giving all the powers access to the islands, but eventually Britain took full control. The Falklands were largely forgotten for two centuries until they reappeared on the world stage in a brief war between Britain and Argentina in 1982.)

Most colonies seemed to offer vast resources for young men to enrich themselves, not to mention prize money divided among the crew when a vessel was seized, so competition for officers' positions was stiff. It paid to have social position or an influential backer in the Royal Navy. Sir Maurice provided both. "Uncle Maurice" shepherded his nephew-protégé throughout his early career. As comptroller supervising the navy's accounts, he could make things happen. Nelson received choice berths that took him to the West Indies, Arctic, and East Indies. He was involved in his first sea battle and prize capture in a campaign against Haidar Ali of Mysore, who was an ally of France in the struggle for control of India. When the American War for Independence came, he was "on the wrong side of the world," he was to say later, and missed the action. Then he came

Previous page: In this famous painting, French and Spanish officers yielded their swords and surrendered to Nelson after he led a boarding party onto their flagship. Nelson Boarding the 'San Josef' on 14th February 1797 after Sir John Jervis' victory off Cape St. Vincent (oil on panel), Barker, Thomas Jones (1815–82) / Private Collection / The Bridgeman Art Library International

down with malaria, one of several episodes of tropical illness in his career. He was sent home for treatment in a leaky old ship that took five months to reach England. Nelson arrived extremely weak, but the disease had subsided, so his uncle immediately arranged for Nelson to be appointed acting fourth lieutenant on the sixty-four-gun frigate *Worcester*.

Nelson now began to study for his permanent lieutenant's examination. To qualify, an applicant had to be twenty years old and to have served six years at sea. Nelson had the required service, but he was still two years short of his twentieth birthday. His uncle managed to get the age requirement waived, arguing that his nephew "looked older" and carried himself with maturity. Sir Maurice volunteered for the three-man examining board that passed Nelson with flying colors. (Uncle and nephew insisted afterward that no influence had been used and that the other panelists did not know of the relationship until the exam had been completed and graded.) Then, Nelson's lieutenant's commission in hand, his uncle had him assigned to the *Lowestoffe*, one of the top frigates in the navy and a most coveted position. Off he went again to the West Indies.

Nelson was obviously a young man of great promise, and he was quickly plucked off the *Lowestoffe* to serve on the flagship of Admiral Peter Parker. In less than a year, not yet twenty, he became first lieutenant, the second in command of a warship. In December 1778, the nineteen year old received his first independent command, the brig *Badger*. Six months after that, he was promoted to post-captain and commander of the frigate *Hinchinbrook*. Inside the navy, it was said that a man who became post-captain by age twenty was a cinch to be admiral, if only by virtue of seniority.

Nelson remained in the West Indies until 1783, when the American War for Independence ended. He led an ill-starred expedition against Spanish-held Fort San Juan in Nicaragua, in which half the force died of yellow fever. Nelson himself was stricken and sent home. That was followed by a second disaster at Turks Island. The only bright spot was that he met Frances "Fanny" Nisbet, the niece of the former president of the island of Nevis. The two were subsequently married and were to become a gossip item and an entry in history books.

Then Nelson received a severe setback. With the American War for Independence ended and no other conflicts in sight, the fleet was cut back from 100,000 men to 40,000. Nelson was sent home at half pay. He spent five bitter years tending his garden in Burnham Thorpe and waiting for a summons to return.

SAVED BY THE REVOLUTION

Britain was at peace, and Nelson was fidgeting at Burnham Thorpe when, on July 14, 1789, a hungry mob of Parisians stormed the Bastille and ignited the French Revolution. The government toppled, and the reigning monarchs, Louis XVI and Marie Antoinette, went to the guillotine. The upheaval alarmed Britain because it occurred just across the channel and also because of its antimonarchical flavor. What king or monarchy might be next?

The British government immediately began remobilizing the fleet. In 1793, at the height of France's Reign of Terror, Nelson was given command of the sixty-four-gun *Agamemnon*, promised a seventy-four-gun vessel as soon as one was ready, and dispatched to the Mediterranean Sea to patrol the French coast. France was engulfed by civil war, Royalists pitted against revolutionaries. Royalists took over the port of Toulon, main base for the French fleet, and appealed to Britain for support. Britain sent sea and ground forces and occupied the port, but Toulon proved indefensible because a young artillery officer named Napoleon Bonaparte so skillfully placed his cannon and barraged the city that the British were forced to evacuate. It was the first matchup between Nelson and Bonaparte, and it would not be the last.

Toulon was the first matchup between Horatio Nelson and Napoleon Bonaparte, and it would not be the last.

Forced out of Toulon, the British chose the island of Corsica for a new base of operations. They captured the island's main port, and the struggle devolved into a land war. Nelson, the man of action, jumped into the ground battle. A near-miss from an artillery shell sent up a shower of stones, one of which struck him in the right eye. Although he could distinguish light and darkness, he effectively lost the sight of the eye. (Although paintings often show him with an eye patch, he never actually wore one, instead using a green eyeshade to shield the eye.)

Nelson spent a frustrating year blockading French ports without engaging in battle. Then Admiral Jervis took command of the Mediterranean fleet, paving the way for the Battle of Cape Saint Vincent and Nelson's Patented Bridge for Boarding First-Rates. The victory brought Nelson public acclaim, which he fostered by publishing his own self-glorifying account. He was awarded a rear admiral's flag and made a Knight of the Order of Bath. The victory also brought a title to Jervis, who became Lord Saint Vincent.

A ONE-ARMED, ONE-EYED ADMIRAL

But Nelson couldn't stay out of action. Nor did the new Lord Saint Vincent want him to. The admiral learned that a Spanish treasure ship was to unload its cargo at Santa Cruz de Tenerife in the Canary Islands. He sent four ships to intercept and capture it, with Nelson in command. A first-night attack on the well-defended port was foiled by heavy seas. The next night, July 25, 1797, Nelson tried again, leading the attack personally.

As the landing boats neared the beach, they were spotted from a lookout tower and shellfire from the citadel's heavy guns trained on them. A shell struck Nelson's right arm, shattering the elbow and severing an artery. Blood streamed from the wound while his wife's brother, Josiah Nisbet, desperately applied tourniquets. Nelson was taken back to the flagship where he refused assistance and insistently clambered aboard using only his left arm. When he arrived on deck, seamen removed their hats in customary salute. Nelson, determined to prove his toughness, lifted his own hat with his free hand. The ship's surgeon immediately amputated the arm above the elbow. In those pre-anesthetic days, the resolute Nelson simply bit his lip and held on until the operation was over, after which he thanked the surgeon.

"Who needs a one-armed, one-eyed admiral?" he cried out despairingly afterward.

Apparently the Admiralty did. Fortified with opium, for six weeks Nelson practiced using only his left hand, laboriously writing in a clumsy scrawl. Three weeks after that, he was returned to England. By December, he was looking for a new command.

Nelson's return was enthusiastically greeted by Lord Saint Vincent, who considered Nelson his most aggressive captain. In Nelson's absence, his nemesis Napoleon had been amassing at Toulon a major fleet of thirteen ships of the line, seven frigates, 300 transports, plus 30,000 men, 2,800 cavalrymen and their horses, 100 guns, and thirteen generals. Napoleon was obviously planning a big offensive somewhere, but where?

Some thought Napoleon aimed to invade Ireland, hoping to capitalize on its deep-seated hatred of London. Others guessed England itself. On May 20, 1798, before the British noticed, the French fleet set sail. It stopped briefly at Malta, then headed directly for its real goal: Egypt. The British cabinet panicked. A French presence in Egypt posed a monstrous threat to India, which was the jewel of the British Empire. Nelson must intercept the French. Posthaste.

The French had long envied Britain's possession of India, which had brought great prosperity to the mother country. Taking Egypt and transforming it into a French colony would position France closer to India and in command of trade routes. Napoleon dreamed of a vast French empire, too. Control of Egypt might give France control of Turkey, the Levant, and the eastern Mediterranean. Starting nearly a week after the French and following several wild-goose chases to Cyprus and Greece, Nelson actually arrived in Egypt before the French, but, believing he was still following them, resumed his search into the eastern Mediterranean.

Meanwhile the French fleet appeared, unloaded a small force that quickly secured Alexandria, then unloaded an additional larger force that drove up the Nile. Napoleon overwhelmed the army of Egypt's ruling Mamelukes in the Battle of the Pyramids. Napoleon began investigating the mysteries of Egyptian civilization, for which he had farsightedly brought thirty scholars and archeologists.

On August 1, 1798, Nelson's fleet unexpectedly came upon the French in Aboukir Bay, 30 miles (48 km) east of Alexandria. The battle began about 2 p.m. and by 7, at dark, it was clear that Nelson had scored a decisive British victory. When three British straggler ships joined the attack, it became a rout. A massive French warship, *L'Orient*, was set afire. When the flames reached the powder magazine, the ship exploded with a roar that rocked buildings in Alexandria. In the waning minutes, a shell struck Nelson's forehead, who had, as usual, exposed himself to danger. Bleeding profusely, he fell into the arms of Captain Edward Berry, exclaiming "I am killed! Remember me to my wife!" He survived to receive more accolades and reapply the Nelson Touch.

The Battle of the Nile ended Napoleon's dreams for Egypt and was applauded all over beleaguered Europe, especially Italy. Some say that Nelson's tumultuous welcome in Naples after the Battle of the Nile turned his head and led to subsequent events that damaged his reputation and raised cries for his dismissal. Certainly it was a welcome far beyond expectations. More than 125 boats greeted his entry into Naples Bay, with tooting foghorns and setting off fireworks. King Ferdinand II of the Kingdom of the Two Sicilies, of which Naples was capital, embraced Nelson at dockside and presented him with a medal.

Nelson's duties in Naples were to be primarily diplomatic: His mission was to persuade the feckless Ferdinand to keep Naples in the struggle against Napoleon. Nelson's first dutiful call was on Sir William Hamilton, the British ambassador, and his wife, Emma, a noted beauty twenty years younger than her husband. Soon Emma and the glamorous naval hero became lovers. Their liaison was to produce a daughter, Horatia, and a scandal that erupted into films (*That Hamilton Woman*, starring Vivien Leigh and Laurence Olivier) and books for two centuries. It also produced a bizarre ménage à trois, with Hamilton, Emma, and Nelson under one roof, and it apparently clouded Nelson's judgment, keeping him in Naples despite orders to leave.

Beauteous Lady Emma Hamilton, wife of an English ambassador, and Nelson became lovers in a scandalous affair that produced a daughter named Horatia. Prints & Photographs Division, Library of Congress, LC-USZ62-97184

Queen Maria Carolina was a sister of the beheaded Marie Antoinette and understandably violently anti-French and anti-republican. Nelson was also, and a confirmed supporter of monarchy. He and the queen persuaded Ferdinand to attack Rome, which was then in French hands. The result was a momentary victory, followed by a disastrous defeat for the Neapolitan army. King, queen, and court fled to Sicily in Nelson's vessels. A new government was proclaimed, based on revolutionary principles, composed of Naples' elite and backed by the French army. However, fighting broke out between Royalist sympathizers and the new government. Cardinal Fabrizio Ruffo negotiated a truce. The monarchy would be restored and republican leaders allowed to go into exile in France.

Nelson, to the cardinal's outrage, renounced the armistice. After the republican leaders boarded, he trained the fleet's guns on their rescue ship and arrested all the passengers. Admiral Francesco Carraciolo, who led the republicans' tiny navy, was brought to Nelson, tried in a drumhead court-martial on Royalist charges of treason, and promptly hanged from the flagship's yardarm. Ninety-nine other republicans were executed, 500 went to jail, and 350 were shipped into exile—the cream of Neapolitan society.

When London heard of the brutal crackdown under British auspices Nelson, until then the national idol, was denounced in the House of Commons. His stock sank even lower the following month. A French fleet had left Toulon, destination unknown, and Lord Keith, Nelson's superior, suspected they were about to attack the British base on Minorca. He directed Nelson to take his fleet and defend the island. Nelson flatly refused. He said it was more important to protect Naples than Minorca, and he was staying put. He was reprimanded for refusing to obey a direct order by Lord Keith, Lord Saint Vincent, the First Sea Lord and the Admiralty. Had Nelson not been the hero of the Nile, he might have been cashiered. Instead he was quietly summoned home.

Nelson converted his return into a triumphal tour and was sumptuously feted at foreign courts along the way. His reception in London was less enthusiastic. The reprimands, the Naples episode, his self-promotion, the fact that he arrived wearing all his foreign medals, and the scandal surrounding Emma (who had accompanied him on the grand tour and with whom he now set up housekeeping in a Surrey cottage) left him without a major command for two years.

Had Nelson not been the hero of the Nile, he might have been cashiered. Instead he was quietly summoned home.

Nelson was too able an admiral to be left on the beach indefinitely. Britain was embroiled in a quarrel with neutral nations about its right to search ships for French-bound contraband. The chief offenders were the Scandinavian nations of Denmark and Sweden. A showdown came in March 1801. Nelson had been appointed deputy commander of the Baltic fleet under Admiral Hyde Parker, a shy man who consistently deferred to Nelson.

Goaded by the anti-British Tsar Paul of Russia, Denmark and Sweden had adopted a policy of armed neutrality, declaring their right to defend their ships against search. Denmark announced an embargo on British shipping and blocked the Baltic ports of Lubeck and Hamburg. Nelson, with twelve ships, decided to force his way into the Baltic past Danish and Swedish shore batteries. The Danes met his twelve ships with eighteen ships of their own, plus some dismasted vessels still equipped with guns. The confrontation began at mid-morning and was still raging at 1:30 p.m. Admiral Parker nervously signaled, "Recall from action." Nelson at first ignored the signal flag, then said whimsically, "I have only one eye. I have the right to be blind sometimes." He raised his telescope to his blind eye and kept fighting. At 4:30 p.m., the Danish flagship *Dannebrog* exploded, and the battle ended with another Nelson victory.

In the summer and fall of 1805, it appeared that Napoleon was now scheduling his long-threatened invasion of England. He recalled his Caribbean fleet and combined it with the Atlantic and Mediterranean fleets. France now had thirty-six ships of the line, augmented by a smaller number from Spain. Admiral Pierre-Charles de Villenueve collected this ungainly force at Cádiz. The British immediately mounted a blockade to keep both fleets pinned in the harbor. Meanwhile, Napoleon had changed his mind. The ships were needed at Naples for a new offensive in Italy. On October 19, Villeneuve tried to make a dash through the Strait of Gibraltar into the Mediterranean. Blocked by weather, he turned back to Cádiz and collided directly with Nelson's fleet. The result was the historic Battle of Trafalgar.

"England expects every man to do his duty," Nelson famously signaled his fleet as the fight began. The fleets met broadside to broadside and within two hours the first Spanish ship, foundering and burning, surrendered. Seventeen other vessels, Spanish and French, surrendered or were captured. Nelson, on the *Victory*, was in the thick of the fighting when, at 1:20 p.m., a sniper's bullet caught him in the lower spine, and he fell to the deck paralyzed from the waist down. Nelson was carried below and lived long enough to learn that he had achieved his final, most memorable and tragic victory.

CHAPTER SEVEN

NAPOLEON BONAPARTE, 1769–1821: HIS PROVING GROUND AT THE SIEGE OF TOULON

Twenty-four-year-old Napoleon Bonaparte realizes that artillery, not infantry, will recapture the French port of Toulon from French royalists and their English allies. It was the beginning of a career that would remake the map of Europe and lead him to an imperial crown.

French Citizen General Jean François Carteaux dismissed the idea that he needed a new artillery commander. It was unfortunate that Captain Elzeár Dommartin, the former commander of artillery, had been badly wounded. But Carteaux didn't think the matter was a calamity.

The general's plan for recapturing Toulon, a city on France's Mediterranean coast, called for seizing the royalists' hilltop forts that encircled the city, one by one. Once they were all in French hands, he would send in his infantry to storm the city. The artillery batteries he had put in place on Montauban hill were sufficient to support the infantry attack. Carteaux was not impressed by Napoleon Bonaparte, the twenty-four-year-old Corsican captain sent to him by two meddlers from the Committee of Public Safety in Paris. The young man stood about five feet, six inches (168 cm) tall. His face was sharp and bony, his complexion was yellow as he if he were suffering from jaundice, his hands were long and thin, and his fingernails were dirty. His hair was barely combed and badly powdered. And Napoleon spoke with such a heavy Corsican accent that some French words and phrases were garbled into unintelligiblity.

Carteaux, by comparison, had a dramatic appearance. At age forty-two, he still looked dashing thanks, in part, to his exaggerated cavalry moustache. He

French General Jean Francois Carteaux rejected the idea that Toulon could be captured only if the French installed artillery on the hills around the city. The Siege of Toulon, 1793 (ink on paper), Constantin, Jean Antoine (1756–1844) / Musee de la Revolution Francaise, Vizille, France / The Bridgeman Art Library

had large eyes, a sweeping brow, broad shoulders, and a deep chest. Yet he was not a professional soldier. Before the revolution, he had made his living as a not-terribly-adept portrait painter. But in revolutionary France, politics was considered more important than experience, and Carteaux was a fanatical champion of the French Revolution. As a reward for his zeal, he was made a general.

Because the government in Paris had sent this new artillery commander, Carteaux could not be rude. Instead, Carteaux invited Captain Bonaparte to remain with him at his headquarters where, after the generals had driven the royalists and their allies out of Toulon, he could share in the glory "without having to exert himself." Napoleon did not take the general's condescending invitation seriously. In his new position, he had virtually absolute authority over the artillery in Carteaux's army. For Napoleon, this was opportunity enough to make history. What was about to happen at Toulon would be the making of him. Bowing to the general, he left headquarters and went out to inspect his guns.

The inspection was brief. Napoleon found only four cannons, two mortars, and insufficient quantities of powder and shells. Furthermore, the batteries were out of range of Toulon. If any guns were fired during the attack on the city, they would likely hit the rear of Carteaux's infantry. Napoleon noticed another flaw in Carteaux's plan. Even if he succeeded in capturing every fort on every hill all around the city, the harbor was still packed with English warships, all of which would train their guns on the French troops the moment they assaulted Toulon. The first order of business, then, was to acquire more artillery to drive the enemy warships from the inner harbor.

RADICALS VERSUS EXTREMISTS

The execution of France's king Louis XVI on January 21, 1793, set off a crisis on the French territorial island of Corsica. Moderates, who had supported the revolution's principles of liberty and equality, were shocked by the regicide, and they became royalists again. They made up the majority of the island's population. Supporters of the revolution and of the elimination of the monarchy—such as the Bonaparte family—suddenly found themselves unwelcome in their own homeland.

In June 1793, Maria Letizia Bonaparte and her six children fled to France where the second-eldest son, Napoleon, was a captain in the army, and her third-eldest son, Lucien, was a prominent Jacobin, an ardent supporter of the French Revolution, in Toulon. Madame Bonaparte and her family had left their home

August 5, 1769
Napoleon Bonaparte is born on the island of Corsica.

1785
Graduates from the Royal Military School in Paris.
December 1793
As commander of the artillery, successfully defeats French royalists and their British allies at Toulon.
March 9, 1796
Marries his mistress, Josephine de Beauharnais.
1796–1797
After a string of military victories in Italy, grants a peace treaty to the Italians.

1798
Captures Malta and Alexandria in Egypt. Wins the Battle of the Pyramids and enters Cairo, but is stranded after Lord Horatio Nelson destroys the French fleet at the Battle of the Nile.
1799
Returns to Paris where he participates in a coup d'état that overthrows the government. Elected first consul.

1804
Proclaimed the emperor of France.
1805
Crowned the king of Italy. Experiences victories at Ulm and Austerlitz, but Lord Nelson destroys the Franco-Spanish fleet at Trafalgar.
1806
Victory at Jena. Installs his brother Joseph Bonaparte as the king of Naples and his brother Louis Bonaparte as the king of Holland.
1807
Signs the Treaty of Tilsit with Tsar Alexander I of Russia, dividing Europe between their two empires. Installs his brother Jerome as the king of Westphalia.

1808
Citizens of Madrid riot against the presence of French troops in their city. Charles IV of Spain abdicates, Joseph Bonaparte is named the king of Spain. Joachim Murat replaces him as the king of Naples.
1809
Divorces Josephine because she has failed to give him a son.
1810
Marries Marie-Louise von Hapsburg, archduchess of Austria.
1811
Marie-Louise gives birth to a son, Napoleon Francis Joseph Charles. The boy is created king of Rome.

1812
Invades Russia. Marches into Moscow to find the city deserted and burning. The campaign and subsequent retreat from Russia costs the lives of 570,000 French troops.
1813
Prussia and Austria declare war on France. The Duke of Wellington drives the French from Spain. France is defeated at the Battle of the Nations outside Leipzig.
1814
Victories at Brienne, Champaubert, Montmirail, Montereau, and Rheims. But then Paris is captured by a coalition army of Russians, British, Austrians, Swedes, Spanish, Portuguese, and Prussians.
April–May, 1814
Led by Marshal Michel Ney, the generals mutiny against their emperor. Abdicates and is exiled to the island of Elba in the Mediterranean.

February 26, 1815
Escapes from Elba and enters Paris in triumph. Raises an army.
June 18, 1815
Crushing defeat at the Battle of Waterloo. Four days later, abdicates for a second time.

May 5, 1821
After six years of exile, dies on the island of St. Helena.

When Corsica fell to the royalists, Napoleon's mother and six of his brothes and sisters fled to France for safety.

Bonaparte family arriving in Toulon (France), when fleeing from Corsica, 17 June 1793, engraved by Motte, Charles (1785–1836) (litho) (b/w photo), Mauzaisse, Jean Baptiste (1784-1844) (after) / Bibliotheque Nationale, Paris, France, Lauros / Giraudon / The Bridgeman Art Library

in Ajaccio in such haste that they arrived with virtually no luggage and almost no money. Compounding her troubles was the political situation in France at the time. In addition to the counter-revolution fomented in the south by the royalists and their British and Spanish allies, the country was in turmoil as the radical Girondins struggled against the ultra-militant Montagnards for control of the government in Paris. The Bonapartes were unprepared for the violence and political extremism that they encountered in France.

Madam Bonaparte chose to settle in a quiet village, La Valette. For living expenses, she borrowed money from her son Napoleon and from her friends in

France. Then she set about tracking down her contacts. She was delighted to find that a fellow Corsican, Antonio Cristoforo Saliceti, was in France and held in high regard by the government of Maximilien Robespierre. It was wise to be a friend of Robespierre: The cold-hearted ideologue saw enemies and counter-revolutionaries everywhere. During the year he was in office, Robespierre, employing the excuse that he was saving the revolution from its enemies, unleashed on France the bloodbath known as the Reign of Terror.

Robespierre had always been a friend of the Bonapartes, and he was an especially generous patron of Napoleon. At Madame Bonaparte's request, Saliceti used his influence to have Lucien Bonaparte appointed quartermaster at the nearby village of Saint-Maximin; Joseph Bonaparte—the eldest son—joined Saliceti's entourage, traveling to Paris where he persuaded the government to release 600,000 livres for the relief of Corsican refugees in France. An old friend of the family, Joseph Fesch, had renounced his vows as a priest, left Corsica, and traveled to France to work for the revolution. Saliceti found him a quartermaster position, too. Saliceti also secured for Napoleon the post as commander of the artillery at Toulon. By this simple act of friendship and patronage, Saliceti launched Napoleon's military career.

THE ANTAGONISTS

The fall of the monarchy and the aristocracy had a ripple effect throughout France that the leading men of every city and town had not foreseen. The Jacobins, the political party led by Robespierre, ejected the local officials, lawyers, merchants and bankers, members of the Masonic lodges, and even army officers from office and all positions of influence. Jacobins took their places, exercising all manner of petty tyrannies over the people that included extorting "loans" from the wealthy, ransacking private homes, and shutting down newspapers and clubs that were critical of the government.

By May 1793, the citizens of Bordeaux, Lyon, Marseille, and Toulon, among other cities and towns, had had enough. They arrested the Jacobins and put their own people back in office. Some were royalists, most were political moderates, but to Robespierre they were all counter-revolutionaries, traitors to the cause of liberty. He sent General Carteaux to put down the insurrection in and around Marseille. On August 24, Carteaux's army captured the city. The soldiers rampaged through the streets, slaughtering approximately 500 civilians. In the days that followed, 1,000 citizens of Marseille were arrested, 412 of whom were executed.

Three days after the bloodbath in Marseille, the inhabitants of Toulon drove out the Jacobin garrison and surrendered their city and their port, along with all the French ships in their harbor—eighteen frigates and many other vessels as well—to the English admiral, Samuel Hood, whose ships had been patrolling the waters along France's southern coast. Admiral Hood ordered his men ashore to take possession of Toulon.

Fresh from his victory at Marseille and armed with orders from Robespierre's Committee of Public Safety in Paris, General Carteaux, assisted by General Jean François Cornu de Lapoype, laid siege to Toulon. Carteaux positioned his army of 8,000 to 10,000 men on the western side of Toulon, while Lapoype's 5,000 men dug in on the eastern side of the town.

Recapturing Toulon would not be easy. More than a century earlier, Louis XIV had sent his finest military engineer, Sébastien Le Prestre de Vauban, to design fortifications that would transform an old port into a naval stronghold. The site was ideal. Toulon lay at the foot of Mount Faron and was flanked by many smaller hills. The large outer harbor tapered down to an inner harbor above which rose a series of promontories that were natural positions for batteries of artillery. De Vauban built a fort on virtually every hilltop, making Toulon the Gibraltar of southern France.

Antonio Cristoforo Saliceti, a fellow Corsican, helped launch Napleon's military career by arranging for the 24-year-old captain to be appointed commander of artillery at Toulon. Antoine Christophe Saliceti (1757–1809) engraved by Carlo Lasinio (1759–1838) (engraving) (b/w photo), Wicar, Jean Baptiste Joseph (1762–1834) (after) / Bibliotheque Nationale, Paris, France, Giraudon / The Bridgeman Art Library

Toulon was defended by 14,000 to 18,000 troops—French royalists, British, Piedmontese, and Neapolitans. The Austrians had promised to send 6,000 troops to reinforce the commanders in Toulon, General Charles O'Hara and Lieutenant General David Dundas, but they never arrived. O'Hara, the illegitimate son of an Irish baron, had made his reputation fighting the Americans during their War of Independence. After George Washington's victory at Yorktown, it was O'Hara who surrendered General Charles

Cornwallis's sword. Dundas was a reformer who advocated military training for all officers in the British military, which was an unorthodox idea at a time when gentlemen who had no military experience at all could purchase commissions.

In spite of their superior numbers and their superior defensive position, the commanders inside Toulon were not pleased with their situation. O'Hara sent complaining letters to London bemoaning the poorly trained troops; the brawls that broke out among English, French, and Italians; and his misgivings about the defensive possibilities of Toulon. Reading between the lines, the government in London wondered whether O'Hara and Dundas were planning to give up Toulon without a fight. The English commanders' mood was not improved by Carteaux's daring seizure of two hills—Montauban and Six-Fours—that commanded the western side of the inner harbor. The defenders had one consolation: The inner harbor was filled with their warships.

"IT IS THE ARTILLERY THAT TAKES THE FORTS"

The warships were the key to Toulon, and Napoleon knew it as well as O'Hara and Dundas. As soon as Carteaux began his assault on the city, his infantry would be caught between fire from the city walls and even more withering fire from the warships' guns. It would be a massacre.

To clear the inner harbor, Napoleon planned to bombard the warships, perhaps with red-hot cannonballs that would set the ships on fire. At present Napoleon did not have the size and number of guns, nor the shells and powder necessary, but he was working on those problems. He had sent out requests for artillery from batteries along the coast and further inland until, in the beginning of October, he had more than 100 guns, including a few long-range mortars, and a generous supply of gunpowder and cannonballs. Nonetheless, what was perfectly clear to Napoleon became a source of derision for General Carteaux and his staff. They called Napoleon "Captain Cannon" and "the Greenhorn." The mockery stung, but Napoleon assuaged the hurt by keeping busy. Besides, he was writing the Committee of Public Safety in Paris about his plan, which he assured the government was superior to General Carteaux's. "It is the artillery that takes the forts," he wrote in October, "and the infantry that only helps."

Napoleon's artillerymen were crude men from the lowest ranks of French society. They and their officers were regarded with contempt by Carteaux and his officers. To raise morale and improve their effectiveness, Napoleon trained his artillery crews, lived with them rather than at headquarters, and taught them that victory was in the hands of the artillery—all of which gave these rough characters a sense of pride. As for the officers, they became devoted to their young commander. Some of them would follow Napoleon throughout his career as his generals and marshals—Auguste de Marmont, Jean-Andoche Junot, Louis-Gabriel Suchet, Louis Desaix, Géraud Christophe Michel Duroc, and Claude Victor-Perrin.

When Napoleon was not with his men, he was urging General Carteaux to attack the fort called l'Eguillette, which commanded the entrance to the inner harbor. Because the representatives of the Committee of Public Safety—among them Saliceti—backed Napoleon in this, Carteaux ordered an attack on the fort. It was a half-hearted effort that General O'Hara drove back easily. A few days later, Carteaux sent some of Lapoype's men against two more forts. They were repulsed, too, and with heavy losses.

Napoleon complained to the government's representatives that Carteaux "does not possess the least notions of the military art." The representatives passed the complaints along to the committee, which responded by sending Carteaux a message that he was relieved of his command. Carteaux was replaced by François-Amédée Doppet, who proved to be almost as bad. After a failed attack on Fort Mulgrave, Doppet resigned.

He was replaced by Jacques Dugommier, a charismatic, energetic commander with forty years of military experience. Dugommier had fought in the American Revolution and with the French revolutionary army in Italy. Napoleon admired him deeply, recalling later that General Dugommier "was an extremely brave man." Making Dugommier even more appealing to Napoleon, the general approved everything the young captain had done with the artillery batteries, and Dugommier gave Napoleon a free hand to continue his excellent work.

"FOR HUMANITY AND DUTY"

In late November, Dugommier and Napoleon agreed everything was in place for a major assault on key forts above the inner harbor, including l'Eguilette. During the assault, Napoleon's batteries would shell other nearby forts as well as Toulon itself, while Lapoype led a diversionary attack on the defenses of Mount Faron at the rear of the city.

So much activity in the French camps alerted General O'Hara that an assault was coming. Rather than wait, O'Hara attacked at five in the morning on Novem-

After Toulon fell to the French, Napoleon's artillerymen turned their guns on ships carrying refugees, many of them women and children, away from the city. Destruction of the French Fleet at Toulon, 18th December 1793, engraved by Thomas Sutherland for J. Jenkins's 'Naval Achievements', 1816 (engraving), Whitcombe, Thomas (c.1752–1824) (after) / Private Collection, The Stapleton Collection / The Bridgeman Art Library

ber 30, targeting one of Napoleon's batteries west of Toulon. O'Hara's several thousand troops drove back the French artillerymen. As they overwhelmed the artillery batteries, the English troops spiked Napoleon's cannons. But Dugommier and Napoleon rode to the rescue, bringing up reinforcements that fought savagely for the possession of the battery. As O'Hara's men fell back, Napoleon led a charge, but the French came to a halt at the fence of sharp wooden spikes that were part of Toulon's defenses. Nonetheless, the French had scored a major coup—the capture of General O'Hara.

At Toulon General Carteaux and his staff had mocked Napoleon as "the Greenhorn." Three years later, when this portrait was painted, Napoleon was a self-assured, successful officer-on-the-make. Napoleon Bonaparte (1769–1821) 1796 (oil on canvas), Lefevre, Robert (1755–1830) / Uppsala University Collection, Sweden / Giraudon / The Bridgeman Art Library International

Two weeks later, Dugommier and Napoleon were ready for another assault. For five days and nights, Napoleon's artillery bombarded a stronghold called Cairo at the entrance to the inner harbor. On December 17, in heavy rain, they mounted a joint attack on the fortress. Dugommier led 5,000 men against Cairo, while Napoleon led 2,000. A horse was shot from beneath Napoleon, but he got up and continued on foot. The French swarmed over the walls of Cairo, where the French army and the Cairo garrison fought hand-to-hand for more than two hours, slashing at each other with sabers until finally the garrison surrendered. Some of the defenders at l'Eguilette nearby were so frightened by the noise of the assault on Cairo that they abandoned their posts. Meanwhile, Lapoype's men had seized the forts on Mount Faron.

Napoleon never flagged during the fight, even after an English sergeant drove his pike deep into the captain's left thigh. Napoleon's new inner circle of friends feared that gangrene would set in and the leg would have to be amputated, but an army surgeon who was skilled as well as sensible, treated the wound and kept it free of infection.

With the French in possession of the most strategic points above the city and the inner harbor, Admiral Hood ordered his fleet to sail out to sea and sent a team of men to destroy the arsenal inside the city. Napoleon hastened their departure by firing volley after volley of red-hot cannonballs at the retreating ships. Meanwhile, all was pandemonium at the docks as the infantry along with hundreds of royalists scrambled into small boats to catch up with the warships and escape to safety.

Once the last English vessels were clear of the inner harbor, Napoleon ordered his gunners to fire on Toulon. For three days he shelled the city. The atmosphere in Toulon was thick with the smoke of burning buildings when the French marched in and took possession of the town. Immediately the troops ran riot, slaughtering an unknown number of civilians. Meanwhile Napoleon's guns fired on and sank four ships bearing refugees, many of them women and children. Then began the mass executions: 200 officers and artillery men were killed on December 20, and 200 civilians were killed on December 21. A Jacobin named Joseph Fouché reported to Robespierre, "We are shedding much blood, but for humanity and duty."

Napoleon had been right about the necessity of artillery in capturing Toulon and chasing away the enemy's fleet. Thanks to endorsements from Dugommier and Saliceti, who sent word to the government in Paris of the shrewdness, courage, and energy of the young commander, Napoleon was promoted to brigadier general. The victory at Toulon marked the beginning of his military career, but to take it to the next stage would require cunning. Robespierre did not tolerate a defeat. In 1793, he sent eighteen unsuccessful generals to the guillotine. In 1794, an even worse year for the French military, he had sixty-seven ineffective generals beheaded. In such a political atmosphere, Napoleon learned that caution was preferable to courage.

CHAPTER EIGHT

SIMÓN BOLÍVAR, 1783–1830: A YOUTH'S OATH TO FREE A COUNTRY

Inspired by an episode from ancient Roman history, twenty-two-year-old Simón Bolívar vowed to liberate his country, Venezuela, from the Spanish Empire. In fact, he did much more, liberating a vast territory that covers the modern-day nations of Venezuela, Panama, Colombia, Ecuador, Bolivia, and Peru.

The two Venezuelans—Simón Rodríguez, thirty-six, and his former pupil, Simón Bolívar, twenty-two—had begun their midday meal late, and they lingered over the table long, so the afternoon was almost done when they decided to take a long walk to the top of Rome's Aventine Hill. The summit promised a panoramic view of the city; but for Rodríguez, a committed revolutionary, the Aventine was also holy ground. It was on the Aventine in 494 BCE that the plebs, the common working people of Rome, threatened to secede and found a new city in which they, and not the aristocratic patricians, would rule. In revolutionary circles of the time—the date of Bolívar and Rodríguez's hike was August 15, 1805—the *Secessio plebes*, ("Secession of the Plebs"), was regarded as significant, the forerunner of the American colonies' defiance of Great Britain and of France's overthrow of the monarchy, the aristocracy, and the Catholic Church.

During August, the heat in Rome is stifling. By the time Bolívar and Rodríguez stopped at last on Monte Sacro, a small promontory on the Aventine where once there stood a shrine to the goddess Diana, they were sweaty and panting. They dropped down onto a block of white marble, a relic from some ruin or other. Once he had caught his breath, Bolívar stood up to survey the skyline of Rome. Then he launched into a lengthy speech that began, "So this is the city of Romu-

Simón Bolívar inherited a fortune in real estate, mines, cattle ranches, and slaves, yet he undermined his own wealth and status to liberate Venezuela from Spain.

lus and Numa, of the Gracchi, and the Horaces, of Augustus, Nero, Caesar and Brutus, Tiberius, and Trajan!"

If Rodríguez's recollection of the speech is accurate—he wrote it down decades later—then Bolívar must have been a long-winded young man. After first reviewing the many advantages Rome contributed to Western civilization, and then denouncing the other side of the coin—the "corrupt Messalinas [and] heartless Agrippinas," Bolívar lamented that to "the emancipation of the human spirit, the enlargement of man and of his reason [Rome contributed] very little— perhaps nothing...The heart of man's problem, freedom, seems to have been ignored. It seems the mystery will not be solved except in the New World."

Simón Bolívar faced his tutor, his eyes moist with tears, his chest heaving as if he were suffering from a high fever, and took an oath. "I swear before you," he said to Rodríguez, "by the God of my fathers and the honor of my country: I will not rest, not in body or soul, till I have broken the chains of Spain."

Then, turning his back on decadent Rome and facing his tutor, his eyes moist with tears, his chest heaving as if he were suffering from a high fever, Bolívar took an oath. "I swear before you," he said to Rodríguez, "by the God of my fathers and the honor of my country: I will not rest, not in body or soul, till I have broken the chains of Spain."

The oath atop the Aventine Hill has come to be seen as the deciding moment in the life of Simón Bolívar and the future of South America. When he returned to his home in Venezuela, Bolívar did join other revolutionaries and spent many years fighting to liberate from the Spanish Empire, not just Venezuela, but also the present-day countries of Colombia, Ecuador, Bolivia, Panama, and Peru.

Yet friends who spent time with Bolívar after his vow on the Aventine had no sense that he had experienced a road-to-Damascus moment that would change the course of his life and human history forever. Nor was he in any hurry to get home to begin his great enterprise. He lingered in Europe, then traveled to the United States to visit some of the battlefields of the American Revolution. He did

July 24, 1783
Simón Bolívar is born in Caracas, Venezuela.

1796
His tutor, Simón Rodríguez, is forced to flee the country when suspected of plotting to overthrow Spanish rule in Venezuela.

May 26, 1802
Bolívar marries Maria Teresa Rodríguez del Toro y Alayza.

January 22, 1803
Eight months after their marriage, Maria Teresa dies. Bolívar is plunged into deep depression.

1804
Makes a grand tour of Europe. In Paris is shocked by Napoleon's coronation as emperor; regards it as a betrayal of the French Revolution.

August 15, 1805
In Rome, swears to liberate his country from Spain.

1807
Returns to Venezuela, after stopping in the United States for an extended visit to the battlefields of the American Revolution.

1810
Caracas city council deposes Spain's viceroy. Sends Bolívar to Great Britain to ask for military assistance. The British government refuses aid, but it promises to remain neutral in Venezuela's war for independence.

July 5, 1811
Delegates of a national congress meeting in Caracas establish a republic. Venezuela is the first Spanish colony to declare its independence. Bolívar frees his slaves.

1812
Spanish and Venezuelan royalists crush the rebellion. Bolívar flees to Cartagena in what is now Colombia.

1813
Bolívar leads a series of successful attacks on Spanish garrisons. Defeats the Spanish at the Battle of Taguanes and enters Caracas, where he is declared dictator.

1814–1815
Spanish and Venezuelan royalists mount a major counter-offensive that recaptures Caracas and drives Bolívar and all his officers into exile. They seek refuge in Jamaica.

1815–1819
Civil war rages across Venezuela and present-day Colombia. On August 7, 1819, Bolívar wins a major victory over the Spanish and royalists at Boyaca.

1817
Invades Venezuela. Establishes a revolutionary government at Angostura (now Ciudad Bolívar), and is elected president of Venezuela.

1819
Defeats the Spanish at the Battle of Boyacá. Organizes a congress that establishes an independent republic comprising the modern-day nations of Colombia, Ecuador, Panama, and Venezuela.

June 24, 1821
Defeats the Spanish at Carabobo, the gateway to Caracas.

1824
Invades Peru and liberates it from the Spanish.

1825
Spanish abandon any hope of holding their colonies of Venezuela and New Granada (present-day Colombia, Ecuador, Panama, and Bolivia, which is named after him). At a national congress, Bolívar writes a constitution and accepts the office of president-for-life.

1825–1828
Infighting between the states and resentment of Bolívar's harsh policies foster a string of insurrections. Survives a failed assassination attempt.

1830
Resigns in April. Dies of tuberculosis at Santa Marta December 17.

THE SECESSION OF THE PLEBS

According to the ancient Roman sources, it was an economic crisis that set off the Secession. Freeborn men, farmers especially, who could not pay their taxes borrowed from moneylenders who charged an exorbitant rate of interest. When these men could not pay back their loans, their creditors seized their farms to pay off the debts. In many cases, the value of the farm did not cover the debt, so the farmer was sold into slavery. One case in particular of what became known as "debt slavery" outraged the plebs: A veteran of Rome's wars was seized and tortured by his creditor because he could not pay what he owed.

As for the patricians, they were not sympathetic to the plight of the debtors, but when the plebs—the craftsmen, shopkeepers, and laborers who were essential to the Roman economy and kept the city running—marched out of Rome to the Aventine where they swore to establish a new city to rival Rome, the patricians realized it was in their interest to come to terms with the lower classes. They created a new political office, the tribune, who would be the plebs' representative in the Roman Senate. In a vote the tribune was vastly outnumbered, but he had the power to veto any piece of legislation that he considered contrary to the interests of his constituents. This concession brought the plebs back to the city.

not return to his palatial house in Caracas until July 1807—twenty-five months after he swore to drive Spain out of Venezuela.

LIFE AT THE TOP

It is one of the ironies of history that Simón Bolívar, an aristocrat, dreamed of overthrowing the aristocracy of his own country. His birth on July 24, 1783, marked the seventh generation of Bolívars in the Americas; in fact, he was named for the founder of his line—Simon de Bolívar, who emigrated from Spain to Venezuela in 1589.

The Bolívars stood at the pinnacle of colonial society for two reasons: They were immensely rich, and they had been careful to marry only within their own race. A large part of the population of Venezuela was of mixed blood—white, Indian, and African. Just as noble families back in Spain prided themselves on having no Moorish or Jewish ancestors, upper class colonial families in Venezuela took pride in having no Indians or Africans in their family trees. The highest positions in the colonial government, the Catholic Church in Venezuela, the professions, and even in commerce were reserved for whites.

A 20th-century mosaic depicts the horrors of the Spanish conquest of the Americas, including summary executions, slavery, robbery, and forced conversion to Christianity. The Conquest, mural in the Avenida de los Proceres (mosaic), Venezuelan School (20th century) / Caracas, Venezuela / Ken Welsh / The Bridgeman Art Library International

The family's fortune began at San Mateo, an estate founded by Simon de Bolívar in the sixteenth century. During the 200 years that followed, the Bolívars acquired more land and estates, in addition to mines, cattle ranches, and slaves to work these large operations. With the profits, they built a luxurious home in Caracas. Like other leading colonial families, the Bolívar men participated in public life as government officials and officers in the militia. And they were loyal to the king. During an uprising in 1749, Simón's uncle, José Bolívar Aguirre, led the soldiers of the king against the rebels and crushed them.

At the time of Simón's birth, Venezuela was a complex country of 800,000 inhabitants, more than half of whom lived in the province of Caracas. At the top of the social ladder were well-born Spaniards newly arrived in Venezuela or sent by the king to govern the colony. A half-step below the Spaniards were the native-born Venezuelan elite known as Creoles—the old, wealthy colonial families such as the Bolívars.

Next came immigrants from the Canary Islands—if they were of pure white blood. Then came the poor and working class whites. Below them were the mixed race inhabitants known as *pardos* who comprised at least half the population of the colony. Below them were African slaves and free blacks. And at the very bottom of the social ladder were the Indians. White Venezuelans rarely saw Indians. The tribes tended to keep to themselves, living in the mountains or forests or around a remote Catholic mission.

Numerically, the mixed race pardos, the blacks, and the Indians had an overwhelming majority in Venezuelan society. There were approximately 590,000 of them. As for the Bolívars and their fellow elite, they totaled 4,048 individuals in 658 families. Although they comprised a tiny percentage of the population, the Creoles owned most of the land, controlled the lion's share of the colony's wealth, and decided what privileges would be granted to the lower orders. For nearly three centuries, the Venezuelan Creoles had controlled the colony, but by the mid-eighteenth century, the lower classes were growing restive.

In 1760, the elite made their first great concession, permitting the pardos to join the military and become officers. In 1795, the elite made an even grander concession, permitting the pardos to purchase a "Certificate of Whiteness." Armed with this document, the pardos could marry a white man or woman, send their children to school, hold public office, or be ordained a Catholic priest. The elite's sudden reversal of policy was purely pragmatic. Frightened by reports of the Reign of Terror in revolutionary France and the slave uprising in the Caribbean colony of Saint-Domingue (modern-day Haiti), the Creoles hoped that by elevating the status of the pardos, they could derail revolutionary sentiment in their own country.

Yet barely three months after this new legislation went into effect, 300 slaves, free blacks, and pardos from the sugar cane fields around the town of Coro rebelled against their masters and employers. They ransacked several haciendas, killed the landowners, and then overran Coro. If all 15,000 slaves and free laborers in the region had risen up, Venezuela might have had a real revolution on its hands.

Instead the army found it a simple matter to defeat the rebels, most of whom were lined up against a wall and shot without the formality of a trial.

Two years later, another revolution flared up, this time led by two white men, Manuel Gual and José María España, minor government bureaucrats who had been reading Rousseau and were impressed by the victory of the thirteen American colonies over Great Britain. In their manifesto, Gual and España called for the elimination of taxes, the abolition of slavery, and the distribution of land to the Indians. Finally, they called for an end to Venezuela's race-based hierarchy, asserting that whites, Indians, blacks, and mixed race persons were all "brothers in Christ and equal before God." Once again the army routed the rebels. Gual fled the country, but España was captured and executed in Caracas' main plaza. The executioner hacked the limbs off his corpse, impaled them on pikes, and displayed them on the main roads leading into the capital.

On June 24, 1821, Bolívar's army defeated the Spanish at Carabobo, the gateway to Caracas, the capital of Venezuela. The Art Archive / Museo Bolivar Caracas / Gianni Dagli Orti

"THE INSATIABLE GREED OF SPAIN"

At a time when colonial leaders in the Americas were beginning to contemplate independence from the mother country, the king of Spain adopted a new policy that curtailed the old privileges of the Creoles. For more than 200 years, the Creoles had governed Venezuela in the name of the Spanish crown. But after 1750, their authority was assumed by a governor or superintendent sent to Caracas from Madrid. He had supreme power in the colony to appoint or remove officials in the government, the military, and the Church, and he could introduce new taxes and do as he wished with the revenue (although most of it was shipped back to the royal treasury in Spain). He did not seek the advice of the Creoles; instead, he required their cooperation and their submission to this new policy.

Being locked out of the government of the colony chafed, but what really antagonized the Creoles was Spain's determination that the colony would not be permitted to develop its resources. Venezuelan's place in the colonial scheme of things was to keep a steady stream of crops, livestock, and gold flowing to the mother country, but under no circumstances would the farms, ranches, and mines of the colony be permitted to compete with the agriculture and commerce of Spain.

As Bolívar wrote years later in his Jamaica Letter, his manifesto in which he envisioned that all of South America is free from European rule, the colonists of Venezuela were obliged "to cultivate fields of indigo, grain, coffee, sugar cane, cacao, and cotton, and to raise cattle on empty plains; to hunt wild beasts in the wilderness; to mine the earth to satisfy the insatiable greed of Spain." But they were forbidden to develop their industries or to trade with any nation other than Spain.

Although Venezuela's full economic potential was being actively stifled, it still generated enough revenue to keep the Creoles wealthy and comfortable. Spain hoped that as long as the top-most tier of colonial society lived in luxury, they would not be tempted to rebel against the king. And in most cases, this was true. During his travels through South America (1799–1804), Alexander von Humboldt, a German naturalist and explorer, remarked that the Creoles of Venezuela "see in revolutions only the loss of their slaves…they would prefer a foreign yoke to the exercise of authority by the Americans of an inferior class."

THE ROAD TO POLITICS

Bolívar's father died when he was two-and-a-half; his mother died when he was nine. His uncles—his mother's two brothers, Esteban and Carlos Palacios—were made his guardians, but because Esteban was almost constantly in Spain, attempting, unsuccessfully, to have the Palacios family formally recognized as members of the Spanish nobility, the duty of raising and educating Bolívar fell on Carlos Palacios, an irritable character who did not like children.

Carlos enrolled Bolívar in a small private academy operated by Simón Rodríguez, a twenty-three-year-old teacher who the year before had been licensed by the Caracas cabildo, or city council, to open a school. In 1792, Rodríguez taught

113 boys, including Bolívar. The curriculum was rudimentary—reading, writing, arithmetic, and the Catholic catechism. Rodríguez hated the work. As for his students, they were as lax about attending classes as their parents were about paying tuition.

Bolívar didn't care for the school either, so his family arranged for him to be taught in the classic fashion of the upper classes—by private tutors in his home. Andrés Bello, at the time Latin America's leading poet and philosopher, taught Bolívar literature. A priest (whose first name is lost to history), Father Andujar, came to the house to teach the boy mathematics. And Rodríguez tutored him in grammar.

Bello and Rodríguez had read John Locke, Rousseau, and Voltaire, and had come to believe in the Enlightenment's principles that reason was the only true basis for any authority and that men ought to be free to govern themselves. It's likely that they discussed these ideas with their pupil. That same year Uncle Carlos enrolled Bolívar in a school for cadets where the boy acquired his first military training.

Between 1799 and 1802, young Bolívar's life leapt from one dramatic event to the next. He traveled to Spain—his first journey outside the Americas, his first experience of the Old World. There he found a mentor in the Marquis de Uztariz, a Venezuelan who had relocated to Spain and made an impressive career for himself serving the Crown; when Bolívar met the marquis, he was minister of the war council. Under the marquis' guidance, Bolívar made the transition from raw, colonial youth to polished young gentleman.

About the same time Bolívar met Maria Teresa Rodríguez del Toro y Alayza, a shy, pale beauty, the daughter of a Venezuelan father and a Spanish mother, and an heiress who would bring a fortune to the man she married. Bolívar described her as "a jewel without flaw, valuable beyond esteem." At Maria Teresa's home in Bilbao, Bolívar proposed marriage to "the lovable enchantress of my soul," and she accepted. On their wedding day, May 26, 1802, Bolívar was eighteen, Maria Teresa was twenty-one. After the wedding, they departed almost immediately for Venezuela.

Maria Teresa was Bolívar's first love, and he was blissfully happy with his wife. Then, only a few months after their arrival home, Maria Teresa fell ill with a fever. Her condition grew worse, and none of the doctors' treatments did her any good. She died, eight months after her wedding day, on January 22, 1803.

Bolívar was inconsolable. In an impetuous moment, he vowed never to marry again. Although he had several affairs during his life, he kept his oath. Years later,

THE LEGACY OF SIMÓN BOLÍVAR

Throughout South America, Simón Bolívar is hailed as more than a hero. He is the object of a patriotic cult, a kind of national saint. What he accomplished in his life is almost miraculous. Although Bolívar had minimal military training and no battlefield experience, he led armies that liberated a vast territory in South America encompassing the countries known today as Venezuela, Colombia, Panama, Ecuador, Bolivia, and Peru. This war of liberation dragged on for fourteen years, during which time Bolívar and the supporters of the independence movement suffered heart-breaking reversals, tragic betrayals, and bloody civil war.

Once Spain withdrew from the war and conceded that she had lost some of her most valuable colonies, Bolívar the commander had to make the transition to Bolívar the nation-builder. Like Jean-Jacques Rousseau in France and Thomas Jefferson in the United States, Bolívar gave the newly liberated people of South America a set of ideals. He held up liberty as "the only object worth the sacrifice of a man's life." He warned against falling under the spell of a dictator, "Only the majority is sovereign; he who takes the place of the people is a tyrant and his power is usurpation."

One of Bolívar's greatest challenges was overturning centuries of privilege and prejudice based on birth and race. Time and again, he asserted that South Americans are not Europeans nor are they Indians, but a mixed people of Spanish, African, and Indian blood. The only way to overcome bigotry was to adopt a constitution that recognized all citizens as equal before the law. Bolívar brought these ideals down from the level of theory to practice by abolishing slavery, recognizing and protecting the rights of Indians, and redistributing land that had been in the hands of the country's wealthy elite.

In spite of Bolívar's principles and good intentions, the transition from colonies to independent nations was not smooth. Racial prejudice and resentments between the classes lingered. Bolívar himself doubted that the vast majority of people were ready for democracy, which explains why he accepted the office of president-for-life. Despite his failures, Bolívar was an extraordinary figure who by his deep commitment to liberty accomplished the impossible, liberating nearly 5 million square kilometers of South America, an area equal to half the size of Europe.

In addition to liberating Venezuela from Spain, Bolívar abolished slavery, recognized the rights of the Indians, and redistributed land that had belonged to the country's wealthy colonial elite. Liberation of Slaves by Simón Bolívar (1783–1830) (w/c on paper), Cancino, Fernandez Luis (19th century) / Casa-Museo 20 de Julio de 1810, Bogota, Colombia / Giraudon / The Bridgeman Art Library International

looking back on the tragic loss of Maria Teresa, Bolívar wrote, "Without the death of my wife, I would not have made my second journey to Europe, and it is probable that the ideas I acquired on my travels would not have root…. The death of my wife propelled me early on the road to politics."

It could not have been an easy visit to Bilbao, but it was necessary for Bolívar to call upon his father-in-law so they could mourn the loss of Maria Teresa together. Once he had fulfilled his family obligations, Bolívar headed north to Paris. At five-foot, six-inches (168 cm) tall, with a build that was so slender he could be described as scrawny, Bolívar did not cut a dashing figure, but he had a handsome face, wealth, and good connections, and he was eager to bury his sorrow in all the pleasures the city had to offer. He rented a house, was reunited with his old tutor, Rodríguez, then began a round of gambling and woman-chasing. He began an affair with Fanny Dervieu de Villars, who presided over a salon where liberal politics was the favorite topic of conversation. De Villars, in her late twenties, had a husband twice her age, but Bolívar pretended the man did not exist. His affair with Fanny lasted two years.

In Europe, Bolívar experienced his political awakening. The bits of Enlightenment philosophy he picked up as a boy, the political banter at Fanny's house, the reunion with the liberal Rodríguez were all working on Bolívar, undermining his placid acceptance of the Creole elite's status quo. He realized how deeply all these factors had altered his outlook when Spain's ambassador to France invited Bolívar to join him at the Cathedral of Notre Dame to witness the coronation of Napoleon. Bolívar refused. He regarded Napoleon's coronation as a betrayal of the principles of the French Revolution. But while he detested Napoleon the emperor, he admired Napoleon the general: He was an example to Bolívar of how much one ambitious man could accomplish. In 1804, Bolívar probably did not see himself as a Napoleonic figure, but in later years, the liberator of Venezuela and Peru and creator of Colombia, Ecuador, and Panama would see himself that way.

All these new, exciting ideas were percolating in Bolívar's mind as he and Rodríguez began their Grand Tour through France, Switzerland, and Italy. And those ideas came fruition at last on a sultry evening in Rome when Bolívar vowed to free Venezuela from the empire of Spain.

CHAPTER NINE

GIUSEPPE GARIBALDI, 1807–1882: THE POLITICAL AWAKENING OF A PATRIOT

A chance encounter with a fellow Italian turned an apolitical seaman into the man who helped unify Italy.

On an April evening in 1833, Giuseppe Garibaldi, mate of the French commercial vessel *La Clorinda*, was strolling along the Taganrog, Russia, waterfront when he met a fellow Italian, a young man from Genoa. When the conversation turned to politics, the Genoese spoke passionately of his desire to work for the unification of Italy. Garibaldi had not given much thought to the condition of his family's homeland, but that chance meeting with a stranger proved to be the transformative moment in his life.

"Columbus can hardly have experienced so much satisfaction at the discovery of a new world," Garibaldi wrote years later, "as I did on finding a man who was actually concerned in the redemption of our country."

Garibaldi wrote about this experience twice, and in the later version, suggested another person also influenced his thoughts about Italian nationhood, but it is clear from both accounts that this is the moment when an apolitical merchant seaman became an Italian patriot. The rest of his life would be devoted to this cause.

A SEAFARING FAMILY

It's odd but not incomprehensible that a Russian town on the Sea of Azov should be the place where Garibaldi experienced his political awakening. Taganrog had been founded in 1698 by Tsar Peter the Great as a naval base to guard the southern extent of his realm against a possible Ottoman invasion. By April 1833, when Garibaldi's ship, *La Clorinda*, entered the town's harbor, Taganrog had lost its mili-

Giuseppe Garibaldi was a pragmatic revolutionary. When it became apparent that Italy was more likely to unite under a constitutional monarchy than a republic, he threw his support behind King Victor Emmanuel.

tary character and become a prosperous center of international trade. It was a lovely town, set on a hill above the harbor, with handsome baroque and neo-classical homes and palaces set along shady, tree-lined streets. Many merchants, diplomats, and émigrés from southern Europe found the town congenial and settled there.

Garibaldi had been to Taganrog several times. An old court document records that during one visit he was fined for smuggling in contraband cigars. But Garibaldi's cargo in April of 1833 was legitimate; he had brought oranges to sell to Russian produce dealers.

Seafaring was the Garibaldi family trade. Garibaldi's father and grandfather had both been ships' captains. The sea did not make the Garibaldis rich, however: Giuseppe's parents, Domenico and Rosa Raimondi Garibaldi, never got far enough ahead financially to own a house, but at least they had the means to provide their four children with educations.

Garibaldi was born on July 4, 1807, in a small house on a tiny alley a few steps away from the Nice waterfront. During the late eighteenth and early nineteenth centuries, control of Nice passed back and forth between France and the Italian kingdom of Lombardy-Venetia. Consequently, in addition to the town's native French population, there was also a large Italian community.

Garibaldi's parents were ambitious for their sons. Giuseppe's brother Angelo made his mother and father proud by becoming Italy's consul in Philadelphia. They hoped that Giuseppe would make a good living as a lawyer, or perhaps fulfill their dreams by entering the priesthood. But Giuseppe was not religious. At age eighteen, Giuseppe accompanied his father to Rome, but while his father followed the pilgrim route to the great basilicas and shrines, Giuseppe visited the shattered remains of pagan Rome.

The sea had always fascinated Garibaldi. When Garibaldi was a young boy, he and several friends "borrowed" a fishing boat for a spur-of-the-moment excursion to Genoa. At age fifteen, Garibaldi went on his first voyage, as an apprentice cabin boy. It appeared that he would follow in the family tradition.

THE "YOUNG" MOVEMENT

In 1833, there was no Italy per se. Instead, the Italian peninsula was carved up into eight separate states: the Kingdom of the Two Sicilies, the Papal States, the Grand Duchy of Tuscany, the Duchy of Lucca, the Duchy of Modena, the Duchy of Parma, the Kingdom of Sardinia, and the Kingdom of Lombardy-Venetia (which

July 4, 1807
Giuseppe Maria Garibaldi is born in Nice, France, to Domenico and Rosa Raimondi Garibaldi, two Italian immigrants from Liguria.

1824–1833
Rejects his parents' wish that be become a lawyer or a priest and makes his living as a sailor.
April 1833
In Taganrog, Russia, encounters a young stranger from Genoa who inspires him to dedicate his life to the liberation and unification of Italy. Joins Giuseppe Mazzini's secret political society, Young Italy.
1834
Implicated in an uprising in Genoa. Flees the country and is tried and sentenced to death in abstentia.
1835–1848
In exile in South America. Fights on the side of independence movements in Brazil and Uruguay. Marries Ana Ribeiro da Silva, and they have four children.

June 1848
Returns to Italy to fight for the establishment of an Italian republic.
1849
Victories at Palestrina and Velletri. Marches north to lift the siege of Venice, but his army deserts him. Escapes Austrian troops and finds safety in Liguria.
1849–1853
In exile, first in the United States, then in England.
1854–1859
Returns to Italy. Purchases land on the island of Caprera for a farm. Angers many of his fellow revolutionaries when he abandons his dream of an Italian republic and throws his support behind a constitutional monarchy.

1859
Defeats the Austrians at Varese. Appointed general of the Piedmont army, but resigns his command when his superiors refuse to let him invade the Papal States.
May–October 1860
Leads 1,000 volunteers to support a revolution in Sicily. Captures Palermo and Naples and repulses the royalist counter-attack at Volturno.
1861
The Kingdom of Italy is established; Victor Emmanuel I is proclaimed king.
1862
Defies government policy and leads 2,000 volunteers in a march on Rome. The Italian army intercepts and arrests him.

1867
Leads another unsuccessful march against Rome. Papal and French troops defeat him.
September 20, 1870
Troops of the Kingdom of Italy march into Rome. The Papal States are abolished.
1871
Fights in the Franco-Prussian War to restore the French republic.

March 10, 1872
Giuseppe Mazzini dies in Pisa.
1875–1879
In Rome, promotes an international league for universal democracy and lobbies the government to make improvements to the city's infrastructure.
1880–1882
Returns to his farm at Caprera. Suffers from severe arthritis and is often confined to his bed.

June 2, 1882
Dies at age seventy-five on his farm. His family and the Italian government refuse to honor his request for a simple funeral followed by cremation, giving him a lavish state funeral with more than 10,000 mourners present. His body is buried beneath a twelve-foot-high (3.6 m) granite pyramid.

was not ruled by an Italian king but by the emperor of Austria-Hungary). The kings, dukes, and of course the pope in Rome, ruled as autocrats, rejected calls for democratic government, and imprisoned political dissidents and executed rebels. But the success of the revolutions in the United States, France, Haiti, and, in 1832, Greece, led Italian insurgents to believe that they could bring down the kings and dukes, strip the pope of his temporal power, and form a united Italian republic.

The unofficial leader of Italy's national revolution was Giuseppe Mazzini, a lawyer and political activist from Liguria, the province where Garibaldi's parents had been born. When Mazzini was twenty-five he joined the Carbonari, an underground political organization that had been founded originally to resist Napoleon's occupation of Italy. Mazzini had been a member for barely a year when the Carbonari called for revolution. It was an utter failure. The force of volunteers who marched on Rome was intercepted and destroyed by an Austrian army. Uprisings in the duchies of Modena and Parma, as well as in various cities of the Papal States, were put down by more Austrian troops.

As an alternative to Catholicism, Giuseppe Mazzini tried to persuade his fellow Italians to adopt a form of Christianity that was less supernatural and more politically progressive. Getty Images

After the Carbonari's ill-fated revolution, Mazzini concluded that Italy needed a new, better organized association for political activists. In 1832 he founded *La giovine Italia*, Young Italy.

The "young" movement was not unique to Italians. At the time there was a Young Austria, Young France, Young Germany, Young Ireland, Young Poland, and Young Switzerland. For activists whose political vision spanned the continent, there was even a Young Europe.

Similar to the Freemasons and the soon-to-be-moribund Carbonari,

Young Italy was a secret society. To safeguard their identity, members adopted new names chosen from the old Italian warrior clans of the Middle Ages. They had a secret gesture of recognition: One Young Italian crossed his arms with the palms of his hand placed over his heart, while the other crossed his arms with the palms of his hands open to his brother Young Italian. Their secret greeting was, "What is the time?" The reply being, "Time for the struggle." And of course there was a secret handshake—a simple interlocking of right index fingers.

Initially the members of Young Italy called themselves "the Good Cousins," then "the Brothers," and finally they referred to themselves simply (if immodestly) as "the Good."

Upon entering the organization—Garibaldi joined late in 1833—the new recruit swore by God and the patriot-martyrs of Italy to fight injustice and tyranny until Italy was free and united. A new member also swore never to reveal any information about Young Italy. If one of the Good betrayed his brothers, all other members of Young Italy were duty-bound to track down the traitor and kill him.

Mazzini instructed his followers that their goal was a united Italy with Rome as its capital. In Rome, they would install a republican government inspired by the republic of ancient Rome. Mazzini never let them forget that their enemies were kings, aristocrats, the pope and the hierarchy of the Catholic Church, and the Austrian troops who had crushed every Italian uprising and hounded every Italian patriot.

Young Italy's membership was a mixed bag. Some were professional revolutionaries. Others were dreamers. A few were dilettantes excited by the thought that they were now heroes. Most however were committed to the cause of the liberation and unification of their country, and they did what they could by collecting arms and ammunition, distributing newspapers and journals that promoted Young Italy's ideals, and teaching the principles of freedom of speech, religion, and the press to ordinary Italians who had never experienced such things.

Almost immediately after Mazzini founded his group, Young Italy was infiltrated by spies who sent back to their various intelligence agencies wildly exaggerated membership statistics. The spies claimed that 140,000 men had joined Young Italy, that there were 40,000 members in the Papal States alone. Most likely Young Italy's membership never exceeded 60,000—a figure that includes cells inside Italy as well as cells organized by Italian immigrants abroad.

MAZZINI'S PROGRESSIVE GOD

The French revolutionaries had tried to obliterate Christianity, and Karl Marx would dismiss all religions as "the opiate of the people," but Mazzini believed that religion could be harnessed to advance the cause of revolution. To Mazzini's way of thinking, the existing churches—the Catholic Church especially—were useless. They propped up the status quo in Europe, and they stood in the way of the enlightenment and liberation of the people. The solution was to introduce a new form of Christianity that was consistent with liberal political principles. "Humanity is, now as ever," Mazzini wrote, "deeply, inevitably religious, and because it is religious, it makes war on the Papacy."

The pope at the time, Gregory XVI (reigned 1831–1846), was everything the anti-papacy revolutionaries would have him be. When uprisings erupted in the Papal States, he brought in Austrian troops to put down the rebellions. He gave his approval to a new volunteer police force, organized by his secretary of state, Cardinal Tommaso Bernetti, to spy on their neighbors and denounce the disloyal. Rebels in Papal States were sentenced to long prison terms or to hard labor, or they were executed. Exiles and refugees from the Papal States spread the word that Gregory was a tyrant, who was so reactionary that he would not permit a railway to be constructed in his dominion.

As an alternative to Catholicism, Mazzini cobbled together a new type of Christianity. His creed asserted that there is a God, but he is remote from his creation, rarely interfering in human affairs. He dwells in heaven where after death the good will join him. On the subject of what happens to the souls of the wicked after death, Mazzini was unwilling to commit himself. His Enlightenment principles would not permit him to openly admit that he believed in the existence of hell.

Mazzini's God did not work miracles. Instead, from time to time, he sent individuals known as "Men of Genius" to guide mankind. Among these were Martin Luther, René Descartes, Sir Isaac Newton, Napoleon Bonaparte, and the Romantic poet George Gordon Lord Byron. As for Jesus Christ, Mazzini portrayed him as a man of the people, a liberator from materialism, and an enemy of tyrants.

In Mazzini's theology, the fundamental divine law was progress—political, social, economic, and religious progress. Mazzini had absolute faith that everything in this world moves forward and improves as it does so.

With this new, politically enlightened form of Christianity, Mazzini hoped to win over the vast majority of the Italian people. By giving his movement a theological cast, he was also elevating his campaign to unify Italy into a crusade in which Young Italy acted in accordance with the will of Mazzini's progressive God.

Whether Garibaldi embraced Mazzini's new Christianity is debatable. At the end of his life, he declared to some visitors, "I am a true Christian!" but he never defined his terms. But even if Garibaldi was not willing to profess Mazzini's form of Christianity, Garibaldi did join him in loathing the Papacy. He wrote that the goal of the revolution was to free the entire world "from the incubus of the Papacy, which everywhere opposes education, protects ignorance, and is the nurse of vice."

Garibaldi's "army" usually consisted of inexperienced volunteers, such as those seen here manning the barricades during an 1848 uprising in Naples.
Getty Images

A BUNGLED UPRISING

Late in November 1833, Garibaldi stepped inside a waterfront tavern in Marseille. At one of the tables sat a group of young men speaking Italian, so he went over to join them. One of the drinkers was praising Young Italy, but he was interrupted by one of his companions who, in a sarcastic tone, asked, "Italy? What do you mean by Italy? Do you mean the kingdom of Naples? Or the kingdom of Piedmont? Perhaps you mean the Duchy of Modena?"

"I mean the new Italy," his friend replied. "The united Italy of all Italians."

Garibaldi was so moved by such patriotic fervor that he could not speak. He rose and shook the young man's hand. It was here in Marseille that Garibaldi joined Young Italy. A few months later, Garibaldi and a few associates tried to lead an insurrection in Genoa. But without popular support, the uprising collapsed almost as soon as it had begun. It appears the authorities were ready for the uprising thanks to Garibaldi, who approached perfect strangers on the Genoa waterfront and in the city's taverns and cafes, urging them to join him in liberating their city.

In 1860 Garibaldi led a successful revolution against the Kingdom of Sicily, capturing Palermo and defeating royalist troops at Volturno.

After the debacle, as soldiers and police fanned out across Genoa to arrest the insurgents, Garibaldi found refuge in the home of a fruit seller. She dressed him in peasant clothes and sent him on his way.

For ten days, Garibaldi followed back roads and rugged footpaths through the mountains until at last he reached his parents' home in Nice. Domenico and Rosa were horrified when their son confessed that he had joined a revolutionary movement, led a failed insurrection in Genoa, and was now a fugitive from the law. At some point he slipped out of Nice and crossed into France. From here he took

passage to South America, settling in Brazil. For the next thirteen years of his life, Garibaldi would be an exile from Italy with a price on his head.

Mazzini was the chief philosopher of the Risorgimento, the political movement to unify Italy, and Garibaldi was its chief commander. After Garibaldi's return to Italy in 1848, he organized one army after another—usually of inexperienced volunteers. Garibaldi suffered defeats and reversals, but time and again, thanks to his genius as a commander, his courage, and his gift for inspiring his troops, he won stunning victories over the trained troops of the kings of Sardinia, Naples, the pope, and their Austrian and French allies.

In politics, he tended toward pragmatism. While purists insisted that Italy must be a republic, Garibaldi threw his support behind a constitutional monarchy because it was more popular with the Italian people. On one point he would not compromise— there could no unified Italy so long as the Papal States existed. In 1870, when Italian troops captured Rome and the pope retreated to the Vatican, the dream Garibaldi first experienced in a remote Russian port was realized at last.

CHAPTER TEN

ABRAHAM LINCOLN, 1809–1865: THE LEGACY OF A SLAVE MARKET ENCOUNTER

A slow raft trip down the Mississippi gave the Great Emancipator a view of slavery he never forgot.

The silent file of black men inched slowly forward, their heads bowed, their eyes downcast, their expressions mournful. The heavy chains shackling them together clank-clanked against the cobblestone New Orleans street. Two nineteen year olds from upriver watched transfixed as a snarling man wielding a whip marched beside them, flicking the whip menacingly to keep the procession moving.

"I will at all times pay the highest prices for Negroes of every description," read a hand-lettered placard posted on a nearby tree. "And will also attend to their sale on commission, having a jail and a yard expressly fitted up for boarding them." Another sign proclaimed: "Wanted! I want to purchase twenty-five likely Negroes between the ages of eighteen and twenty-five years, male and female, for which I will pay the highest prices in cash." Still a third declared, "For sale: Several likely girls from ten to eighteen years old, a woman twenty-four, a very valuable woman twenty-five, with three very likely children."

The procession shuffled past a row of enclosures, walled off from the street by fences two stories high. "T. Hart, Slaves," a hanging sign advertised. "Charles Lemarque, Negroes," read another. Then the two youths saw the black men herded into a large open area and forced, one by one, to step up on a platform in the center, where their bodies and their lives would be offered for sale. It was a horrifying picture that would remain with one of the youths, Abraham Lincoln, for the rest of his life.

A gangly Lincoln (in blue trousers at left) watches as an auctioneer offers a "comely young mulatto woman" for sale in the New Orleans slave auction, painted later by Joseph Boggs Beale. Getty Images

The New Orleans slave market was the largest in North America, dwarfing those in Charleston, Savannah, Baltimore, and Richmond. Situated where the mighty Mississippi poured its waters into the Gulf of Mexico and thence the Atlantic Ocean, New Orleans opened a riverine highway into the vast rich agricultural heartland of the continent and connected it to the markets and lands across the sea.

In the early nineteenth century, vast tracts of the inland United States were being subdivided into large farms and plantations, cultivating rice, cotton, tobacco and sugar cane. Their burgeoning fields had an almost insatiable demand for bent-back labor. Crops must be planted, tended, weeded, hoed, harvested, and prepared for market—demanding work from dawn to dusk and performed under a merciless summer sun. Plantation housewives needed female help to cook, clean, plant gardens, wash clothes, mind children, milk cows, and collect eggs.

The demand for humans was endless. Almost daily, sailing vessels tied up at New Orleans docks to disgorge a cargo of African men and women bound for involuntary servitude.

The demand for humans was endless. Almost daily, sailing vessels tied up at New Orleans docks to disgorge a cargo of African men and women bound for involuntary servitude. According to one estimate, two million African slaves passed through the slave markets in the forty years before the U.S. Civil War of 1860. And that figure did not include the children of slaves condemned to slavery by accident of birth.

A FRONTIER BOYHOOD

Abraham Lincoln was born in the slave-holding state of Kentucky in 1809, when the territory was mostly wilderness and small towns and villages carved out of the brush, not plantations. Few of Lincoln's neighbors had slaves. The 1810 census for Hardin County, where Thomas Lincoln had settled his family in a hand-hewn log cabin in 1806, counted 940 Negroes in a population of 7,531, most of whom

February 12, 1809
Abraham Lincoln is born in a log cabin near Hodgenville, Kentucky, to Thomas and Nancy Hanks Lincoln, second child and first son.

December 1816
Lincoln family moves across the Ohio River to the Pigeon Creek settlement in Indiana.

October 5, 1818
Nancy Hanks Lincoln dies of "milk sickness." Thomas remarries one year later to Sarah Bush Johnston. Abraham develops great affection for her.

April 1828
Along with neighbor Allen Gentry, takes homemade flatboat of farm produce on three-month, 1,000-mile (1,600 km) trip to New Orleans.

March 1830
Lincoln family moves again from Indiana to the Sangamon River area of Illinois, 200 miles (325 km) away.

March 1832
Black Hawk War breaks out in Illinois. Lincoln volunteers and is chosen captain of his militia company. Serves three one-month hitches.

August 4, 1834
Runs for Illinois State Assembly as the Whig candidate and is elected. Serves four two-year terms and becomes the leader of the Illinois Whig party.

November 4, 1842
After several off-and-on engagements, marries Mary Todd of Kentucky and moves to Springfield, Illinois. Studies law and sets up a law practice.

August 3, 1846
Elected to the U.S. House of Representatives. Serves one term, speaking against the U.S.-Mexican War.

May 29, 1856
Leaves the Whig party to join the new Republican Party.

May 1858
Nominated as the Republican candidate for U.S. Senate, opposing Democrat Stephen Douglas. Conducts seven debates with Douglas on slavery issue that are followed nationwide and bring Lincoln to national prominence.

November 1858
Illinois legislature chooses Douglas senator by a vote of 54–46.

May 18, 1860
Nominated as the Republican candidate for president to oppose Douglas.

November 6, 1860
Elected president over Douglas and two pro-slavery opponents. Receives 180 of 303 possible votes.

December 20, 1860
South Carolina secedes from the Union and is followed by six other "Cotton Belt" states in the Deep South, forming the Confederate States of America with Jefferson Davis of Mississippi as president.

April 12, 1861
Confederate forces fire on Fort Sumter, a U.S. installation in Charleston, South Carolina Harbor. Civil War begins.

April 17, 1861
Virginia, North Carolina, Tennessee, and Arkansas join the Confederacy.

July 21, 1861
First Battle of Bull Run, near Washington, opens land hostilities and ends in the defeat of Union troops.

April 16, 1862
Abolishes slavery in the District of Columbia by executive order.

May 20, 1862
Signs the Homestead Act, granting 160-acre (650,000 m²) freeholds to homesteaders and opening the West for settlement.

May 30, 1862
General George McClellan fails to take Confederate capital of Richmond in the Seven Days Campaign and is replaced by General John Pope, who loses the Second Battle of Bull Run.

September 17, 1862
Union and Confederate armies clash at Antietam, Maryland, in the bloodiest day of fighting in U.S. history. McClellan, restored to command, halts the Confederate drive north, but he is fired again by Lincoln for failure to follow up.

June 28, 1863
After crushing Union defeats at Fredericksburg and Chancellorsville, Virginia, General George Meade is named the new commander of the Army of the Potomac.

July 3, 1863
Meade's army holds off the Confederate northern offensive in a three-day battle of Gettysburg, Pennsylvania. On the same day, General Ulysses S. Grant takes Vicksburg, Mississippi, giving the Union complete control of the vital Mississippi waterway and cutting the Confederacy in two. The twin victories constitute the turning point in the war.

November 19, 1863
Lincoln delivers the famous Gettysburg Address, consecrating the battlefield as a national cemetery.

March 12, 1864
Appoints General Grant general in chief of all U.S. armies.

June 8, 1864
Lincoln is nominated for reelection on the Union ticket of Republicans and War Democrats.

September 2, 1864
General William Tecumseh Sherman captures Atlanta and begins the infamous destructive March to the Sea.

November 8, 1864
Lincoln is reelected with 212 of 233 possible electoral votes and 55 percent of the popular vote.

April 9, 1865
Confederate General Robert E. Lee surrenders the Confederate army to General Grant at Appomattox Court House, Virginia.

April 14, 1865
While attending a Washington theater, Lincoln is shot by John Wilkes Booth.

April 15, 1865
Lincoln dies at 7:22 a.m. without regaining consciousness and is succeeded by Vice President Andrew Johnson.

were freed slaves. But by 1816, the number of slaves in the county had grown to 1,238; one landowner alone had 58 slaves.

Abraham's parents, Thomas and Nancy Hanks Lincoln, attended the Little Mount Baptist Church, whose members had strong antislavery convictions, which the Lincolns shared. "Partly because of slavery," his son was to say later, in 1816, Thomas Lincoln chose to move his family across the Ohio River to the free state of Indiana. With the eight-year-old Abe also wielding an axe, the family hacked out a plot of land near Little Pigeon Creek. There, with the help of neighbors and Abe's growing muscles, they constructed an 18-by-20-foot (5.5-by-6.1 m) cabin.

As an adult, Lincoln, the village wit and raconteur, liked to tell audiences that he understood the toils of slavery. He had been a slave himself, he said, but he had been set free "and now they let me practice law." The joke was always good for a laugh, but Lincoln was half serious. The young Lincoln had been compelled by his father to work the family fields and also those of his neighbors as a hired hand. Ironclad custom required that all of Lincoln's earnings be turned over to his father to support the family.

It was this form of "slavery" that took the nineteen year old 1,000 miles (1,600 km) down the Sangamon, Ohio, and Mississippi rivers to New Orleans in 1828.

James Gentry, the largest landowner in the Pigeon Creek settlement, had a bright idea that spring. He had harvested bumper crops on his land in the fall. His hogs had fattened, thrived, and multiplied. But other farmers in this part of Indiana had prospered, too, meaning that the market for corn and pork might be glutted, driving prices down.

Pigeon Creek was a tributary of the Sangamon, which fed into the Ohio, which in turn joined the Mississippi, eventually reaching New Orleans and the export markets beyond. The Gentry property abutted the Ohio River. Why not build a flatboat and ship his produce downriver, where his son, Allen, could look for buyers? That sounded like a capital idea to Tom Lincoln. He immediately volunteered his own nineteen-year-old son, Abe, to come along as a deckhand—for wages, of course, that would be paid to his father.

The two youths immediately set to work chopping timber for a flatboat, cutting the logs into thick oak planks for a stout double bottom. They rigged two pairs of long oars at bow and stern and a steering post. Lincoln constructed a small deck shelter where they could store possessions and provisions and take refuge from the weather. There was a small earthen firepit amidships for cooking.

The result was a seaworthy craft 80 feet (24.4 m) long and 18 feet (5.5 m) in the beam. It would be their floating home for nearly three months.

In April, the rivers were running full and moving swiftly. Lincoln and Gentry loaded the boat with barrels of cured pork and corn and herded some live hogs aboard. Then they shoved off on the first leg of the long journey south.

SHADES OF HUCKLEBERRY FINN

Not unlike Huckleberry Finn and the runaway slave Jim in the Mark Twain novel, Lincoln and Gentry drifted lazily downriver, 4 to 6 miles (6 to 10 km) a day, tying up to the riverbank at night to watch the stars overhead. It was not always an easy trip. They had to avoid the proud white steamboats, plowing arrogantly upriver heedless of smaller craft. Other flatboats, sometimes as many as six in a line, canoes, and small vessels must be dodged. Lincoln, in the bow, had to watch for treacherous or changing currents that might drive the boat ashore or onto shoals, and to combat the sudden shift in direction with the oars and sweeps. Strong crosswinds or abrupt bends in the river also threatened to hurl the boat into the riverbank.

As a sixteen year old, Lincoln had built a small scow that he used to ferry passengers, one or two at a time, from Indiana river towns to the river steamers in midstream, or alongshore from village to village. But neither Lincoln nor Gentry were experienced rivermen or navigators. Their trip could have ended disastrously only a few miles from home.

Rounding a curve in the Sangamon, the vessel became hung up on the lip of the Camron milldam. The forward one-third of the vessel slanted downward over the edge of the dam and slowly began filling with water. Pork barrels slid down the deck and further overweighted the bow. Much of the nearby town of New Salem came out to look at their plight and offer advice, while Lincoln sat on the shore and studied the situation. Then he lifted some of the cargo onshore. Then he borrowed tools and cut a hole in the bow to let the water out. After plugging the hole—and with the help of some residents—he dropped the boat over the dam, reloaded the cargo and pushed off again on the southward course, to the admiration of spectators.

Along the way, Lincoln and Gentry stopped at plantations or small villages to sell some of their produce. One day they tied up along Louisiana's "Sugar Coast," below Baton Rouge, where cane fields marched down to the Mississippi. They went ashore and visited the plantation of a Madam Duchesne and to explore a

Lincoln manned the steering oar to maneuver his flatboat around a Mississippi snag in this later painting by Joseph Boggs Beale. Getty Images

small village. Returning to the flatboat after dark, they soon fell asleep, then awakened to find the vessel being ransacked.

Seven thugs—Lincoln identified them as "Negroes" in his campaign autobiography—were methodically grabbing cargo, food, clothing, utensils, whatever could be carried off. Lincoln, now nearly six feet, four inches (193 cm), tall and hard-muscled from swinging an axe and manning a steering oar, picked up a timber as a club and knocked one man overboard. Another came at him, but Lincoln, victor in New Salem village wrestling matches, threw him to the ground. Then Lincoln and Gentry chased the others into the woods. Both of them emerged with gashes on the forehead. Lincoln carried a scar above his right eye the rest of his life.

WELCOME TO THE BIG EASY

Lincoln and Gentry arrived in the humidity of New Orleans in late July. They were greeted by sights unlike anything a small-town youth had ever seen or imagined. So many flatboats like Lincoln's were moored in the port that he could only reach shore by stepping carefully from one deck to another.

New Orleans in 1828 was a city of 40,000. Since European settlers came in the 1600s, it had flown the flags of France, Spain, Britain, and now the United States, and was cosmopolitan as well as polyglot. Lincoln was wide-eyed at the sights and sharp-eared at the sounds. Seamen from everywhere mingled on the sidewalks, speaking—and cursing each other—in a babel of tongues: French, Spanish, Portuguese, Jamaican, and Barbadian mixed with the Southern and Midwestern accents of Americans.

Rows of taverns, wreathed in tobacco smoke, throbbed with music, singing, laughter, shouting, jeering, and epithets. Lipsticked women beckoned from windows to the males on the street below. Elegant ladies shielded by parasols sat in equally elegant carriages that rumbled across the cobblestones. To nineteen year olds barely beyond adolescence and whose quiet streets at home were mere dirt tracks and mud, it was a different world.

And then their explorations took them to the slave market. A young woman—Lincoln's former law partner and biographer, William Herndon, was to describe her later as "a vigorous and comely young mulatto"—was being offered for sale. The young men could not take their eyes away as she was forced to climb up on the platform for all to eye and assess. Tearful and trembling, she was ordered to turn this way and that, to open her mouth to display her teeth, to bend and twist. She was told to trot up and down the platform like a horse, presumably to show how smoothly she moved, and whether she was healthy and supple enough for a hard day's work as a field hand. Laughing, the auctioneer patted and pinched her bottom, and he invited bidders to do the same, while the stricken girl tried to wriggle away.

Lincoln turned to Gentry with a look of anger and disgust. "By God, let's get out of here," he said.

That was the first of two flatboat trips Lincoln made down the Mississippi. What else, if anything, he said during the visit to the slave market remains controversial, even nearly two centuries later. His cousin John Hanks later insisted that Lincoln had said, "If I can ever hit that thing," meaning the institution of slavery,

"I'll hit it hard." Former law partner Herndon repeated the story in his memoir, saying he had heard it directly from Hanks during an interview. But Hanks only traveled to St. Louis on the second flatboat trip and never reached New Orleans. He was also known to embroider his memories of Lincoln and their times together.

Lincoln never mentioned the incident publicly, and only a few other friends recall Lincoln ever referring to the market, or expressing the shame and horror he is said to have felt. As a political candidate and as president, though, Lincoln could not afford to sound antislavery or abolitionist themes. Throughout Lincoln's career, as the country fractured into free states and slave states, and violent quarrels broke out over whether new territories should be free or slave, his foremost aim was to keep the Union together with or without slavery.

Lincoln's views were succinctly summed up in a letter to Horace Greeley of the *New York Tribune* in 1862: "If I could save the Union without freeing any slave, I would do it; if I could save it by freeing all the slaves, I would do it; and if I could save it by freeing some and leaving others alone, I would also do that." Lincoln's famous Emancipation Proclamation in 1862 took some 700 legalistic words to grant freedom to slaves in those states "in rebellion," but only in those states. It said nothing about the horrors of slavery, and it did not even imply that slavery was wrong. It did not even hint that slaves were individuals, or humans.

Yet Lincoln's circle of intimates and advisers were convinced that he considered slavery evil and inhumane, and that his policies were partially driven by what he had seen of its horrors. That included his wife, Mary Todd Lincoln, the daughter of slave-holding Kentuckians, some of whose family served with the Confederacy and all of whom despised Lincoln. A rift developed in the family as Mary lectured her Confederate relatives on the evils of slavery.

After Lincoln's death, a letter came to light that he wrote in 1855 to his slave-owning friend Joshua Speed in Kentucky. Lincoln recalled a steamboat trip the two had taken on the Ohio River in 1841. "You may recall," Lincoln wrote, "as I well do, that there were on board, ten or a dozen slaves shackled together with irons. That sight was a continued torment to me." He went on, "I confess I hate to see the poor creatures hunted down and carried back to their stripes, and unrewarded toils, but I bite my lip and keep quiet."

Herndon and Lincoln retained their law partnership throughout Lincoln's presidency, and they remained close friends and confidantes. Even in 1889, when Herndon's three-volume biography of Lincoln was published, Herndon was firm

Our stock for the present Spring trade will be found to embrace, in extent and variety, the most complete assortment of any stock of FANCY DRY GOODS ever offered to the trade of Louisville, to which we particularly invite the attention of merchants visiting this market.
f20 d&w2mis

FOR SALE OR RENT.

For Sale.

A NEGRO BOY, aged about 12 years, quite likely. Sold for no fault. Address Box 1,406.   123 d4*

For Sale.

A NEGRO MAN, 28 years old, an excellent and reliable dining-room servant (sold for no fault), also a good WASHERWOMAN, on reasonable terms. Apply to
WM. ROSS,
At the Washington Insurance Office,
f17 dtf   Over B. P. Scally, Main, near Second st.

For Rent,

TWO FARMS 3½ and 4 miles from the city, on Seventh street plank road—200 acres cleared and in a fine state of cultivation, with new improvements on each. Said farms are highly suitable for dairy or gardening purposes. Will rent for a term of years.   JOHN JONES, JR.,
fe9 dtf   No. 4 Court Place.

For Rent.

THE three-story business house on the east side of Wall street, formerly occupied by Crittenden & Co. It is a large and well ventilated house; has a dry and well paved cellar, and is a very desirable house for a grocery or commission business.
For terms, apply to   WM. B. REYNOLDS
or CRITTENDEN & CO.,

WANTED.

Partner Wanted,

THE writer of this wishes a PARTNER to unite with him in the DRUG BUSINESS in the interior of Kentucky. The house is well established and doing a first-rate business. The person answering this must be a first-rate Druggist, well recommended, and possessed of a capital of $2,500. For further information apply to
HARVEY, KEITH, & CO.,
f23 d6*   On Main, bet. Sixth and Seventh.

Wanted.

A GOOD COOK AND WASHER, without incumbrance, who can come well recommended, can find an excellent home on application to
f22 dtf   FIELDING & TRUMAN, 408 Main st.

300 NEGROES WANTED.

I have leased the house on Sixth street, between Main and Market, for a term of years, known as the "Powell House." I wish to purchase Negroes of both sexes, for which I will pay the highest cash prices. Persons having negroes for sale will give me a call, as I am anxious to buy. I have at all times Negroes for sale, and can at all times found at my premises.
f7 dis2m&w9   W. P. DAVIS, Agent.

WINCHESTER & CO.

Slave-market posters like these greeted Lincoln when he arrived in New Orleans at age 19.

in his belief that the New Orleans episode had been instrumental in shaping Lincoln's principles.

"In New Orleans for the first time he beheld the true horrors of slavery," Herndon wrote. "He saw Negroes in chains, whipped and scourged. Against this his humanity rebelled and his mind and conscience wakened to the realization of what he had often heard and read." Citing Lincoln's presidential reputation for upholding humane principles even toward enemies, Herndon and others believed that Lincoln never forgot the humiliation and fright he saw in that young woman's face in 1828.

ULYSSES S. GRANT, 1822–1885: HOW PERSISTENCE IN THE FACE OF GRINDING POVERTY SHAPED A LEADER

"Sam" Grant quit the army to be a farmer—and failed. The experience made him a victorious general.

The bedraggled man was standing on a cold street corner in St. Louis that winter day in 1857, holding up a log of firewood to passersby. He wore a threadbare, badly faded military greatcoat with buttons missing. A battered slouch hat was pulled low on his forehead. His sun-bronzed face was fringed with a scrabbly beard, and his hands were gnarled and calloused.

Behind him stood a patient but tired-looking mule, tethered to a decrepit wagon. The wagon carried a full bed of firewood, like the stick he was displaying. He offered it for sale to an approaching pedestrian.

The man waved him off disdainfully. He was immaculately dressed in a military uniform, every button gleaming, trousers pressed, boots polished. Suddenly the man swung back with a startled expression. He walked closer and peered at the firewood salesman's face. "Great God, Grant!" he exclaimed. "What are you doing?"

Ulysses S. Grant, former U.S. army captain, smiled ruefully and nodded in recognition. "I am solving the problem of poverty" he replied with chagrin.

True. The decade of the 1850s was not being kind to Grant. His was a long and difficult struggle after he resigned from the army with a damaged reputation in 1854, amid charges of being drunk on duty. He was destitute and dispirited. Then came the great war that was to transform the country. The same quali-

Artillery officer "Sam" Grant played a key role in the Battle of Chapultupec, the decisive American victory in the Mexican-American War. Prints & Photographs Division, Library of Congress, LC-USZC4-6207

ties of determination, perseverance, and doggedness that saw Grant through the tough 1850s propelled him to leadership and the status of hero in the 1860s.

THE HOWITZER IN THE CHURCH TOWER

Grant had made a modest name for himself in the Mexican-American War of 1846–1848. Second Lieutenant Grant, a West Point graduate and artillery specialist, wrestled a mountain howitzer to the belfry of San Cosme Church, over the protests of San Cosme priests. The belfry overlooked the San Cosme *garita* ("gate"), one of several gates guarding the fortress of Chapultepec and Mexico City. From Grant's lofty perch, the artilleryman and his battery poured a devastating fire onto Mexican troops in the courtyard below. U.S. infantry under General Zachary Taylor stormed the gate, and the guards surrendered. The capitulation opened the way to capture of the Mexican capital and brought the two-year-old war to an end.

"You will find me a better farmer than a soldier," twenty-six-year-old Grant told his comrades when the war ended, declaring he planned to return to civilian life. His heroics at Chapultepec, however, earned him a promotion to the permanent rank of first lieutenant and a temporary captaincy, so he decided to make a career of the army. He returned to the United States and served at posts in the east before being assigned to California in 1852. The Gold Rush state and former Mexican territory had just been annexed to the Union.

On August 22, 1848, the shy, taciturn Grant had married the vivacious Julia Dent. She was the sister of his West Point roommate, the daughter of "Colonel" Frederick Dent, a wealthy, slave-owning plantation owner, and had grown up on the family estate, White Haven. Dent hoped his daughter would marry up the social ladder and certainly not to an army officer; four years passed before he consented to the marriage. Grant's Ohio family refused to attend the wedding because they disapproved of slaveholding. (The best man was Julia's cousin and Grant's fellow officer, Lieutenant James Longstreet, who would be second-in-command to Robert E. Lee facing Grant fifteen years later.)

California in 1852 was not a place for an impecunious army officer to set up housekeeping for a young bride used to crinoline gowns and jeweled dancing slippers. Not when a single egg sold for $5 and even the most humble lodging cost a small bag of gold dust. Nor was it a place to save money for a future and build a family; the couple's first child, Frederick, had been born in May 1850. Their second child, Ulysses Jr., who was nicknamed "Buck" because he had been born

April 22, 1822
Hiram Ulysses Grant is born in Point Pleasant, Ohio.

March 3, 1839
Appointed to the U.S. Military Academy at West Point. Erroneously listed as Ulysses Simpson Grant. He retains the name.
June 1843
Begins military service as a second lieutenant.
1846–1848
Serves in the Mexican-American War.
August 22, 1848
Marries Julia Boggs Dent of Saint Louis, Missouri.
June 2, 1854
Resigns from the army to begin farming.

November 8, 1860
Abraham Lincoln elected president of the United States.
December 20, 1860
South Carolina secedes from the Union. Six other deep Southern states follow to form the Confederate States of America.
April 12, 1861
Confederate artillery fires on Fort Sumter, South Carolina, triggering the Civil War. Four additional states secede and join the Confederacy.
April 19, 1861
Grant is named a lieutenant colonel of the Illinois militia.
August 9, 1861
Grant rejoins the U.S. army as a full colonel.

February 16, 1862
Grant's troops capture Fort Donelson.
July 3, 1863
Grant captures Vicksburg on the Mississippi after a protracted siege, cutting the Confederacy in two.
January 1, 1864
Grant is named the commander in chief of all Union armies. Headquarters are with the Army of the Potomac.
April 9, 1865
General Robert E. Lee surrenders the Confederate armies to Grant at Appomattox Court House, Virginia.

May 21, 1868
Nominated for president as Republican candidate; elected in November and reelected in 1872.

July 23, 1885
Dies in Mount McGregor, New York, of throat cancer.

in the Buckeye state of Ohio, arrived while his father was en route to California. Grant longed for his wife and family. He was desperately lonely and desperately poor. His $480-a-year captain's pay had been raised by $197 to offset inflationary California costs, but that was not nearly enough for his family's passage and a place to live. Grant set out to do something about it.

When two workers found gold in the American River in the California foothills, the news quickly spread across the nation, and around the globe. "The world rushed in," in the words of one book title about the Gold Rush. More than 200,000 fortune-seekers swarmed into California, lured by the misguided notion that they could just step into a watercourse and pluck gold nuggets out of the streambed. And that was only in the first year. Only a few became rich. But all had to be fed, clothed, housed, and entertained. Obviously money-making opportunities abounded. Grant and other enterprising officers saw their chance.

After a brief stop in San Francisco following an excruciating ocean trip by steamer and across the tropical isthmus of Panama, Grant was ordered north to isolated, remote Fort Vancouver at the mouth of the Columbia River in the Oregon Territory. It was cheaper than San Francisco, but he still needed money. He teamed up with Lieutenant Henry Wallen, who was also eager to bring his family but lacked the wherewithal.

TWO NAÏVE BUSINESSMEN

"Neither of us had the slightest bit of business experience, or business sense," Wallen was to say later of the pair's naivete. Nonetheless, they seized on a capital, money-making idea. They would cut 100-pound blocks of ice from the nearby ponds and lakes and ship it by sailing schooner to San Francisco, where ice was a precious commodity. Unfortunately the ship became becalmed en route, the trip took six weeks, and the two men's investment melted away before reaching its destination.

But Grant had grown up on a farm, and the soil in the Columbia Valley looked black and rich. Potatoes were selling for $8 to $9 a bushel in San Francisco. They would plant potatoes and sell them to feed the hungry hordes of gold-seekers. Grant, with his wry sense of humor, wrote a friend: "Our crop was enormous. Luckily in June the Columbia River rose to a great height and overflowed and killed most of our crop. This saved digging them up, for everybody else on the Pacific Coast seemed to have come to the conclusion at the same time that agriculture would be profitable. The only potatoes we sold were to our own mess."

But the gold-seekers still had to be entertained. Grant, Wallen, and two other officers leased the Union Hotel in San Francisco for $500 a month as a "sort of club billiard room," and hired an agent to run it. The agent was either "derelict or dishonest," friends said. He absconded, leaving the officers with a mountain of debt that took years to pay off.

Then Grant received what appeared to be a promotion. His captaincy was made permanent, and he was given command of Company F, Fourth Infantry. But he was transferred to another remote location, the newly built, raw Fort Humboldt, 300 miles (485 km) north of San Francisco in the rainy, foggy forests of giant redwoods. Humboldt was even lonelier, mail from Julia came at best once a week, and there was little for the officers to do, except complain. And drink. And drink.

Stories abound about Grant's drinking, then and later. Many of Grant's friends insisted throughout his career that he didn't drink as much as was depicted; he just showed its effects more. He would have one or two sips, the friends maintained, and his words would slur, and he couldn't walk straight or think straight. He drank more and more. "The habit had become confirmed in him," one friend declared.

The fort's commander, Colonel Robert Buchanan, was a martinet, firmly opposed to alcohol in any form. He repeatedly warned his officers about drinking and encouraged them to take a temperance pledge.

"HE WAS SLIGHTLY UNDER THE INFLUENCE"

One of Grant's duties as a company commander was to supervise payment of the enlisted men under his command and to sign the payroll voucher, showing that they had been paid. On payday in April 1854, the payment table had been set up in the orderly room of Company F. The first sergeant and paymaster sat behind the table. The soldiers lined up, and each man stepped forward, saluted, and stood at attention while his monthly pay was handed to him. Then he signed the payroll, pocketed the money, saluted, and left. Then Captain Grant arrived. The men came to attention and looked at Grant. He was unsteady, his eyes bloodshot, and his words slurred as he spoke to the first sergeant. He leaned on the payroll table for support. "He was slightly under the influence of liquor," Lieutenant Henry Hodges reluctantly reported later.

The next day Buchanan summoned Grant. The two men differed afterward in their recollections. Buchanan considered Grant a good, competent officer, liked by his men, but he had been warned again and again. It was a disciplinary question. He gave Grant a choice: Resign or face charges of being drunk on duty. In Grant's version, he simply offered to resign, despite Buchanan's wish to keep him. The unhappy Grant had been considering resigning, anyway, and this was his excuse. He quit the army next day.

By autumn 1854, Grant was back in Missouri, determined to prove himself as a farmer. Colonel Dent had given his daughter and son-in-law 60 acres (242,000 m²) on White Haven to farm and build a home for his growing family. The land was hardly the plantation's most productive. It was hilly, rocky and included some dense woods, which Grant, ever the optimist when his financial prospects were concerned, saw as a bonanza. The trees could be logged and sold as cordwood, given him an additional source of income. They could also be used to build the Grants a dwelling. He immediately set to work, clearing the land for planting and preparing a construction site for a house.

Because Ulysses S. Grant had always been opposed to oppression of other races, he did most of the farm work himself, even though the plantation had slaves.

Because Grant was still scrupulously paying off his debts from his bad California investments, the first growing season he had little money for seed or farm implements. Grant was too proud to ask his father-in-law for an advance or loan. He simply planted what he could afford, mostly oats, corn, and vegetables to feed the family, and reaped a meager harvest. In autumn, however, he saw a brighter light ahead. Firewood was in demand, and Grant concluded that he could rely on firewood sales for income, at least temporarily. He earned enough to purchase seed for spring planting and even to buy a pair of scrawny, bony horses to pull the plow. Grant studiously fattened the animals until they were ready for spring.

Grant did most of the work himself, even though the plantation had slaves. He had always been opposed to slavery and oppression of other races. In Grant's military career, he had stood up for the rights of Indians and Mexicans. He called the Mexican-American War in which he fought "one of the most unjust wars ever fought" to the outrage of fellow officers. In California, Grant protested the influx of

Chinese to work the gold mines, not because he opposed immigration but because their lives were "little more than bondage." Colonel Dent declared that the slaves "imposed" on the goodhearted Grant by letting him tackle the hardest and heaviest jobs. When Grant hired freed slaves for logging, neighbors complained that he "spoiled" them by paying 10 percent more than the going rate.

That summer Grant and neighbors raised his new log house. He quixotically named the place "Hardscrabble," some believed in a sly dig at the Colonel's mansions with their columns and pretentious names. Grant needed the house: A third child, a girl named Julia for her mother, arrived to join Buck and Frederick. However the harvest was rewarding, if not spectacular. Farming seemed to be paying off, and Grant looked forward to a banner year in 1857.

It began that way. Grant put seeds in the ground, the weather was good, the rains adequate. Then in early June came a deep and lasting freeze that devastated his crop. Vegetables froze in the ground. Wheat fields turned brown. Corn shriveled on the stalk. At harvest time, Grant totaled up the damage. He had expected to glean 400 to 500 bushels of wheat. Instead he harvested a mere 75 bushels. Oats and corn did better, but every farmer had the same problem and was frantically trying to sell his crop at fire-sale prices. Grant decided that taking the grains to market would be wasted time.

"BREAD OR DEATH!"

And then came the financial panic of 1857. Banks closed or suspended payments in specie, businesses went bankrupt or simply closed their doors, workers were fired or furloughed, and protesters shouting "Bread or Death!" swarmed through St. Louis streets. And Julia was pregnant again. Needing money to buy Christmas presents for his wife and family, Grant went to a pawnshop and hocked his treasured gold watch and chain. He wrote to his successful father for money, but there was little to lend.

Spring 1858 was no better. Colonel Dent's second wife died, and he decided to move from White Haven into St. Louis. He leased the plantation to Julia and Grant, and they put their 60 acres up for sale. Grant wrote his father again, trying to be upbeat. The winter wheat was promising, and he was planting Irish potatoes, cabbage, beets, cucumbers, and melons, which he expected to sell at a premium in St. Louis. "Every day I like farming better," he assured his father, "and I do not doubt that money is to be made at it." Meanwhile, could he borrow $500 at 10 percent interest?

Things looked less rosy in June. Another wave of cold weather destroyed his crops. Grant decided he must give up on the farming "experiment," as Julia called it. After those dogged years of backbreaking toil and dashed hopes, he must take a job in the city.

If Grant wouldn't go to her father for help, Julia would. Her cousin, Colonel Dent's sister's son Harry Boggs, operated a small real-estate and rent-collecting firm in St. Louis. Real estate, it was said, was going to boom in the spring because the financial panic was subsiding. Julia pressed her father to ask Boggs to take Grant into the firm. So one day in 1858 Grant climbed down from a wagonload of wood and accosted Boggs. "The old gentleman thinks I should learn the details and that my large acquaintance among army officers would bring additional customers to make it support both our families," he told Boggs. Soon a new sign went up over the small office. "Boggs and Grant, General Agents." With no money to invest, Grant was more a clerk than a partner. Taking the final steps to acknowledge his failure as a farmer, he auctioned off his horses, grain, and implements, helped Colonel Dent arrange a tenant farmer for the following growing season, and swapped Hardscrabble for a house in town.

Vivacious Julia Dent Grant was a popular figure in St. Louis and Washington society.

It was another case of Grant's being ruled by hope rather than experience. He was clearly not born to be a real-estate salesman, and he was too much of a softie to pressure dilatory tenants for rent, especially if the tenants were army personnel. He spent his time with them talking about Mexican-American War experiences or remembering the old days around the barracks and ignoring the purpose of the visit. Then the deal for Hardscrabble fell through. Julia and the children moved back to White Haven, while Grant occupied an unheated room behind the real-estate office. Grant walked 12 miles (19.3 km) each way every weekend to see his family. He was not bringing money into the firm and he knew it, so he quit. Friends recommended Grant for county engineer, a $1,500-a-year

Frantic depositors storm a failed bank at the height of the financial panic of 1857.

position for which his West Point education qualified him. But the choice was made by five county commissioners on partisan grounds, and Grant, unaffiliated with either party, lost to a Democrat, three votes to two.

Finally, Grant decided to swallow his pride and do what he had always sworn he would never do: Ask his father for a job. Jesse Grant's tanning and leather business had prospered under the business acumen of Grant's two younger brothers. The brothers had just opened a new leather-goods store in Galena, Illinois, upriver from St. Louis. Jesse persuaded his son Simpson to hire Ulysses at $800 a year, "until something better should turn up in his favor." In 1860, Grant and his family arrived by river steamer to start a new chapter in their lives, Grant marching down the gangplank carrying the family's favorite chairs.

Grant wasn't cut out to be a leather-goods salesman, either, it was quickly evident. He was too diffident to serve customers, often telling them to wait until a clerk was available. What he was good at was relating his army experiences and adventures in the Mexican-American war. Although people insisted that Grant steadfastly refused to drink, the army veteran soon became known in the gathering places about town.

DOGGED PERSEVERANCE UNTIL THE END

In 1860, the issue of slavery was dividing the country, nowhere more so than in Illinois. As a direct replay of their famous debates, Abraham Lincoln, the folksy Republican lawyer from Springfield, and Senator Stephen A. Douglas, the Democrat, were contending for the presidency. There was talk of a rebellion by Southern states if Lincoln were elected and a possible breakup of the Union. Grant had never voted. In the presidential election of 1856 pitting Democrat James Buchanan against Republican General John C. Frémont, Grant famously said, "I didn't vote for Buchanan, because I didn't know him, and I didn't vote for Frémont because I did." But now the country seemed to be arming for rebellion and possibly all-out war, and Grant the military expert was the center of curbstone discussions, his opinions repeatedly sought and listened to. If Lincoln were elected, he predicted flatly, "The South will fight."

This time Grant was right. Lincoln defeated Douglas and two other candidates in November. South Carolina seceded from the Union, followed by the Deep South states of Georgia, Florida, Alabama, Mississippi, Louisiana, and Texas. After Lincoln was inaugurated, on April 12, 1861, South Carolina troops bombarded Fort Sumter, a federal installation in the Charleston, South Carolina harbor. The key state of Virginia, plus North Carolina, Tennessee, and Arkansas, seceded too, forming an eleven-state Confederate States of America with its capital at Richmond, Virginia, and Jefferson Davis as president. A man came rushing into the leather-goods store on Galena's Main Street shouting the news to Grant, who was up on a ladder stocking shelves. "Jefferson Davis ought to be hung," Grant said, "and the others with him." When Grant came down from the ladder, he said to brother Orvil, "I think I should go into service again." "I think you should," Orvil said.

The next day, Grant volunteered for a militia unit that was rapidly being formed in Galena, and he was elected captain. Days later, Grant was named a lieutenant colonel as Illinois mobilized a makeshift militia for three months' service and war. Grant quickly whipped the raw recruits into some sort of fighting shape, and Governor Richard Yates appointed him to command the new militia. Backed by river gunboats and applying his farm-honed qualities of relentlessness and refusal to quit in the face of adversity, he captured first Fort Henry on the Tennessee River and then Fort Donelson on the Cumberland, opening the way to Nashville and the central South. After a series of tough, stubborn victories in the West he assumed command of all Union armies and by his willingness to accept heavy losses but keep pushing forward, he finally forced the Confederate surrender at Appomattox Court House on April 9, 1865. The phrase, "Like Grant took Richmond," became standard jargon for dogged perseverance toward a goal until it was achieved.

Grant's wife and eldest son Frederick visited the commander-in-chief's Virginia headquarters in the closing days of the Civil War. General Grant with his wife Julia Dent and their son Frederick Dent Grant, at City Point (b/w photo), American Photographer, (19th century) / Private Collection, Peter Newark Military Pictures / The Bridgeman Art Library

CHAPTER TWELVE

THEODORE ROOSEVELT, 1858–1919: "THE FOUR-EYED DUDE FROM NEW YORK"

After the heartbreaking death of his wife, Theodore Roosevelt headed for the wide-open West to start a new life. Two years as a rancher toughened him for war and a landmark nation-changing presidency.

It could have been a scene from a John Wayne Western. On a chilly night in 1884, a young man in buckskins pushed through the swinging doors of a dingy saloon in the United States' "Bad Lands," the rugged country straddling the Dakota and Montana Territories. Twenty-five-year old Theodore Roosevelt, fresh from New York, had been out searching for lost horses from his newly acquired Elkhorn Ranch. Nolan's Hotel in Mingusville (now Wibaux, Montana, population 567), had a well-earned reputation as one of the toughest, roughest watering holes in the West. Roosevelt was a confirmed teetotaler, but he was to say later, "It was a cold night, and there was no place else to go."

The young man cut a strange figure in those surroundings. Although dressed in standard Western garb and dusty from an all-day ride, his buckskin tunic, elaborately beaded and decorated with fringe, had obviously been custom-made. His calfskin boots with gleaming silver spurs looked new, too, and so did his broad-brimmed sombrero, pushed back on his head. His face was sun-bronzed, and his thick reddish-brown mustache, flecked with gold, set off a row of prominent, projecting teeth. He spoke in a high-pitched voice. And firmly planted on his nose were rimless pince-nez, giving him an owlish expression.

"Hey, Four-Eyes!" a voice called out, a voice obviously thickened by whisky.

Waving his sword triumphantly, Rough River Roosevelt legendarily leads his cavalrymen up San Juan Hill in this famous 1898 lithograph. Theodore Roosevelt leading the 'Rough Riders' during the Spanish-American War, detail of a painting by W.G. Road, 1898 (colour litho), American School, (19th century) / Private Collection, Peter Newark American Pictures / The Bridgeman Art Library

The few customers and the bartender cowed or smiled nervously. A tall man brandishing a revolver in each hand strode across the barroom. He fired one of the pistols and put a bullet through the barroom clock. "Hey, Four-Eyes! Four-Eyes is going to treat!"

Ignoring the challenge, Roosevelt smiled, stepped across the room and took a chair behind the stove, near the end of the bar. Menacingly, the armed man pursued him, pushed up against Roosevelt's chair. He sneered and challenged the young man again. "You're going to treat, Four-Eyes!"

Roosevelt, frail and asthmatic as a youth, had learned to box as part of a self-directed program to build himself up. He had been successful; he was thick-muscled in the shoulders and arms and carried nearly 200 pounds (91 kg) on his 5-foot-8-inch (173 cm) frame. He had fought for the lightweight championship at Harvard, where boxing was considered part of a well-rounded, manly education. The snarling gunman repeated his challenge, calling on him to treat. "Well, if I've got to, I've got to," Roosevelt said and rose from the table. As Roosevelt stood up, he suddenly lashed out with his right fist, catching the man on the point of the jaw, followed up with his left, then swung again with his right. As the man toppled, he fired both guns harmlessly. His head hit a corner of the bar, and he dropped to the floor, senseless. Roosevelt scooped up the guns while the onlookers picked up the man and hustled him outside. Roosevelt sat down again to the admiring murmurs about "that dude from New York."

Roosevelt had come West to put behind him tragedy and heartbreak and in an effort to carve out a new life for himself. That new life was to mold him into a hero and earn him a sculpture on Mount Rushmore.

WE CALL HIM "TEEDIE"

Roosevelt was born just before the Civil War into one of the United States' patrician families. The Roosevelts were among the early Dutch settlers of New Amsterdam, arriving in 1644 and rapidly building a fortune in shipping, banking, and foreign trade. They remained to prosper after the colony became English in 1660 and New Amsterdam was renamed New York.

Young Theodore Jr.—"Teedie" to the family—was the second of four children. Sister Anna—"Bamie"—was three years older, sister Corrine—"Conie" —three years younger, and brother Elliott—"Ellie"—fourteen months younger. (Elliott was to become the father of Eleanor, who married distant cousin Franklin and became something of a heroine herself.) The family lived in a large mansion

October 27, 1858
Theodore Roosevelt is born on East Twentieth Street, New York City, to Theodore Roosevelt Sr. and Martha "Mittie" Bulloch Roosevelt.

September 1876
Matriculates at Harvard College.
February 9, 1878
Theodore Roosevelt Sr. dies.
October 18, 1878
Meets Alice Hathaway Lee and vows to marry her.

June 30, 1880
Graduates from Harvard College.
October 27, 1880
Marries Alice Hathaway Lee.
November 8, 1881
Elected to New York State Assembly, age twenty-three. Serves three terms and is chosen minority leader.
1882
First book, *The Naval War of 1812*, is published. Writes thirty-eight books during his career.

September 18, 1883
Visits the Dakota Territory and makes his first investment in cattle ranching.
February 12, 1884
Alice Roosevelt gives birth to their first child, Alice Lee.
February 14, 1884
Mother Mittie Roosevelt dies of typhoid fever. Wife Alice Hathaway Roosevelt dies later the same day of Bright's disease.
May 1884
Leaves New York and moves to Dakota Territory to enter ranching.

June 1886
Returns to New York and politics.
November 2, 1886
Defeated as the candidate for New York City mayor, running third.
December 2, 1886
Marries Edith Carow in London and sets up home on Sagamore Hill, Long Island, New York.

September 12, 1887
Theodore Roosevelt Jr., his first son, is born.
May 7, 1889–May 5, 1895
Serves as the U.S. civil service commissioner.

May 6, 1895–April 19, 1897
Serves as police commissioner and president of the board of police commissioners, New York City.
April 19, 1897–May 6, 1898
Serves as assistant secretary of the navy.

February 15, 1898
Battleship *Maine* is blown up in the harbor of Havana, Cuba. The Spanish government is blamed.
April 23, 1898
U.S. declares war on Spain.
May 15, 1898
Resigns from the navy and organizes a volunteer cavalry regiment known as the Rough Riders.
July 1, 1898
Leads the Rough Riders in a charge up San Juan Hill, Cuba.
December 10, 1898
Treaty of Paris officially ends the Spanish-American War.
November 8, 1898
Elected governor of New York.

November 6, 1900
William McKinley elected president of the United States; Roosevelt elected vice president.
September 14, 1901
Assumes presidency after the death of McKinley. Reelected in 1904.
May 4, 1904
Work begins on the Panama Canal authorized by Roosevelt. The canal opens in 1915.

December 10, 1906
Awarded the Nobel Peace Prize for helping to end the Russo-Japanese War of 1905.
November 1912
Runs for president on the Progressive ticket. Defeated by Democrat Woodrow Wilson. President William Howard Taft is a distant third.

January 6, 1919
Dies of a coronary embolism at Sagamore Hill.

in the then-fashionable neighborhood of Broadway and Fourteenth Street. Their capacious walled garden featured ornamental peacocks.

Teedie, 8½ pounds (3.9 kg) at birth, was an extremely energetic and inquisitive child who "made a lot of noise," his father said, but not at first a healthy one. He suffered repeated asthma attacks and was confined to bed or a "tassel chair" in the library while tutors schooled him in English, French, German, Latin, history, logic, and literature. Roosevelt quickly taught himself to read, lugging around a huge book of natural history and demanding that adults point out the words applying to each illustration until he finally learned to decipher them for himself. Having discovered the magic of books, he quickly immersed himself in reading, especially the classics. By the time Roosevelt attended small private classes at age thirteen, he was reading two or three books a day. A friend of the time described him as "the most studious little brute I ever knew in my life."

But Roosevelt's real passion was the wonders of nature. He collected birds' nests, feathers, and furs, followed animal tracks in the snow, and kept so many mice, hedgehogs, frogs, and snakes in his room that the upstairs maid finally rebelled. The "Roosevelt Museum of Natural History" set up with brother Elliott was banished to the attic, over his furious protests.

THE GRAND TOUR OF EUROPE

When Roosevelt was ten, the whole family went to Europe and traveled for more than a year. He was introduced to London and Paris, cruised down the Rhine, attended the opera in Vienna, climbed in the Swiss Alps, and spent Christmas in Rome. Throughout, the ten year old diligently kept a journal, writing in it every day of the 377-day trip with the exception of five days of illness. The journal, complete with ten-year-old misspellings, is still in print. He duly noted when he first set foot "in Briten" (cq) and reported that at the Tower of London "I put my head on the block where so maney (cq) had been beheaded." But the trip itself he pronounced "boring" except for the natural history museums and zoos visited and the birds and animals sighted. He carefully noted each sighting and birdcall in the journal and a notebook he called his "science log."

When Roosevelt was twelve, his father bought him his first gun—a double-barreled breech-loading weapon. He had persuaded his father to hire someone to tutor him in taxidermy, and he used the gun primarily to add bird specimens to his collection. To Roosevelt's astonishment, though, he found that he could not hit anything no matter how carefully he squinted down the barrel. One day out hunting with Elliott, he heard his brother reading from a distant sign. Teedie not only could not read the sign, he could not even distinguish the letters. An examination disclosed that he was profoundly nearsighted and had diminished vision in one eye because of a childhood accident. Outfitting him for the first time with spectacles "literally opened an entirely new world to [him]." The spectacles, usually in the form of a pince-nez, were to become his trademark and bring the "four-eyes" jeers that followed him through his youth.

Roosevelt's early ambition was to become a renowned naturalist, a new Audubon discovering and enumerating new species. Indeed at the age of fourteen, two of his articles on birds had been published in a scientific journal. His father had taken Teedie aside and assured him of that if he chose such an unremunerative profession Theodore Sr. would provide a yearly income of $8,000, which was a comfortable if not princely amount in 1876.

As Roosevelt prepared to enter Harvard, however, the young man disappointedly recognized that biological scientists were apt to spend all their time indoors, peering through laboratory microscopes and disdaining those whose focus was outdoors. Theodore wanted to confront wildlife in its natural setting, breathing the fresh air that an asthmatic craved. Accordingly, when he left for Cambridge armed with high entrance-examination scores in languages, science, history, and philosophy, he put ornithology aside.

In 1877, his idealistic father was chosen collector of customs by new President Rutherford B. Hayes, only to be humiliated when the corrupt New York Republican machine boss Roscoe Conkling blocked the appointment in favor of one of their own. Theodore Sr. died suddenly after this defeat, and his son blamed the machine. Roosevelt vowed that instead of science he would choose public service and direct all his energy into vigorous anticorruption reform.

SHE WAS SWEET, PRETTY, AND PLEASANT

Like most young men his age—eighteen when he entered Harvard—young Theodore was very much aware of girls, as his journal revealed. But he seemed to have no true favorites. Edith Kermit Carow, a neighbor and seeming intellectual soulmate of the bookish but exuberant Roosevelt was a frequent visitor to the Roosevelt household. There was some family whispering—especially by "Mittie" Roosevelt, his mother—that a love match might be in the making. At

LESLIE'S WEEKLY

Vol. XCIV. No. 2421   New York, January 30, 1902   Price 10 Cents

MISS ALICE ROOSEVELT.

THE CHARMING DAUGHTER OF THE PRESIDENT, WHO HAS BEEN ASKED BY EMPEROR WILLIAM TO CHRISTEN HIS NEW YACHT—HER LATEST PHOTOGRAPH, TAKEN IN HER DEBUTANTE GOWN, AND WEARING THE NECKLACE WHICH WAS THE GIFT OF THE PRESIDENT—Copyright 1901, Frances Benjamin Johnston

Alice Hathaway Roosevelt, named for her late mother, grew up a much-photographed figure in Washington society, as shown in this 1902 magazine cover. Frances Benjamin Johnston Collection, Prints & Photographs Division, Library of Congress, LC-USZ62-88700

Cambridge, the young man launched a voluminous and detailed correspondence with the young woman back in Manhattan. But others caught his eye, too. His journal abounds with names of young women he met and admired. But he was discreet about his feelings for the opposite sex. Roosevelt limited his appraisals to "sweet," "pretty," or "pleasant." Then on Friday, October 18, 1878, the twenty-year-old Harvard junior was invited home for a weekend by his best friend, Dick Saltonstall.

The Saltonstall name still resonates through Massachusetts society and history. The Saltonstalls were the elite of the elite, the crème de la crème. Their estate in Chestnut Hill, 6 miles (10 km) southwest of Boston, was a huge, rambling structure fronted by a vast sweep of lawn and set in a forest of chestnut trees. The Saltonstall mansion shared the eminence with another home, that of George Cabot Lee. Only 20 yards (18 m) separated the two buildings. Dick Saltonstall explained that the Lees were family; Mr. Lee was Dick's uncle by marriage. He also "happened to mention" that Alice Hathaway Lee, seventeen, was his sister Rose's closest friend, and Alice was in the Saltonstall house almost as much as her own.

Saturday afternoon, Roosevelt walked through the woods with the girls, attended church on Sunday, and went "chestnutting" alone with Alice. His journal entry, as usual, was noncommittal and guarded. He termed Alice "sweet" and "pretty," and Rose who was admittedly less attractive, "pleasant." But Roosevelt was back at Chestnut Hill on November 11, describing Alice in the journal as "sweet as ever." At Thanksgiving, he and Alice managed to be alone together repeatedly and emerged dropping the Victorian formality and calling each other the more intimate "Alice" and "Teddy." As Roosevelt left Chestnut Hill, the twenty-year-old college junior vowed he would marry her. And he did, on October 27, 1880.

"THE DEAREST LITTLE WEDDING" AND MORE

But before what a friend called "the dearest little wedding" could take place, the young man in a hurry had other matters to deal with. First, Harvard. He threw himself into his studies, graduating magna cum laude and being elected to Phi Beta Kappa. Deciding the road to a political career lay through law, Roosevelt enrolled in Columbia Law School. And he made a long-promised trip West with brother Elliott. The two spent six weeks ranging across the prairies, living a frontier life and hunting. At the end, Theodore noted that he had bagged 205 "items," Elliott 201. Meanwhile, Roosevelt had been bitten by a snake, thrown headfirst out of a wagon, soaked in a rainstorm, half-frozen by cold, and suffered repeated bouts of asthma and diarrhea. But the trip and the immensity of the country imbued Roosevelt with a love for the wide-open West, and he vowed to return again and again.

Back in New York, Roosevelt plunged into reform politics and quickly took leadership roles. Only twenty-three, the brash young man was elected to the state Assembly. There he established himself as a "fighting cock," his piercing "Mis-tah Speak-ah" introducing vigorous reformist objections to pending legislation and demanding investigations of purportedly corrupt officeholders. In Roosevelt's second term, he was nominated as Republican candidate for Speaker of the Assembly. It was a pro forma nomination, because the Democrats were the majority party, but it automatically made him minority leader. In this role, Roosevelt cut a wide swath guiding reform legislation and launching investigations, to the dismay of party bosses.

While maintaining a home in Manhattan and buying property for a planned Oyster Bay estate to be named "Leeholm" in Alice's honor, the young couple lived in married quarters in Albany, the state capital, during the legislative year. In 1883, a hunting trip to the Dakota Territory inspired Theodore to buy land and establish a ranch. And, to her husband's great delight, Alice had become pregnant. She remained in New York while he commuted each weekend to Albany. During the week, he threw himself into his work, putting all his weight and persuasive powers behind a controversial "Roosevelt Bill" that completely reorganized New York City government and emasculated the role of aldermen, whom he regarded as citadels of corruption.

Then, on February 13, 1884, as the Assembly was opening its morning session and beginning debate on the bill, he received a telegram informing him that Alice had given birth to a daughter. While his colleagues were still congratulating him, he received a second telegram summoning him back to Manhattan posthaste. He was greeted by his brother Elliott. "There is a curse upon this house," Elliott intoned mournfully. "Mother is dying, and Alice is dying, too." Mittie Roosevelt succumbed to acute typhoid fever at 3 a.m. on February 14. At 2 p.m. on St. Valentine's Day, the anniversary of the date when Roosevelt had first proposed marriage, his twenty-two-year-old "little pink bride" died in his arms, a victim of kidney failure associated with childbirth.

"THE LIGHT HAS GONE OUT OF MY LIFE"

The twin tragedy devastated Roosevelt, leaving him stunned, haggard, stumbling through a blur of funeral, burial, mourning, memorial services, and condolences, none of which relieved his grief and loss. Roosevelt scarcely looked at his newborn child, a little blonde girl in her mother's image who had been named "Alice Lee" in her mother's honor. In Roosevelt's diary for February 14, he drew a large cross and wrote, "The light has gone out of my life."

Roosevelt returned to Albany to see through final passage of the Roosevelt Bill. In May, he left the baby in the care of his two sisters and boarded a train for his ranch in the Dakota Territory. This became his refuge, where he could escape from the trauma of recent months and put the "house with the curse upon it" behind him.

One of Roosevelt's first moves on arriving was to summon two Maine backwoodsmen, Bill Sewall and Wilmot Dow, who had been his hunting guides, to come and work on the two ranches, now named the Elkhorn and the Maltese Cross. He promised them a share of the ranch profits. Then Roosevelt began to throw himself fully into frontier life, helping the two men chop trees for the new building, herd the cattle, and dig wells. Alone, Roosevelt ventured off on a hunting trip into the Big Horn Mountains of Wyoming. He "bagged" small game such as grouse, sagehens, prairie chickens, and jackrabbits, and also two grizzly bears, blacktail deer, an elk, and antelope. Roosevelt triumphantly hauled them all home to be mounted as trophies. Returning after forty-seven days, he wrote his sister Bamie, referring to the tragic events of the previous spring, "At last I am able to sleep well at night."

Deputy sheriff Roosevelt and two employees arrest boat thieves after a wintry pursuit in the ice-choked Little Missouri River. Theodore Roosevelt Collection, Harvard College Library

DUDE ON A ROUNDUP

Roosevelt was now an established rancher and cattleman. When 1,300 new head of cattle were delivered, he personally and with help of only one cowboy, herded them, weathered a stampede, and brought them safely into Elkhorn. With sixty other men riding 300 horses, Roosevelt participated fully in the spring 1885 roundup, sometimes spending as long as forty consecutive hours in the saddle, wearing out five horses, diverting another stampede, and winning grudging admiration from the hard-bitten cowboys who rode with him.

Roosevelt became something of a celebrity in the frontier town of Little Missouri, which had now grown to eighty-five buildings. He was elected chairman of the Stockmens' Association and named a deputy sheriff of Billings County. He still found time to write. His new ranch home had been completed, and his library shipped west. There he completed the popular *Hunting Trips of a Ranchman* and undertook a biography of pioneer-senator Thomas Hart Benton.

But Roosevelt was becoming restive. The ranches were not prospering, and he missed the intellectual stimulation of his circle in New York. Moreover, he had kept up his correspondence with Edith Carow, and it had become increasingly intimate. On one of his New York trips, Roosevelt took her to see his Oyster Bay property. There he proposed to her, and she accepted. They kept the engagement a secret, but he was eager to marry.

Roosevelt had one last adventure ahead of him, however. In March 1886 the frozen Little Missouri River became choked with chunks of ice, only a narrow

stream rushing between the floes. Roosevelt, to the merriment of the landlubbin'
cowboys, had equipped himself with a flatbottomed boat that he kept tied up at
riverside. One morning he emerged to find that the boat was gone.

Roosevelt was furious. Not so much by the loss of the boat—it was inexpensive
and easily replaced—but by the temerity of the crime itself. He was, after all, a
deputy sheriff, sworn to uphold the law. He was certain he knew who had taken
the boat—three drifters, one of them a vicious gunman, Red Finnegan, who had
erected a makeshift camp a few miles upstream. There was only one way the mis-
creants could escape—downriver. Roosevelt set Sewall and Dow to work building
a scow and set off in pursuit. Three fruitless days followed. Then on the morning
of April 1, he spotted smoke from a campfire around a bend in the river.

Roosevelt found one man cowering on the riverbank; the other two were off
hunting. When they returned, Deputy Sheriff Roosevelt and his little posse confronted them with drawn rifles. They surrendered quickly, even gunman Finnegan
dropping his weapon after a few seconds. Roosevelt rejected suggestions that he
merely shoot all three; he was determined to bring them to justice, even though the
next big town, Mandan, was 150 miles (240 km) away. There followed eight days of
steady poling while the three were kept under guard around the clock. Food ran out
until they had only dry flour for sustenance. At last Roosevelt reached a cow camp
where he stocked up on food, then borrowed a horse and rode 15 miles (24 km) to a
ranch where he hired a prairie schooner and two horses. He piled the three prisoners into the wagon and set off for the sheriff's office in Dickinson, sending Sewall
and Dow to continue with the boats. Staying up for 36 straight hours lest his prisoners flee, he finally turned them over to the sheriff (collecting some $50 in sheriff's
fees for the arrest and his expenses). Then he hopped a train back to New York.

FROM ROUNDING UP CATTLE TO ROUNDING UP VOTES

With all Roosevelt's explosive force, he jumped full tilt into New York City politics, a late entry in the 1886 race for mayor. He finished third. He announced his
engagement to the patient Edith by notes written on shipboard en route to London, where they were married in a small, out-of-the-way church on December 2.
After a brief European honeymoon, Theodore installed Edith in the mansion at
Oyster Bay, now called Sagamore Hill.

In 1889 Republican President Benjamin Harrison (whom Roosevelt dis-
paraged as a "coldblooded, narrow-minded, prejudiced, obstinate, timid old

psalm-singing Indianapolis politician") named him to chair the Civil Service Commission, where he immediately set out with his usual reformist zeal to rid government hiring of political favoritism. In 1895, he became police commissioner of New York City, repeatedly grabbing headlines for accompanying officers on arrests of bribe-bestowing racketeers.

When Republican William McKinley was inaugurated as president in 1897, Roosevelt was appointed assistant secretary of the navy, under John D. Long, a somnolent and ailing veteran politician, who left administration of the department to his bumptious young aide. "I am having such fun running the navy!" Roosevelt exulted to a friend as he ordered new battleships, bought ammunition, revamped training procedures, and sought to make the United States a global naval power.

When war with Spain began after the sinking of the U.S.S. *Maine* in Cuba in 1898, Roosevelt, thirsting for action, resigned to recruit a cavalry regiment known as the Rough Riders and made up of fellow Western ranchers and cowpunchers and Eastern bluebloods who rode to hounds. Waving his hat ostentatiously, Lieutenant Colonel Roosevelt famously led a charge up San Juan Hill. The war ended soon thereafter. An exuberant sensationalist press proclaimed Roosevelt a genuine hero, propelling him into the New York governorship, and in 1900, making him McKinley's vice-presidential choice. In September 1901 McKinley was assassinated and "that damned cowboy," as one angry Republican leader termed Roosevelt, became president of the United States. After nearly eight years of his environmental and trust-busting policies, Roosevelt was on his way to Mount Rushmore. His days of seeking escape were now in the past.

EXPUNGING THE PAST

But the newly minted president never forgot his sojourn in the West or his frontier friends. To their dismay, White House staff were warned that cowboys, no matter how dusty or foulmouthed, were to be ushered into the Executive Office. Once when Roosevelt's old partner Sylvane Ferris was refused entry, "T.R." was outraged. "The next time that happens, Sylvane," he said, "you shoot out the windows."

Alice, his "sweet little bride," however, was erased from memory. The early love letters that had poured from Harvard to Chestnut Hill and all correspondence between them were tracked down and destroyed, and pictures of the once-happy couple were removed from walls and ripped out of albums. Oyster Bay would only be referred to as "Sagamore Hill." Roosevelt never spoke of Alice Hathaway Lee again.

CHAPTER THIRTEEN

EDITH COWAN, 1861–1932: A CHILD OF TRAGEDY BECOMES A CHAMPION FOR ALL CHILDREN

When Edith Cowan was seven, her mother died in childbirth. Eight years later, in 1876, her father was hanged for murdering her stepmother. These experiences of sorrow, shame, and loneliness—she spent almost her entire childhood and adolescence in boarding school— instilled in Cowan a lifelong commitment to improving living conditions for Australia's women and children.

The Browns started quarreling early in the day, and their bickering continued off and on all afternoon. The topic was always the same: Kenneth Brown accused his new wife of infidelity; the outraged wife answered that Brown was a drunk. As they squabbled, Brown did drink heavily, which gave his wife more ammunition. The fighting ended abruptly a little before six in the evening when Brown grabbed his gun and shot and killed his wife.

News of the murder came as a shock but not a surprise to Brown's family and neighbors. The couple had been unhappy almost from the beginning of their marriage. Brown's younger brother, Maitland, suggested they separate for a time; Kenneth could move in with his brother while Mrs. Brown remained in the couple's cottage. But the Browns rejected Maitland's offer.

At the time of the murder, Kenneth Brown's two oldest children by his first marriage, sixteen-year-old Blanche and fifteen-year-old Edith, were away at a boarding school in Perth. The murder affected the girls deeply, especially Edith. Seven years earlier they had lost their mother, and now it was almost certain that their father

In addition to fighting for women's right to vote, Edith Cowan lobbied the government of Western Australia for day nurseries for the children of working mothers, free schools, and better access to medical care. National Library of Australia, nla.pic-an23351616

would be executed. The girls would be orphaned under the most terrible, most disgraceful circumstances.

Kenneth Brown's trial at the courthouse in Perth, however, was not the open-and-shut case many expected. Although Brown stood in open court and admitted to murdering his wife, saying, "I did it. I will pay for it," the jury could not agree on a verdict. Maitland and other members of the Brown family had tried to persuade the judge to dismiss the case on the grounds of diminished capacity, because Brown's heavy drinking and business and financial troubles had deprived him of sound judgment.

There was truth to the Brown family's argument. After the death of his first wife, Mary Eliza Dircksey Wittenoom, Brown lost interest in his children and his sheep raising station, Glengarry in Western Australia. He sent his daughters to the Perth boarding school, leased Glengarry, and traveled to Melbourne in eastern Australia to try his hand at some new business. A few years later he returned home with a new wife but no sign that he had prospered in the eastern colonies. The Browns settled in a cottage in Geraldton, a town on Champion Bay, just a few miles from Glengarry, which was still being leased. Brown was not working; he spent his days and nights sitting in his house, drinking and squabbling with his wife.

There may have been a second reason why the jury failed to reach a verdict in the case: Brown was a local celebrity. Between 1852 and 1863, Brown had been a member of at least four expeditions that explored Western Australia, including Mount Magnet and the Murchison River.

Whatever their reasons, two separate juries failed to reach a verdict in the Brown case. But when the case was tried a third time, the jury convicted Brown of murder. Except for telling the court that by the time of his second marriage "the joy of life had long since gone," Brown did not try to excuse himself. His one regret, he added, was the shame he had brought to his family.

On June 10, 1876, Brown was hanged for the murder of his wife.

The Brown family could barely stand the grief and disgrace of the murder and then Kenneth's execution. At school, young Edith became quiet and introspective as she sought some way to distract her mind from her family sorrows.

August 2, 1861
Edith Dircksey Brown is born at the sheep raising station of Glengarry near Geraldton, Western Australia.

1868
Her mother dies in childbirth and Cowan's father sends her and her elder sister, Blanche, to a boarding school in Perth.

June 10, 1876
Her father, Kenneth Brown, is hanged for the murder of his second wife.

November 12, 1879
Marries James Cowan, registrar and master of the Supreme Court.

1880s and 1890s
Becomes increasingly involved in volunteer organizations to improve the lives of women, children, immigrants, and the poor.

1894
A founding member of Perth's Karrakatta Club and is elected its first secretary. Club members work for the educational improvement of women and for the recognition of their political and civil rights.

1906–1909
As the founding member of the Children's Protection Society, establishes a day nursery for working mothers.

1909–1917
Through the Women's Service Guild, lobbies successfully for a women's hospital. The King Edward Memorial Hospital for Women opens in 1916; Cowan serves on the advisory board.

1915
Is the first woman appointed to the bench of the Children's Court where criminal cases involving minors are adjudicated.

March 12, 1921
Is the first woman elected to the Western Australian Parliament.

1921–1924
Introduces legislation to improve the health and education of infants, children, and women, and to open the law and other professions to women. Proposes a housewives' union and sex education in state schools.

1924
Bid for re-election fails, due largely to a falling-out between two of Western Australia's largest women's organizations.

1926
Establishes the Royal Western Australian Historical Society. Her eldest daughter, Dircksey, is named the first keeper of records.

November 12, 1929
Edith and James celebrate their fiftieth wedding anniversary.

April 1932
After a meeting at the Historical Society, collapses and is taken to the hospital.

June 9, 1932
Edith Cowan dies and is buried in the Anglican section of Karrakatta Cemetery.

A LONELY CHILD

It is not known if Edith ever met her stepmother. The year her mother died, 1868, Kenneth Brown sent his daughters to Perth to a boarding school operated by Agnes Cowan. Brown may have sent his girls away simply to further their education because there was no girls' school anywhere near Glengarry. But it is also possible that he sent them to Perth because he was already becoming emotionally distant from his family.

Edith Brown met James Cowan when she was a 16-year-old student at the boarding school operated by his sisters. At the time of Edith's death, the couple had been married for 53 years. Courtesy State Library of Western Australia, The Battye Library

The move to Perth was a wrenching experience for seven-year-old Edith. As an adult she would mention in passing that one of her most vivid memories of her early years at school was a profound sense of loneliness. Yet the move to Perth was in many ways the making of Edith Brown. It gave her opportunities to learn that she would never have had at Glengarry, and she encountered teachers who encouraged her, particularly her tutor, the Reverend Sweeting, former headmaster of Bishop Hale's School in Perth.

Edith's years at the Cowan boarding school were fortuitous in other ways as well. Agnes Cowan had a brother, James, who often visited the school. He was making a career as a government administrator, but he wished he could have remained on his family's farm at York. He was an enthusiastic outdoorsman who rode his horse almost every day. It was a life-long passion. James Cowan was still riding through the streets of Perth long after horses had been replaced by automobiles. It was while visiting his sister Agnes that James, twenty-nine years old, met Edith Brown, sixteen years old.

In 1878, James was appointed registrar and master of the Supreme Court, a position that paid an annual salary of £100 and permitted him to keep his job as clerk to the Bench of Magistrates. With two salaries to ensure his financial security, James Cowan was ready to propose marriage to Edith. On November 12, 1879, the couple married in Perth's St. George's Cathedral. Their first child, a daughter, was born the following year. The couple went on to have three more daughters and one son.

THE FOUNDING OF THE KARRAKATTA CLUB

In October, 1894, American physician and lecturer Dr. Emily Ryder was on her way to India when she stopped at Perth. During her visit, she agreed to address the women of the St. George's Reading Circle. The caliber of books the women studied impressed Dr. Ryder, and in her speech she expressed the opinion that it is "the duty of every woman to make the most of herself in all ways. Contact with other women and interchange of thought will widen her mental horizon." She urged her audience to banish gossip from their meetings and dedicate themselves to transforming their reading circle into a women's mutual help and improvement society.

Inspired by Dr. Ryder's speech, twenty-five women came together to form a new organization that became known as the Karrakatta Club (named for the Perth suburb where the first clubhouse stood). Thirty-three-year-old Cowan was elected secretary.

This was the first women's club in Australia, and its goals were ambitious. The women wanted to bring about changes in Australian society that would alter the status of women and children. In the years that followed, they lobbied the government for day nurseries for the children of working mothers, shelters for unmarried mothers, access to free schools, and the right of women to vote. When the first members discussed their ambitions with Dr. Ryder, she told them candidly, "Ridicule would be cast upon [the club] and evil spoken of it, but you must make up your minds to live down opposition and to ignore ridicule."

The bridge between the reading circle and the club was education for women; Cowan and Lady Madeline Onslow, the club's first president, encouraged women to read books and newspapers, to keep up with the latest ideas and important political and social events. "When we get the franchise," Lady Onslow said on one occasion, "we shall cut a sorry figure if we are not well up in all that is happening."

Even before Australian women could vote, Cowan would find a way to enter public life. She served several terms as a member of the North Fremantle Board of Education, one of the very few offices in which women could serve. But she wanted more. The memory of her mother who lived, gave birth to children, and died without access to a doctor or a hospital; the tragedy of her stepmother who had no place to go to escape an alcoholic husband; her own loneliness as a little girl sent to school far from home because there was no decent school in the neighborhood, all worked together to inspire Cowan to work for dramatic changes in the basic structure of Australian society. In the Karrakatta Club, Cowan found women who shared her vision.

During the last years of the nineteenth century and the first years of the twentieth century, Cowan was busy with all manner of volunteer and public service work. She served on the North Fremantle Board of Education; she helped found the Children's Protection Society, then successfully lobbied the government to overturn old legislation that tried children as adults. In 1916, the Anglican bishops in Western Australia asked Cowan to serve on the church's Social Questions Committee; she was the first female member. And in 1920, Cowan became a justice of the peace.

THE AUSTRALIAN SUFFRAGISTS

Australia in the 1890s was part of the British Empire, and its vast territories were carved up into four colonies. Throughout the country there were women's organizations such as the Karrakatta Club that lobbied for more protections and better opportunities for women and children, while also demanding that women enjoy the same political and civil rights as men.

To illustrate the basic unfairness of denying women these civil rights, women's suffragist groups distributed flyers that spelled out the inequality of their situation. The Victorian Women's Suffrage Society published a leaflet that followed a question-and-answer format.

The Karrakatta Club, the first women's club in Australia, was named for the Perth suburb where the first cluhbhouse was located. This photograph, taken circa 1920, shows club members in the sitting room. Courtesy State Library of Western Australia, The Battye Library

"Are Women Citizens?

"Yes! when they are required to pay taxes.

"No! when they ask to vote."

"Does Law concern Women?

"Yes! when they are required to obey it.

"No! when they ask to have a voice in the representation of the country."

"Is Direct Representation desirable for the interests of the people?

"Yes! If the people to be represented are men.

"No! if the people to be represented are women."

As Dr. Ryder had warned Edith Cowan and her fellow members of Karrakatta Club, men would use scorn and ridicule to undermine their insistence on entering political life. In political speeches and in the press, opponents described women as unsuited to government because they were emotionally unstable, obsessed with trivialities, and intellectually inferior to men.

In spite of such opposition, in 1894 South Australia became the first colony to recognize a woman's right to vote. This was followed by Western Australia—Cowan's home colony—in 1899, New South Wales in 1902, and Victoria in 1908. It was not a complete victory, however: Aboriginal women were not allowed to vote, and women were barred from running for the individual colonial parliaments, a policy that remained in force until 1920.

In the election of 1921, four weeks before men and women went to the polls, Cowan surprised everyone by announcing that she was running to represent West Perth in the Western Australian Parliament. She was fifty-nine years old. Cowan didn't expect to win, not least because her opponent, T.P. Draper, was the incumbent and also an ally of the women's movement. He had introduced the bill that admitted women to Parliament.

To advance her candidacy, Cowan took out a nearly full-page newspaper ad that listed all of her work and accomplishments during thirty years of social service in Western Australia. And like other political candidates of the time, Cowan also took her campaign directly to the voters. She spoke on street corners and rented halls, and she even went door-to-door to drum up support.

Cowan's platform highlighted the things that had been important to her all her life—issues that concerned women and children. She told voters she wanted to reform legislation regarding divorce, the guardianship of children, and the rights of inheritance, all of which still favored men. She wanted to break down more barriers. Women still could not practice law, nor were they admitted as observers in the Speaker's Gallery in Parliament. She wanted day nurseries for working mothers, kindergartens in every school district, and cooperation between the schools and the Health Department to ensure that children would receive proper medical attention and had a healthy diet.

On March 12, 1921, when residents of West Perth went to the polls, political pundits still expected Draper to win. When the votes were tallied Draper had 1,109 votes, and Cowan had 1,164. By this narrow victory, Cowan became the first woman elected to an Australian Parliament.

In Cowan's first address to her fellow members she said, "I stand here today in the unique position of being the first woman in an Australian Parliament. I know many people think perhaps it was not the wisest thing to do to send a woman into Parliament. It is a great responsibility to be the only woman here." Although her maiden speech was modest, Cowan's goals were ambitious. She set about at once advancing her agenda—clinics for infants, more schools, and legislation that compelled men who had deserted their families to contribute a fair amount to the support of their wife and children. Cowan opened up the legal and other professions to women, established service organizations for immigrants, and even tried to found a union for housewives. Unfortunately Cowan served only one three-year term; bitter rivalry between two competing women's organizations in Perth undermined her base.

T.P. Draper was the incumbent in the 1921 parliamentary election. He lost his seat to Edith Cowan by 55 votes. Courtesy State Library of Western Australia, The Battye Library

Outside Parliament, Cowan continued working for political and social causes. She was a delegate to the 1925 International Conference for Women in the United States. Only in the year of her death, 1932, did illness force her to retire from all her committees. Two years after Cowan's death, friends and admirers erected in Perth's Kings Park a clock tower as a memorial to "Her Many Good Works for Humanity." Not long afterward, Western Australia opened its first college, naming it for Edith Cowan. Very likely, this is the monument that would please her best.

CHAPTER FOURTEEN

MOHANDAS GANDHI, 1869–1948: THE TRANSFORMATION OF A SHY BARRISTER INTO A HUMAN RIGHTS LEADER

Indian-born Mohandas Gandhi hoped to make a living as a successful barrister, until a fateful business trip to South Africa and a racial slur changed his life —and the course of history.

Mohandas Gandhi didn't notice the curious looks on the faces of his fellow passengers on the train. The twenty-four-year-old Indian was too preoccupied with his impending business meeting. It was 1898, and the young barrister was en route to Pretoria, the capital of Transvaal in the Union of South Africa, to represent a client in a contentious lawsuit against a business competitor. Gandhi wore a dark gray suit, starched shirt with wing collar, and striped cravat. He spoke English with a proper British intonation, picked up in a London law school.

Intellectually, Gandhi was up to the task. He had graduated from University College at London and was a thoughtful, introspective man. However, he was extremely shy, and he was often uncomfortable speaking in public. On the train, he nervously went over his notes on the case—notes he already had committed to memory. He had been traveling much of the day, but the accommodations in the first class compartment made the journey bearable. Except for the frequent butterflies in his stomach, it had been an uneventful day.

The train pulled into the Pietermaritzburg Station at 9 p.m. Several new passengers boarded. A white European man entered the first class section and spotted

A champion of Indian civil rights, Gandhi was given the title *Mahatma*, an honorific meaning "great soul," by his countrymen. Portrait of Mohandas Karamchand (Mahatma) Gandhi (1869–1948) (oil on canvas), Rao, V.R. (20th century) / India House, London, UK / The Bridgeman Art Library

Educated in London, Gandhi became the first Indian barrister permitted to practice law in South Africa. Mahatma Gandhi (1869–1948) as a barrister in South Africa, c.1900 (b/w photo), English Photographer, (20th century) / Indian Embassy, Paris, France, Archives Charmet / The Bridgeman Art Library

Gandhi sitting quietly, studying his notes. The dark-skinned barrister's presence clearly agitated the European. Seconds after entering, the man abruptly exited the train car. Gandhi was vaguely aware of someone moving past him as he pored over his legal documents. Moments later the man returned, accompanied by the train conductor. "Come along," the conductor told Gandhi. "You must go to the van compartment." Gandhi was nonplussed. He had purchased a first class ticket. Was there a problem? He stared up at the two men standing over him in confusion. "Coolies," explained the conductor, were restricted from traveling in first class.

Gandhi's face grew hot with humiliation. Originally used by Europeans to describe manual laborers, the term *coolie* had become a catchall racial slur for Indians. But for the dark pigmentation of his skin, and his turban, Gandhi might have passed for the quintessential English barrister. He was an educated, well-dressed, professional—a member of the legal profession no less—and all the two men could see was the color of his skin.

A peaceful man by nature, Gandhi dreaded conflict. This aspect of his personality made him an effective negotiator; he worked hard to settle his legal cases out of court, thereby avoiding a contentious public fight. Normally reluctant to cause a scene, Gandhi could not allow the insult to stand uncontested. His humiliation quickly turned to rage—rage born not out of personal vanity but of national pride. Angry, he soon overcame his natural shyness. Gandhi refused to give up his seat, explaining that he had paid for a first class ticket and was legally entitled to sit in that section. The conductor was unimpressed by the Indian's argument and had him forcibly removed from the train by a police constable while the European passenger looked on in triumph.

Gandhi spent the night in the railway station. The incident on the train left him rattled and incensed. He considered abandoning his business trip to Pretoria and returning to India. But he realized he had a duty to represent his client—and he decided, an even greater duty to discover what types of mistreatment his fellow

October 2, 1869
Mohandas Karamchand Gandhi is born in Porbandar in Gujarat, India.

1883
Weds Kasturba Makhanji in a marriage arranged by the couple's parents.
1888
Leaves India to study law in London.
June 11, 1891
Sworn in and accepted as a member of the British Bar Association.
June 12, 1891
Returns home to India.

May 24, 1892
Begins practicing law in Bombay.
April 1893
Sets sail for South Africa to represent a client in a civil lawsuit.
June 1893
Forcibly removed from a train at the Pietermaritzburg Station after refusing to yield his seat to a white passenger.

August 1894
Founds the Natal Indian Congress to fight racial discrimination.
September 1894
Becomes the first Indian to be accepted as an advocate of the Supreme Court of Natal, South Africa.
1899
Organizes the Indian Ambulance Corps to tend to British forces during the Boer War. Receives a medal for his contributions.

1903
Enrolled as a barrister in the Supreme Court at Transvaal. Founds the Transvaal British India Association in South Africa.
1906
Holds a meeting in Johannesburg where he proposes his satyagraha—civil disobedience—campaign to protest discrimination.
1907
Meets with interior minister of Transvaal and presents him with a list of resolutions.

1908
Arrested and jailed for three months for not carrying an Indian registration card.
1909
Visits England to publicize and drum up support for the Indian cause in South Africa.
1913
Leads 3,000 Indians on a protest march into the Transvaal. Gandhi is arrested along with the protesters.

1914
Returns to India after championing the rights of Indians in South Africa for twenty-one years.
1920
Elected president of All-India Home Rule League.
1932
Undertakes a "fast unto death" to protest the British government's mistreatment of India's lowest caste, the so-called "untouchables."

1934
Announces decision to retire from politics.
1942
Appeals to the British government to grant India its independence.
August 15, 1947
Largely due to Gandhi's unwavering commitment to establishing an independent nation, India is granted its independence from British rule at midnight on August 15, 1947.

January 30, 1948
Is assassinated by a Hindu extremist on the way to evening prayer.

countrymen were subjected to in Pretoria. If a well-dressed professional Indian man could be evicted from a train, discrimination against the poor indentured Indians living in the area must be far worse.

The following day, Gandhi boarded a stagecoach and was immediately told that he could not sit inside the coach with the other passengers. As a "coolie," he had to sit up front with the coachman. Insulted but determined to reach his location, he reluctantly acquiesced, taking a seat next to the driver.

Some time into the trip, one of the white passengers sitting inside the coach demanded that Gandhi vacate his seat up front so that he could enjoy a cigarette in the open air next to the driver. The man tossed a filthy piece of cloth onto the footboard and ordered Gandhi to sit on that. "Here, sami, you sit on this. I want to sit beside the leader," the man said. Gandhi refused. The man attacked him, hitting him repeatedly in the face until the other passengers intervened. Afterward, Gandhi learned from fellow Indians that he had been lucky to escape with his life.

LIFE AND HARDSHIP IN SOUTH AFRICA

The incidents on the train and in the stagecoach had a lasting and monumental effect on Gandhi. The shy barrister who loathed the adversarial environment of the courtroom became a passionate advocate for his people. He was appalled at the way his fellow countrymen were treated in South Africa. Indians living in South Africa were subjected to a curfew, forced to pay an imposing poll tax, and were victims of frequent racial attacks. Indian marriages were declared invalid because they were not performed in accordance with Christian rites.

Emboldened by his newfound nationalism and determined to correct the appalling injustices faced by his countrymen, Gandhi became a voice for Indians in Africa. News of the brave Indian barrister spread quickly though the Indian enclaves and soon dozens of Indians were calling on him for advice, and to sound off about their woes.

After much negotiation, Gandhi successfully settled the lawsuit in his client's favor without taking the matter to court. This was most fortuitous, as Indians were barred from practicing law in South African courts. His employer was pleased; the company's associates in Pretoria held a dinner in Gandhi's honor the evening before he was due to return to India.

During dinner, there was talk of the pending "Indian Franchise Bill." Currently being considered by the Natal Congress, the bill would deprive Indians of the right to vote in government elections. In addition, Indians would still be required to pay an oppressive poll tax. Gandhi was dismayed that no one had come forward to oppose the bill. Instead of returning to India, he decided to remain in South Africa in the hopes of preventing the bill from passing.

When Gandhi arrived in South Africa, more than 60,000 Indians were living there. The promise of steady work and high wages had lured thousands away from their homeland. Many were former serfs—plantation workers—who remained after their terms of servitude had ended. Others were free Indians who had emigrated on their own accord.

The territory was divided into four distinct regions, ruled by two separate powers. The Cape Colony and Natal were under British rule, while the Orange Free State and the Transvaal were Dutch colonies. Although the population was predominantly non-white, the white minority ran the government.

Gandhi's first order of business was to be admitted into the Supreme Court of Natal. The local barristers' association opposed his admittance, stating outright that an Indian could not be permitted to practice law. Fortunately, the chief justice overrode the association and swore Gandhi into the bar—with one caveat: Gandhi must abandon the turban he regularly wore. Realizing he had bigger battles to fight, he agreed. Although his efforts to quash the Indian Franchise Bill failed, they were not in vain. He managed to draw much-needed attention to the plight of Indians living in South Africa, and founded the Natal Indian Congress in 1894.

SOWING THE SEEDS OF SATYAGRAHA

In 1896, Gandhi's wife and sons joined him in South Africa. For the next twenty years, he remained in South Africa fighting injustice and working to better the living conditions of Indians. It was in South Africa that he began to promote his policy of passive resistance, or mass civil disobedience, to fight government oppression. He called the action *satyagraha*, a Sanskrit word meaning "truth and firmness." Practitioners were called *satyagrahi*. The term later came to be known as civil disobedience.

Satyagraha, which aims to win over an opponent by self-sacrifice, was embraced by Gandhi's fellow Indians. "A satyagrahi must be afraid neither of imprisonment nor of deportation," Gandhi would later write. "He must neither mind being reduced to poverty, nor be frightened, if it comes to that, of being mashed into pulp with a mortar and pestle."

In 1906, the Transvaal Government enacted the Asiatic Ordinance, which banned Indian immigration, enacted segregation laws that dictated where Indians could live and work, and required all Indians over the age of eight to be fingerprinted and carry a registration card at all times. Supporters viewed the ordinance as "the first step to end what may mean the extinction of the white races in this country by immigration from the East." Many whites decried what they believed was an influx of new Asiatic immigrants. In reality, many of the Indians were returning to the homes they had fled from when the Boer War broke out in 1899.

On September 11, 1906, Gandhi called a meeting at the Empire Theatre in Johannesburg in response to the Ordinance. Some 3,000 people attended, most of them Indians. Gandhi stepped onto the stage and greeted the audience. He explained that he had drafted a proposal stating that no Indian would ever acknowledge the legality of the Asiatic Ordinance if it were passed. He vowed to oppose the Ordinance at all costs. He read from the pledge of resistance he had drawn up:

> In the event of the Legislative Council, the local Government, and the Imperial Authorities rejecting the humble prayer of the British Indian community of the Transvaal in connection with the Draft Asiatic Law Amendment Ordinance, this mass meeting of British Indians here assembled solemnly and regretfully resolves that, rather than submit to the galling, tyrannous, and un-British requirements laid down in the above Draft Ordinance, every British Indian in the Transvaal shall submit himself to imprisonment and shall continue so to do until it shall please His Most Gracious Majesty the King-Emperor to grant relief.

Inspired by Gandhi's resolve, members of the audience voiced their approval. Gandhi introduced the audience to the concept of satyagraha and the importance of militant nonviolence. He spoke truthfully, making the audience aware that the journey ahead would be a difficult and dangerous one. "If someone asks me when and how the struggle may end, I may say that, if the entire community manfully stands the test, the end will be near," he explained. "If many of us fall back under storm and stress, the struggle will be prolonged. But I can boldly declare, and

Mohandas Gandhi (second from right, standing) founded the Natal Indian Congress in 1894 to fight discrimination against Indians living in South Africa. DINODIA

with certainty, that so long as there is even a handful of men true to their pledge, there can only be one end to the struggle, and that is victory."

By the end of the meeting, nearly all 3,000 members of the audience had declared their allegiance to the cause and pledged to resist the ordinance. Gandhi had persuaded the various Indian sects to put aside their differences and present a unified front. Together, they would defy the ordinance at all costs—even if meant being sent to prison.

The Indian community refused to register with the Transvaal government as directed. Members lit a bonfire and burned their immigration certificates. Undocumented and thus prohibited from entering Transvaal, dozens of Indians defiantly crossed the border into the capital city of Pretoria. They were arrested and sent to jail. Undeterred by these arrests, Gandhi and his associates organized strikes in the coalfields and sugar plantations and marches through Transvaal.

For eight years, the satyagraha campaign continued. Thousands of Indians were imprisoned for disobeying the Asiatic Ordinance; at one point 2,000 of the 10,000 Indians in the Transvaal community were incarcerated. (The majority of Indians resided in the British-controlled Natal region.) Gandhi was arrested and jailed several times, as were members of his family. The Indian resistance was made up of Indians from all castes and classes; these brave men and women included the young as well as the elderly. Subjected to prison, beatings, increasing repression, and killings, the members of the satyagraha remained true to their pledge of nonviolent civil disobedience.

Gandhi met with government officials numerous times in the hopes of reaching a compromise. Interior Minister General Jan Smuts begrudgingly agreed to work toward an agreement with Gandhi, but progress came to a halt when the Transvaal government refused to repeal any part of the Asiatic Ordinance. Meanwhile, support for the satyagraha was growing in England. Many British citizens and public officials decried the appalling treatment of Indians in South Africa, Indians who were technically British citizens.

In addition to the severe restrictions of the Asiatic Ordinance, the Transvaal government also imposed an unbearably high poll tax on Indian laborers. The meager salaries the laborers were paid made it impossible to support their families and pay the required poll tax. In October 1913, Gandhi and 6,000 Indian laborers protested the poll tax by marching into the restricted city of Transvaal. Thousands of workers went on strike, virtually shutting down the coal mines and sugar planta-tions. Once again, scores of Indians were arrested, Gandhi among them.

Transvaal was ill equipped to deal with such a well-organized, massive pro-test. With pressure mounting from England, and productivity at a standstill in the mines and plantations, the Transvaal government finally conceded to the Indians' demands in 1914, abolishing the poll tax, recognizing Indian marriages, and lifting many of the restrictions enacted by the Asiatic Ordinance.

Gandhi had successfully employed nonviolent mass civil disobedience to eradicate government-sanctioned racial discrimination. "Truly speaking, it was after I went to South Africa that I became what I am now," Gandhi wrote in his autobiography. "My love for South Africa and my concern for her problems are no less than for India."

FIGHTING FOR FREEDOM IN INDIA

In July 1914, Gandhi returned to his native India. There, he continued to fight oppression and champion the civil rights of Indians for the remainder of his life. He was instrumental in helping India win its independence from British rule. Considered the Father of India, Gandhi was given the title Mahatma, an honor-ific meaning "great soul," by his countrymen. He was assassinated by a religious Hindu extremist in 1948.

On April 25, 1997, nearly one hundred years after Gandhi was thrown off a train, a crowd gathered at Pietermaritzburg Railway Station in his honor. South African president Nelson Mandela conferred the Freedom of Pietermaritzburg award posthumously to the great Indian leader. Present at the ceremony was Gopalkrishna Gandhi, Gandhi's grandson and India's high commissioner to South Africa.

"When Gandhi was evicted from the train," he told the crowd, "an Indian visiting South Africa fell, but when Gandhi rose, an Indian South African rose."

CHAPTER FIFTEEN

WINSTON CHURCHILL, 1874–1965: LEARNING EARLY ABOUT THE HORROR OF WAR

Winston Churchill wanted to be a soldier, a hero, and a member of Parliament. He achieved all three by age thirty, and he became one of the most revered men in history.

Young Winston Churchill snatched a rifle from a nearby Sikh warrior and began firing. A British army subaltern doubling as a news correspondent, the rookie officer carried only a pistol for personal defense. He was twenty-two years old, and "embedded" with Britain's Malakand Field Force on the frontier between British India (now Pakistan) and independent, tribal Afghanistan. It was the same hostile territory where, more than a century later, NATO forces would contest with Taliban fighters from Afghanistan. In 1897, as in 2008, borders were porous and meaningless. Twenty-first-century Afghan fighters readily crossed over and took refuge in the tribal lands of Pakistan; in 1897, traffic moved the other way.

Churchill realized that his small unit was dangerously isolated, far ahead of the Field Force's main column. With him were four other British officers and some eighty nervous Sikh soldiers—"sepoys," Indian troops paid by the crown. British officers didn't fully trust the sepoys, recalling the bloody Sepoy Mutiny of 1857.

Now, storming down on the little company from the rocky hilltops ahead came a wave of Pathan tribesmen, screaming, shouting, stumbling, and falling in their haste, waving and firing their rifles menacingly. Churchill raised the rifle, took careful aim, and squeezed the trigger. He was gratified to see one of the oncoming horde clutch his chest and topple from his mount. It was the first

New York World-Telegram and the Sun Newspaper Photograph Collection, Prints & Photographs Division, Library of Congress, LC-USZ62-126509

time he had shot at another human being, he realized, the first one he had killed, and he kept firing. He gave thanks for the new Lee-Enfield repeating rifle, which allowed ten shots without reloading. The repeating rifle, along with the Maxim gun, a primitive machinegun, had revolutionized frontier warfare, particularly against mounted opponents. A jingle by the poet Hilaire Belloc was popular and reassuring in the army:

"Whatever happens

We have got

The Maxim gun

And they have not."

Churchill hit three, perhaps five, and kept firing, as the Sikh whose rifle he had taken handed him more cartridges. He discovered his troops were melting away. British officers maintained that in battle native troops ran. The Sikhs had repeatedly proven themselves tenacious fighters, but this time the scuttlebutt was correct.

The regimental adjutant, Lieutenant Victor Hughes, rode up in a cloud of dust. Churchill and the others must withdraw. "The Buffs are coming," he announced. The Buffs were a crack cavalry unit of the 31st Kent Regiment, who had been summoned from their station nearby. Lieutenant Hughes, a corpulent, slow-moving veteran, wheeled his horse. As he did so, a bullet caught him from the rear and exited in front. Bleeding profusely, he fell heavily from the saddle.

It was a point of honor on the frontier that the wounded must be immediately removed from the battlefield. Brutal and angry tribesmen were known to mutilate and kill the British fallen, leaving them to the wolves. Another verse dolefully chanted by soldiers was from Rudyard Kipling:

"When wounded and left on Afghanistan's plains

And the women come out to cut up what remains

Just roll to your rifle and blow out your brains

And go to your Gawd like a soldier."

Churchill watched in horror as the verse played out before his eyes. Four Sikh soldiers struggled to lift the bleeding adjutant and carry him away, but gave up and fled as Pathan tribesmen rode up. Pathans wielding long knives slashed at the wounded man. Mercifully, Churchill heard the bugles of the oncoming Buffs, and the knife-wielders scattered. As he left the battlefield, he carried with him a vivid image of war's horrors, coupled with a conflicting realization that war and

November 30, 1874
Winston Churchill is born in Blenheim Palace, Oxfordshire, son of Sir Randolph Churchill and Jennie Jerome Churchill.

April 1888
Enters the Harrow School.
September 1, 1893
Admitted to the Royal Military Academy at Sandhurst, on his third try.
January 24, 1895
Father, Sir Randolph Churchill, dies.
February 1895
Commissioned a second lieutenant in the 4th Hussar Regiment.

September 5, 1897
Joins the Malakand Field Force on the India–Afghanistan Frontier. Remains for six weeks and writes dispatches for the *Morning Post.*
September 2, 1898
Participates in the "last great cavalry charge" by the 21st Lancers at Omdurman, Sudan.

July 2, 1899
Stands as the Conservative Party candidate for Parliament from Oldham, but is defeated.
October 1, 1899
War breaks out between Britain and Boer republics in South Africa.
October 14, 1899
Sails to South Africa as a foreign correspondent. Captured, he escapes by hiding in a bale of sheep wool.

November 3, 1900
Elected to Parliament from Oldham.
1906
Leaves the Conservative Party, joins the Liberals.
August 15, 1908
Marries Clementine Hozier.

July 11, 1911
Becomes the first lord of the admiralty.
February 19, 1915
Anzac forces land at Gallipoli, Turkey, as suggested by Churchill as first lord.
January 1916
Anzac troops are withdrawn from Gallipoli. Churchill is blamed for the disaster and resigns.
October 1916
Leads the 6th Battalion, Royal Scots Fusiliers in battle in France.

1917
Becomes the minister of munitions in the David Lloyd George cabinet.
November 11, 1918
Armistice is declared, ending World War I.
1922
Loses Parliamentary seat in the general election.
1924
Leaves the Liberal Party to return to the Conservative Party and is named chancellor of the exchequer.

1930s
Although out of office, he repeatedly warns of the German military buildup and threat to Britain.
September 1, 1939
German army invades Poland, beginning World War II. Prime Minister Neville Chamberlain forms the war cabinet with Churchill as first lord of the admiralty.
May 10, 1940
Germany invades the Low Countries and France. Chamberlain resigns. Churchill replaces him as prime minister.
July-September 1940
Repeated German air raids devastate cities in the Battle of Britain; Churchill rallies people with defiant speeches: "We shall not flag nor fail. We shall go on to the end…We shall defend our island, whatever the cost. We shall fight on the beaches, we shall fight on the landing grounds, we shall fight in the fields and in the streets, we shall fight in the hills…We shall *never* surrender."

December 7, 1941
The Japanese bomb Pearl Harbor, and the United States enters the war.
June 6, 1944
Allied troops land in Normandy in France.
May 8, 1945
Germany surrenders to the Allies.
July 26, 1945
Churchill's Conservative government is defeated at the polls. He is replaced as prime minister by Clement Attlee.
September 2, 1945
After the U.S. atomic bombing of two cities, the Japanese sign the surrender treaty on the USS *Missouri.* World War II ends.

October 26, 1951
After a Conservative election victory, becomes prime minister again.
August 27, 1955
Resigns as prime minister and is succeeded by Anthony Eden.

January 24, 1965
Dies in his London home, age ninety, after the most severe of a series of strokes.

killing for cause and comrades can be justified. The twin views persisted through fifty years and wartime leadership that saw a 2002 BBC poll proclaim him "The Greatest Briton of Them All."

BORN TO BE A HERO

Churchill was born March 30, 1874, with the genes of a hero. His birthplace, Blenheim Palace, had been built for and presented to his ancestor, John Churchill, the first Duke of Marlborough, in gratitude for his victory at the Battle of Blenheim in 1704. The now largely forgotten battle was a great victory in the War of the Spanish Succession, a Europe-wide struggle designed to keep a royal French Bourbon off the throne of Spain and thus uniting the two into one powerful nation. Churchill's father, Sir Randolph Churchill, was the third son of the sixth Duke of Marlborough. His mother, Jennie Jerome, was a U.S. heiress known for her great beauty and her numerous lovers, said to number more than 200. Neither Churchill's mother nor his aloof father had much time for the boy, leaving parenting primarily to his nanny, Elizabeth Everest, whom he adored and called "Woom." Even as prime minister, he still kept her portrait in his office. While scarcely the traditional mother, Jennie remained close to her son throughout his life and was a major supporter, indefatigable adviser, and correspondent during his military and political careers.

Sir Randolph went to Parliament at age twenty-four and quickly became a leader of the Conservative Party. He was a dynamic speaker and policy maker, whose "Tory democracy" appealed to working-class Britons as well as the traditional wealthy and titled Conservative backers. He rose to become chancellor of the exchequer at thirty-seven, the second highest post in the British cabinet. Then he began to behave strangely, slurring his words, stumbling when he walked, slobbering, and given to sudden outbursts that caused other members of Parliament (MPs) to jeer and make fun of him. He was diagnosed with advanced tertiary syphilis and died at forty-five. His son did not know the true nature of the illness until his father's final weeks. Churchill later published a flattering biography of his father and declared that he had entered politics to pursue his father's ideas and to vindicate his memory.

Previous page: The English-officered Malakand Field Force overwhelmed rebellious Pathan tribesmen in the still-contested frontier between Afghanistan and what is now Pakistan. Getty Images

Churchill was not a good student, clearly not Oxford or Cambridge material. He attended Harrow, but courses such as Greek and Latin defeated or bored him. Deciding that a military career was the best pathway to Parliament, he applied three times for Sandhurst, the military academy, and failed each time. The second time he barely scored 50 percent in English and couldn't qualify even for cavalry, which had the lowest requirements. Churchill took a year of cram courses and did better, but was still admitted only because of Jennie's formidable clout. At Sandhurst, he graduated twentieth in his class, scoring high in tactics, gymnastics, drill, and riding, but poorly in Classical languages and French. He learned polo, which he played with passion until he gave it up at fifty-two. Meanwhile, he educated himself by reading history and the great classics. Churchill's final ranking qualified him for the cavalry. He was commissioned into the elite 4th Hussar Regiment, which was an appointment that dismayed his father, who considered an infantry command more prestigious and a better training ground for politics.

Winston Churchill learned how to play polo at Sandhurst, and he played it with passion until he was in his fifties.

The Hussars were ordered to India in 1896 for a routine tour of seven years. They were given ten weeks' leave for farewells. Churchill decided to make good use of the time. A Sandhurst professor had admired his clear and precise writing style and encouraged him to write for London newspapers while in India. Churchill didn't want to wait to try his hand at journalism. He wanted to witness war and write about it. He hopped a ship for Cuba, where local rebels had risen up against their Spanish colonial overlords. He stayed for two weeks, saw several skirmishes, and found himself under fire, an experience he called "exhilarating." He sent accounts back to London's *Daily Graphic* for which he was paid five guineas each.

Returning home, Churchill learned that an expedition was planned for India's North-West Frontier Agency and that it would be headed by Sir Bindon Blood. He had met Blood at a garden party the previous year in which Blood had casually promised that if he ever commanded another expedition, he would invite Churchill to join him. Churchill immediately cabled Blood that he was en route to India and

reminded him of his "promise." Churchill had almost given up hope of reply when he received a terse cable, "Very difficult. No vacancies. Come up as correspondent. Will try to fit you in." Next day he was off to India, and after the sea voyage and a creaky seven-day train ride in blistering heat, he joined the Malakand Field Force.

Churchill spent a month with the Malakand, primarily on a punitive expedition against the rebellious Pathans, all of which Churchill described for readers of the *Daily Telegraph*. Churchill then decided that his dispatches were too good to waste on a daily newspaper, and he sat down to expand them into a book. The result was *The Story of the Malakand Field Force*, his first book. (He was eventually to write more than 100.) The book gave an unvarnished account of the expedition, spiced with bits of humor (some of it poked at the leaders), vivid descriptions of blood and gore, and some sharp criticisms of the tactics and generalship of the leaders. The force had lost 150 men, and it had devastated the Pathans' homeland in the Mamund Valley, burning houses, uprooting crops, and killing bystanders to avenge the military deaths. "Whether it was all worth it, I cannot tell," he wrote sharply. "At any rate, at the end of a fortnight, the valley was a desert, and honour was satisfied."

Thanks partly to Jennie's energetic promotion and despite numerous proof-reading errors, the book was an immediate bestseller. Even the crown price, the future Edward VII, told a friend, "Everybody's reading it." But Churchill's trenchant comments, sometimes phrased as jokes, rankled army brass and political figures. They found it "bumptious" of a subaltern with no genuine experience of war to publicly criticize his superior officers. Who does he think he is? was a steady refrain. And why did his Hussar officers permit him leave to go off with another unit and then take time from his duties to write about it? Even among the other young officers, Churchill was scarcely popular.

THE LAST GREAT CAVALRY CHARGE

The London newspapers were also filling up with angry articles about the Sudan, an African territory south of Egypt and bisected by the Nile. In 1885, General Charles Gordon, known as "Chinese" Gordon for his earlier Far East exploits, had been tortured and killed in the embassy residence there by fanatic followers of a

General Sir Bindon Blood, commander of the Malakand Field Force, invited young Churchill to India as a correspondent in 1897. Getty Images

fundamentalist Muslim sect, the Mahdists. The papers and voices in the House of Commons called out for revenge, even though the incident was a decade old.

Britain was also in the process of building a colonial empire in Africa from north to south. Imperialists in Commons urged construction of a Cape-to-Cairo railroad to tie the colonies together. That meant following the Nile, and that in turn meant clearing the great river's course of hostile tribes and sects. The papers disclosed that General Horatio Herbert Kitchener would lead an expedition up the Nile toward Khartoum, where Gordon had been killed, avenging his death in the process. Churchill, looking for new wars and perhaps another book, wanted to go along. But

The Dervishes were completely destroyed. Churchill wrote his mother that he personally had killed "three for certain, two doubtful, one very doubtful."

that required approval from Kitchener. And Kitchener had read *The Story of the Malakand Field Force*. In a fury. He wanted no part of that "presumptuous medal-hunter."

However, the crown prince had also recommended the book to his prime minister, Lord Robert Arthur Talbot Gascoyne-Cecil Salisbury. Salisbury, chortling over the barbs thrown at the brass hats, complimented Churchill and declared, "If there is ever anything I can do which would be of assistance to you, please do not hesitate to let me know." Churchill mentioned his unsuccessful request to Kitchener. When Churchill applied again for permission, he was told Kitchener was too busy to personally deal with the matter, but a spokesman hinted that Churchill should go ahead with his plans. Churchill then learned that an officer of the 21st Lancers had died, creating a vacancy in Kitchener's ranks. A few days later, Churchill headed for Africa.

Churchill was still a cavalryman at heart; the idea of the Lancers appealed to him. He arrived fully equipped, having bought a horse and acquired a commission for articles from the *Morning Post*. He appeared at the 21st Lancers' camp just in time to join one of the last—and most chronicled—cavalry charges in British military history. Forty thousand Mahdists, referred to by the British as "Dervishes," were drawn up in a 5-mile (8 km) wide line of battle in the desert at Omdurman, near Khartoum. Facing them were 26,000 British and Egyptian soldiers. The British also boasted massed artillery, twenty Maxim guns and thousands of repeating rifles, which was an enormous edge in firepower. The Dervishes attacked and died in the thousands. Kitchener then called in the cavalry, the 21st Lancers, to clear the battlefield and make his victory complete.

With Churchill waving a pistol instead of a lance, 310 Lancers charged at a gallop across the open desert at the remaining 3,000 Dervishes. It was a slaughter. The Dervishes were completely destroyed. They scattered and melted into the desert. The Lancers lost seventy killed and wounded. Churchill wrote his mother that he personally had killed "three for certain, two doubtful, one very doubtful." After trumpeting the gallantry of the charge, he saw no point in staying longer in the Sudan. Omdurman had given him enough action to launch another book, *The River War*, and he set out to write it.

IN AND OUT OF JAIL

Churchill's dispatches from Omdurman, emphasizing his own role, made him even more a celebrity. Now might be the time to cash in on his fame. He resigned from the army and stood for Parliament. As a Conservative candidate following in his father's footsteps, he chose a by-election to fill a vacancy in an industrial London suburb, Oldham. His campaign focused almost exclusively on his war experiences. His Liberal opponent gibed that *he* "had not been a swashbuckler around the world." Churchill replied, "And I do not belong to a party composed of prigs, prudes, and faddists." Working-class Oldham was not ready for a Conservative candidate, however. Churchill made a respectable showing, but lost.

In the mid-1800s, British settlers and Boer settlers of Dutch ancestry had conducted a spirited colonial rivalry in South Africa. Britain's colonies consisted of two self-governing states, Cape Colony and Natal, bequeathed to Britain after the Napoleonic wars. The Boer republics were Transvaal and the Orange Free State. Britain had briefly annexed Transvaal, stoking the competition, but the Boers succeeded in wresting it back. Then in 1886, rich gold and diamond deposits were discovered in the Transvaal and "the world rushed in," as in California in 1849. Fortune-seeking *uitlanders*, as the Boers called them, swamped the previously placid agriculturalist society. By 1899, according to one estimate, uitlanders outnumbered Boers 70,000 to 44,000—almost two to one, yet could not vote. Uitlanders petitioned for voting rights. Transvaal President "Oom Paul" Kruger decreed that they could neither vote nor own property in the republic. The uitlanders, mostly English-speaking, asked Britain to intercede, and the British colonies backed the immigrants. Transvaal militia entered the Cape Colony in pursuit of agitators and were held prisoner; a group of wealthy Cape colonists staged the "Jameson raid" in an attempt to overturn Kruger's government. Outright war between Britain and the Boer republics began on October 1, 1899.

On October 14, armed with a contract from the *Morning Post* for the princely sum of 250 pounds a month, Churchill was on a boat for South Africa. He was accompanied by sixty bottles of wine and brandy, which he estimated would see him through the first four months.

When Churchill arrived in South Africa, he quickly learned that the Boers were far more aggressive and skilled warriors than the British had believed. Born to the saddle and backed by German-made Krupp artillery plus up-to-date Maxim guns, they embarrassed the British in a series of battles, invading Natal and besieging the key rail town of Ladysmith. Fierce fighting was going on around Ladysmith, and Churchill and other correspondents wanted to be there. They set out by rail but discovered that Boers had cut the line 30 miles (48 km) south of the besieged city. Stymied, the correspondents pitched their tents in the railway yards at Estcourt, where 2,000 British troops were bivouacked. There Churchill met an old friend from Makaland days, Captain Aylmer Haldane, and they spent the evening tapping into Churchill's mobile wine cellar.

The next day, the area commander, Colonel C.J. Long, called Haldane in and assigned him a reconnaissance mission. He was to take an armored train and two companies of men and probe north along the rail line to gauge the Boers' whereabouts and strength. Haldane invited Churchill to accompany him. Neither man liked the idea of an armored train, and events were to prove them right. To them the armored train had some of the later virtues of a tank (which had not been invented yet), but it was wedded to the rails. With its noise and giveaway puffs of smoke, it was easily spotted and a vulnerable target. It was particularly ill suited for a scouting mission, which could have been accomplished by a few men on horseback. You could hardly see out the windows, Churchill complained.

Churchill's daughter-in-law and the prime minister's 20-month-old namesake enjoy a wartime stroll in 1942. New York World-Telegram and the Sun Newspaper Photograph Collection, Prints & Photographs Division, Library of Congress, LC-DIG-ppmsca-04652

Sure enough, the train had barely advanced when it rounded a downhill curve at full speed and slammed into a mountain of boulders piled on the tracks. Three cars were derailed, and the track was damaged. Back in his combined role of correspondent and army officer, Churchill rounded up a crew of volunteers and labored to get the engine back on the rails and the tracks cleared. When they finally succeeded and the engine resumed running, Churchill helped to carry wounded into the engine cab. Then he rode with it for a few miles, jumped off, and trudged back toward Estcourt. Churchill had not gone far when he met two Boers on horseback, pointing rifles directly at him. Alone and without his pistol, which he had left in

---

After escaping from a prisoner-of-war camp, Winston Churchill hid at the bottom of a mine shaft with only a revolver, water, a little food—and a bottle of whisky—for six days.

---

the cab, he saw no chance of escape. "What could I do?" he recalled afterward. He raised his hands and surrendered for the only time in his adventuresome life.

Haldane had surrendered, too, and the two were taken to a makeshift officers' prisoner-of-war camp in the State Model School in Pretoria, where they immediately began plotting escape. They recruited Regimental Sergeant Major A. Brockie, who had posed as a lieutenant to get into the officers' camp. Brockie spoke Afrikaans, the Boer language, and the native dialect. He would be an important asset on the outside. Neither Haldane nor Brockie wanted Churchill to join the escape, because his celebrity would surely bring on a search. Churchill persuaded them, and the three worked out a simple plan. A prisoner's latrine was located at the back of the camp against a corrugated iron fence. One by one, they would go to the latrine and when all were together, would help each other clamber over the fence and flee. They entered the latrine, unopposed by a nearby sentry, and then waited for the sentry to move. After an hour with the sentry still in place, Haldane and Brockie left the latrine, deciding to return the next night. Churchill stayed, waited until the sentry was distracted, and then scrambled over the fence unaided.

Unable to speak either Afrikaans or the local Kaffir dialect, with no clue where he should go, and without food or water, Churchill stumbled about in open country for a day and a half, nodding wordlessly at passersby. Then in the midnight darkness, he spotted lights at a distance. Approaching, he saw they were the fires at a coal mine. If there were mines, there should be homes nearby. Exhausted, footsore, and hungry, Churchill nervously knocked on a door, unsure whether he might be greeted in Afrikaans or Kaffir. Instead, a man pointing a revolver at him opened the door and spoke in English. Churchill pleadingly described his plight. "Thank God you've come to this house!" exclaimed miner John Howard. "Any other house would have been dangerous. Here we are all English."

For the next six days, Howard secreted him at the bottom of a mine shaft with only a revolver, a bottle of whisky, water, and a little food. On the sixth night, he led Churchill to a farm wagon loaded with bales of wool. Howard and his friends had scooped out a cave in the baled wool for Churchill. He barely fit inside and could scarcely breathe. He endured three days of jostling and bouncing until one morning he looked out and saw signs in a foreign language. He had reached safety in neutral Portuguese East Africa.

He had a gripping story to tell, and he quickly wrote it for *Morning Post* readers. Then he went home to London and to another Parliamentary by-election. This time, his unmistakable hero status won handily. Churchill was on his way to a statesman's career that ranged from disaster at Gallipoli (see Chapter 17) to the dark days of World War II, when his stentorian voice and defiant oratory galvanized an embattled nation and rallied them to an epic victory. It was Churchill's "finest hour," for which he had been preparing all his life.

CHAPTER SIXTEEN

ALBERT EINSTEIN, 1879–1955: A COMPASS POINTS THE WAY FOR A YOUNG GENIUS

Albert Einstein was an apathetic, almost dull boy until the gift of a magnetic compass aroused his curiosity and awakened the sleeping genius inside him. His greatest contributions to science were the result of his lifelong quest to understand the hidden forces that controlled the compass—and the universe.

The child was restless. He had been cooped up for several days and longed to go outside and breathe the fresh air. His mother, Pauline, felt his forehead: It was warm, possibly from fever. She marched him back to his bed where he reluctantly scrambled back under the covers.

Since his birth, Pauline and Hermann Einstein had worried about their son, Albert. The child was born with a strangely shaped, elongated head, and he did not learn to speak until he was three years old. Albert was quiet and withdrawn; at times, he seemed rather dull, almost as if he were mentally deficient. The Einsteins feared that the boy might be mentally retarded. A family doctor assured them that Albert was simply a late bloomer.

But at five years old, Albert still had not bloomed. He spoke now but employed a strange pattern of speech, starting a sentence only to abandon it midway through and then begin all over again. He lost focus easily and seemed lost in his own world. This quality would later lead several schoolteachers to label young Albert Einstein as a hopeless case, both unreachable and unteachable.

Additionally, Albert seemed uninterested in childhood pursuits or in other children. Games of tag and hide-and-seek did not hold his interest. He disliked

The future Father of Modern Physics was a late bloomer who did not begin speaking until the age of three. Hebrew University of Jerusalem Albert Einstein Archives, courtesy AIP Emilio Segre Visual Archives.

sports and avoided rigorous physical activity. When Albert's cousins dropped by for visits, he refused to play with them, retreating instead to a quiet room where he'd spend hours playing alone with his building blocks. Albert's only companion was his younger sister, three-year old Marie, whom everyone called "Maja."

A socially withdrawn boy, Albert Einstein preferred to spend time alone, or with his younger sister, Maja. Hebrew University of Jerusalem Albert Einstein Archives, courtesy AIP Emilio Segre Visual Archives

The introverted young Albert was far less restrained with tantrums than words. Exploding in violent rage over trifles, he threw chairs and toys across the room. Maja often bore the brunt of her brother's anger. On one occasion, he hit her with a garden hoe, on another he hurled a bowling ball at her, narrowly missing her head. Hoping to redirect Albert's energy, Pauline arranged for the boy to learn to play the violin. The first instructor fled the house after Albert flew into a rage and flung a chair at the wall. It quickly became apparent that Albert did not like being told what to do. This was an early glimpse into Albert's rebellious nature and his distrust of authority.

Gradually, Pauline and Hermann accepted the fact that Albert was an unusual child. They decided to foster a sense of independence in the boy and allow him to develop at his own pace. When Albert was four, the Einsteins took him into downtown Munich and allowed him to cross the street by himself. By the time he turned five, he was roaming through the streets on his own, gazing in awe at the cathedrals and architectural wonders that dotted the city. Albert was the only child of his social class to be allowed such freedom at such a tender age. Devoted but permissive guardians, the Einsteins realized they needed to adopt an unusual parenting approach to raise such an unusual boy.

The Einstein house was frequently filled with music, poetry, and laughter. Hermann ran an electrochemical company with his brother. During his time off, he liked to read German poetry to his wife and children. Pauline was a gifted pianist who enjoyed performing for the family. The music sometimes calmed Albert down when he was in one of his terrible moods.

On this dreary day, a bad cold kept Albert confined to the house. He was too weak and too depressed to throw one of his famous temper tantrums. To cheer the boy up, Hermann bought him a present: a magnetic compass. The small device mesmerized Albert. He sat up for hours playing with the compass, flipping it over and over. No matter which way he turned the compass its tiny magnetic needle remained

March 14, 1879
Albert Einstein is born in Ulm, Germany.
June 21, 1880
The Einstein family relocates to Munich, Germany.
1884
Receives the compass that sparks his intellectual curiosity.

March 31, 1885
Enrolls in a local elementary school.
Autumn 1889
Begins independently studying science and philosophy.
June 1894
The Einstein family moves to Milan, Italy.
October 1896
Graduates from high school and enrolls in the Federal Polytechnic School
(the ETH) in Zurich, Switzerland.

July 28, 1900
Graduates from the ETH and begins working on his doctoral thesis.
June 16, 1902
Accepts a position with the Swiss Patent Office.
January 6 1903
Marries Mileva Maric.

March 1905
Publishes a series of groundbreaking scientific papers, one of which
introduces the special theory of relativity.
January 15, 1906
Receives his doctorate from the University of Zurich.
February 28, 1908
Begins private tutoring sessions in physics for Bern University.

January 30, 1912
Appointed professor of theoretical physics at the
Federal Polytechnic School in Zurich.
December 1913
Relocates to Germany where he is appointed director
of the Kaiser Wilhelm Institute in Berlin.
June 1914
Separates from his wife.
1915
Completes his formulation of the general theory of relativity.

June 2, 1919
Officially divorced from Mileva, Einstein marries Elsa Löwenthal in Berlin.
November 9, 1922
Awarded the Nobel Prize in Physics.
1928
Begins working on a unified field theory.

October 1933
Immigrates to the Unites States where he is hired as a professor at the
newly founded Institute of Advanced Study in Princeton, New Jersey.
October 1, 1940
Becomes a U.S. citizen.

April 18, 1955
Einstein dies from heart failure at the age of seventy-six,
in Princeton, New Jersey.

pointing north, as if influenced by some hidden force field. He realized that there was something larger than life at work, an unseen mysterious force that was pulling the strings. The epiphany awakened an insatiable curiosity that hitherto had been sleeping inside the quiet, seemingly dull boy. That curiosity would later drive him to discover one of the greatest theories in science, the theory of relativity.

Years later, Einstein would credit that compass for igniting his lifelong passion for science. "Something deeply hidden had to be behind things," sixty-seven-year-old Einstein noted in his autobiography. "What man sees before him from infancy causes no reaction of this kind; he is not surprised over the falling of bodies, concerning wind and rain, nor concerning the moon or about the fact that the moon does not fall down, nor concerning the differences between living and nonliving matter."

The childhood discovery left a "deep and lasting impression" on him. In turn, Einstein, with his brilliant mind and charmingly enigmatic personality, would leave a deep and lasting impression of his own on history.

DISAPPOINTMENTS, THEORIES, AND DISCOVERIES

Born in Ulm, Germany, on March 14, 1879, Einstein is as dominant a thinker in the twenty-first century as he was in the twentieth. He was just twenty-six and working as a patent technician when he introduced his groundbreaking special theory of relativity, which paved the way for the development of modern physics. The theory, which included science's most famous equation $E=mc^2$, posited that time and space are relative, rather than absolute, concepts, and that motion must be defined relative to a frame of reference. The scientific community was slow to embrace Einstein's theory, which challenged accepted notions established by Isaac Newton two centuries earlier that space and time are absolute.

Aside from contradicting existing concepts, the theory was also written by an outsider, a low-level patent clerk who had failed to find gainful employment in the scientific field. Einstein's attempts to secure a position in academia were rebuffed time and time again. During his school years, the brilliant young man ruffled quite a few feathers. Einstein's distrust of authority, independent nature, and quirky, often tactless personality alienated many of his professors. This pattern followed Einstein from elementary to university classes. "You'll never amount to anything," an elementary teacher informed a preteen Einstein.

Skilled in math and science, Einstein performed poorly in most other subjects. He was unable to pass the entrance exam for his university of choice, Zurich's vaunted Federal Institute of Technology. Professor Heinrich Weber recognized Einstein's aptitude for mathematics and science, and he invited the young man to attend his lectures at the institute. Weber hoped that with serious study Einstein might successfully pass the exam. With his help, Einstein eventually was accepted into the institute. However, Einstein's truculent behavior and refusal to toe the line caused Weber to withdraw his support.

"You're a clever fellow," he told Einstein, "But you have one fault. You won't let anyone tell you a thing!" Believing Weber to be an inferior scientist, Einstein refused to address him as professor. Weber developed an immense dislike for his student and was largely responsible for blacklisting Einstein in the academic community. With anti-Semitic fervor growing in Europe, Einstein's Jewish heritage served to further limit his already limited prospects.

"You'll never amount to anything," an elementary teacher informed a preteen Albert Einstein.

Unable to procure the letters of recommendation necessary for a decent job, Einstein floundered and worried about his prospects. The future Father of Modern Physics was even turned down for a job teaching high school science. By that time, he had a wife and child to support. Einstein wrote to prominent scientists in the hope of landing an assistantship. To famed chemist Wilhelm Ostwald he wrote, "I venture to ask you whether perhaps you might have use for a mathematical physicist who is familiar with absolute measurements. I am taking the liberty of making such a request only because I am without means and only such a position would give me the possibility of further education." Ostwald did not reply.

THE MIRACLE YEAR

A friend of Einstein's eventually helped him obtain a job with the Swiss Patent Office. The job was beneath the fledgling physicist, but Einstein was grateful for the financial security the paycheck brought. When business was slow, Einstein turned his attention to his true passion: physics, making calculations, and working out theories. Einstein longed to be accepted into the field and make a lasting contribution to science. He wouldn't have to wait very long.

In 1905, the year now considered his "miracle year," Einstein published four articles that changed accepted views of space, time, and matter. The fourth article presented the special theory of relativity. In *Relativity*, a book that Einstein wrote in 1916 to explain the theory to nonscientists, he said, "The nonmathematician is seized by a mysterious shuddering when he hears of 'four-dimensional things,' by a feeling not unlike that awakened by thoughts of the occult. And yet there is no more common-place statement than that the world in which we live is a four-dimensional space-time continuum."

Einstein's work consumed him. As his professional life thrived, his personal life devolved into shambles. To the detriment of Einstein's family, he spent countless hours searching for answers to explain the mysteries of the universe. His wife, Mileva, complained that Einstein lived only for science. She also accused him of having an affair with his distant cousin, Elsa Löwenthal. The Einsteins divorced, and Mileva moved away with their two sons.

Einstein's theories opened the long-closed doors of academia. In 1914, Einstein was appointed director of the Kaiser Wilhelm Institute and professor of theoretical physics at the University of Berlin. A year later, Einstein refined his early formulations and introduced the general theory of relativity. The new theory included the effect of gravitation on the curvature of a space–time continuum. "My relativity theory reduced to one formula all laws which govern space, time, and gravitation," he told a reporter. "The purpose of my new work is to further this simplification and particularly to reduce to one formula the explanation of the field of gravity and the field of electromagnetism."

Ironically, when Einstein was awarded the Nobel Prize, it was not for his theory of relativity, which was not fully accepted at the time, but for his work in quantum physics.

In 1919, Einstein married Elsa Löwenthal. A divorcée with two daughters, Elsa doted on her new husband. Einstein, in turn, treated her as a housekeeper and cook. If Elsa resented her new role, she kept it to herself. She was his constant companion and seemed content to play second fiddle to Einstein's real love: science. Although Einstein provided financial support for his sons, he saw them infrequently. For all Einstein's accomplishments, he was still very much the awkward, socially inept young child whose imagination was sparked by an ordinary compass.

Einstein married twice. He's seen here with his second wife, Elsa, and her daughter Margot. Getty Images

AN INTERNATIONAL CELEBRITY IS BORN

While Einstein pored over his mathematic calculations inside a classroom, political tensions were mounting outside in the streets of Berlin as Adolf Hitler and his Nazi party rose to power. Einstein's Jewish heritage and radical new scientific ideas made him a convenient—and very public— target for a new regime that eschewed modernity and foreign influence. In Germany, the theory of relativity was dismissed as "Jewish physics." In 1933, Einstein and his family fled his homeland for the United States, where he accepted a position with the prestigious Institute for Advanced Studies in Princeton, New Jersey.

Einstein received a hero's welcome in his new country. Despite the fact that few laypersons were able to understand the theory of relativity, Einstein had become an international celebrity. His revolutionary ideas impressed scientists around the world. But it was Einstein's irrepressible personality and his eccentric appearance that endeared him to the public. With his slightly disheveled clothing and mop of wild hair, Einstein resembled the quintessential absentminded professor. Journalist A.V. Lunacharsky described Einstein as "a jolly fellow" whose "remarkable simplicity is so charming that one feels like hugging or squeezing his hand or slapping him on the back—which in no way detracts from one's esteem for him. It is a strange feeling of tender affection for a man of great defenseless simplicity mixed with boundless respect."

It was Albert Einstein's irrepressible personality and his eccentric appearance that endeared him to the public. With his slightly disheveled clothing and mop of wild hair, Einstein resembled the quintessential absentminded professor.

But the smiling, bumbling image Einstein presented belied his personal failings as a man. The charming scientist was aloof with those closest to him and viewed his family as a distraction from his work. An emotionally distant husband, he neglected his first wife, and treated his second as a household servant. "I can love humanity, but when it comes to close relationships, I'm a horse for single harness," Einstein admitted. "I failed twice, rather disgracefully." Einstein was also an ineffectual father who spent little time with his sons, and never sought out the illegitimate daughter he fathered with Mileva Maric and gave up for adoption before the couple married.

Movie stars, artists, writers, politicians, and intellectuals clamored to befriend the guileless, good-natured scientist. Einstein viewed his popularity with bemusement. He never understood his appeal to the public. Arriving to deliver a lecture at Princeton, he was surprised to find the auditorium filled to capacity. In addition to scientists and students, dozens of laypersons had turned up to see the famed genius. Bewildered by the large crowd, Einstein remarked, "I never knew physics was so popular." One of the most brilliant minds in history was also one of the most child-like and naïve. It was that paradoxical mix of brilliance and naiveté that drew so many people to Einstein.

Einstein was also a humanitarian and a pacifist dedicated to promoting world peace. He advocated the creation of world government that had the power to enact and enforce global laws designed to keep the peace and prevent war. Einstein spent the last two decades of his life working on a unified field theory linking electromagnetism with light. His efforts to create the theory were unsuccessful. Ill and confined to bed, Einstein spent his final hours scribbling equations in a notebook. He died on April 18, 1955.

In 1940, Einstein and his family immigrated to the United States from Germany. The physicist is seen here accepting his certificate of American citizenship. New York World-Telegram and the Sun Newspaper Photograph Collection, Prints & Photographs Division, Library of Congress, LC-DIG-ppmsca-05649

Einstein's legacy and his celebrity live on. In 2000, *Time* magazine named him the leading figure of the twentieth century. Today, his name is synonymous with genius, and his iconic image is etched into the popular imagination.

A modest man, Einstein didn't consider himself particularly gifted intellectually. Instead, he ascribed his scientific discoveries to his inexhaustible curiosity. For Einstein, curiosity was the great motivator. He never lost his sense of wonder at the world. "The most beautiful experience we can have is the mysterious," he wrote in later life. "It is the fundamental emotion that stands at the cradle of true art and true science. Whoever does not know it and can no longer wonder, no longer marvel, is as good as dead."

CHAPTER SEVENTEEN

KEMAL ATATÜRK, 1881–1938:
A YOUNG TURK GROWS UP

An eight-year-old schoolboy started early to reform Turkish society. Forty years later, he succeeded, and he brought the medieval country into the twentieth century.

Mustafa was upset. It had been a bad day at the civil preparatory school he attended in Salonika in the Ottoman empire. Not just a bad day, maybe his worst day since his father died months before. The year was 1887, and Mustafa's mother had recently moved the family here to further her son's education.

Mustafa was gifted with figures, and he could add and subtract instantly. But today's lesson involved speech and grammar. These were not his strengths. Called upon to recite, Mustafa hesitated, cleared his throat, and mumbled his answer. Teacher Kaymak Hafiz rapped his stick and told Mustafa to speak up. A classmate smirked and snickered. Mustafa shouted at him. The other boy shouted back. Hafiz, known for his harsh methods, pushed them apart, then raised his stick and brought it down on the eight-year-old's shoulders—whack, whack, again and again.

Beatings were commonplace. The crowning indignity was the old-fashioned costume that school rules required Mustafa to wear—white, billowing trousers with a sash at the waist. By Turkish tradition, Mustafa, the oldest son, was now head of the household. He felt that a male in that position should not be subjected to such disrespectful treatment. Nor should he be dressed like a child. Mustafa decided he would not return to the civil preparatory school again.

Right up the street was another school where a neighborhood friend studied. A military preparatory school, it educated boys for service in the imperial army.

Turkish President Kemal Atatürk dressed in traditional Turkish military costume, which he had deplored as a schoolboy and later abolished along with the sultanate.

Young Kemal Atatürk was proclaimed a hero and heavily decorated after the Gallipoli campaign in 1915.

Mustafa's friend's father was an army officer. Students there got to wear smart, trim, modern uniforms and boots. Mustafa had recently become extremely conscious of his appearance and the impression he made on others. His mother noted that he spoke differently, with slower cadence and deeper register, more like a grownup. He wanted to wear a uniform like his friend, and become an officer. His days of balloon-shaped trousers at the civil preparatory school were over.

That night, Mustafa announced his decision to the family. His paternal grandmother, who by tradition had the last word in such matters, was all in favor. She hadn't wanted him to attend the school at all. Education should be limited to studying the Koran, she said. His mother was aghast. She had envisioned his supporting the family in a reliable civil-service job. She was definitely opposed to a military career. She didn't want her son to enter such a dangerous profession.

Demonstrating the persuasive powers that would serve him well later, Mustafa convinced his mother and had his way. Within a few days, the boy—who would later change his name and enter history under the triple-barreled name Mustafa Kemal Atatürk—had donned the cherished uniform and enrolled in the military school. That simple firm step at age eight launched an outstanding military career that made him the founder and first president of modern Turkey, and redrew the map of Europe and the Middle East.

AN ILLNESS IN ISTANBUL

In the last decades of the nineteenth century, when Mustafa was beginning his education, Turkey was derisively described as "the sick man of Europe." In 1453, the furiously expanding and proselytizing Muslim Turks had reached the walls of Vienna, causing Christian Europe to shake in its shoes. Much of the Mediterranean basin, North Africa, the Tigris–Euphrates valley, Syria, Arabia, and southeastern Europe had come under Ottoman sway. Lands comprising the modern states of Bulgaria, Albania, Greece, Macedonia, Moldavia, Bosnia, and Montenegro had been swallowed up.

But by the 1800s, these countries were getting restless. Greece rebelled and with British support freed itself by 1830. Egypt was nominally Ottoman but was

Winter 1880/81
Mustafa is born in Salonika, Macedonia, part of Ottoman Empire.
1893
Enters military preparatory school in Salonika.
1895
Enters military high school at Manastir.

September 13–October 8, 1912
Sent to Cyrenaica (now Libya) in the Italo-Turkish War. Promoted to major.
First Balkan War between Balkan provinces and Ottoman Turkey begins.
January 3–October 27, 1913
CUP seizes power in Constantinople. Second Balkan War begins. Assigned
to Sofia, Bulgaria, as a military attaché.

January 20–August 6, 1915
Takes command of 19th Division on Gallipoli peninsula. Allied (Anzac)
troops land at Ari Burnu (Anzac Cove). Kemal's troops check their advance.
Promoted to colonel. Allies land at Suvla Bay on Gallipoli. Kemal's troops
stop them from reaching heights.

September 16–November 13, 1918
British drive Ottoman troops out of Syria/Palestine. Ottomans sign an
armistice with the Allies in Syria/Palestine. Returns to Constantinople.

April 23– August 20, 1920
Elected the president of the Grand National Assembly in Ankara. Greek
troops invade. Treaty of Sevrès is signed, awarding parts of Ottoman
provinces to Greece, Serbia, and Italy. Sultan signs treaty, despite protests.

August 1922
Turks launch a final offensive against the Greeks and win a decisive victory.
November 1, 1922
Assembly abolishes sultanate; he flees on British warship.

March 3, 1924
Caliphate abolished.
April 20, 1924
Assembly votes the first republican constitution.
February 17, 1926
New civil code is passed, giving women full civil and voting rights.
November 1, 1927
Elected for a second four-year term.
August 9, 1928
Latin alphabet is adopted; Kemal teaches the first language class.

March 13, 1899
Enters War College in Constantinople.
February 10, 1902
Commissioned an infantry second lieutenant. Enters the Staff College.
c.1904
Joins the "Young Turk" movement, Committee for Unity and Progress (CUP).
January 11, 1905
Promoted to staff captain and assigned to the cavalry in Syria.

June 28–November 2, 1914
World War I begins. Ottoman Empire signs a secret alliance with Germany.
Ottoman navy under German command shells Russian Black Sea ports.
Russia declares war on the Ottoman Empire.

January 9–April 1, 1916
Allies abandon the Gallipoli expedition. Transferred to Caucasus, in
command against Russians. Appointed brigadier general.
July 7, 1917
Appointed commander of the 7th Army in Syria.

April 30– July 8, 1919
Appointed the inspector of armies in Anatolia. Meets nationalist commanders
in Anatolia and proclaims resistance movement. Resigns from the Ottoman
army.
September 4–11, 1919
Nationalist congress meets and elects Kemal its leader.

January 9– October 20, 1921
Turks win the first battle of the Turko-Grecian war. Assembly passes the
constitution for the new Turkish republic. Turks win the second major battle
of the war. Greeks launch a major offensive and capture two Turkish cities.
Kemal takes full command of nationalist troops, throws back the Greeks at
the Battle of Sakarya. Assembly awards Kemal the rank of marshal. French
sign accord with Turkey and withdraw the occupation force.

July 24– October 29, 1923
Treaty of Lausanne is signed, revoking Sevres, returning lands, and
recognizing Turkish sovereignty. Allied occupiers evacuate Constantinople.
Ankara officially becomes the Turkish capital. Turkey is proclaimed a
republic; Kemal is elected president unanimously.

May 4, 1931
Elected for the third time.
June 21, 1934
Surnames are made compulsory for all Turks. Kemal chooses "Atatürk"
("Father of the Turks").
March 1, 1935
Elected for the fourth time.
November 10, 1938
Dies at 9:05 a.m. in his palace bedroom.

controlled by Great Britain. Bosnia-Herzegovina was Ottoman in name only, administered by Austria-Hungary. By 1913, little remained of the once-grand Ottoman domain except for Constantinople and a few adjoining territories.

Turkey had fallen behind its neighbors in other ways. While parts of Europe were rapidly industrializing, Turkey remained a medieval state. Its customs and traditions, like Mustafa's trousers, dated from an earlier time. Even Mustafa's name—a single name, with no surname—was anachronistic. Although areas such as Syria and Macedonia had limited autonomy, the empire was ruled absolutely from Constantinople by the sultan and the caliph, head of the Muslim faith. Muslim and governmental authority were inextricably intertwined.

In 1876, under pressure from merchants and oligarchs, Sultan Muhammad V allowed Turkey's first constitution to be drawn up. It provided for a representative assembly, an executive, and courts. Within two years, the sultan junked it and ruled without a legislature. The constitution had for the first time officially authorized a Turkish army, but it was starved for funds. Even after humiliating defeats that cost the empire all its Balkan territory, the military was still equipped with ancient flintlock muskets and outdated artillery.

A simple firm step at age eight launched an outstanding military career that made Mustafa Kemal Atatürk the founder and first president of modern Turkey and redrew the map of Europe and the Middle East.

Young officers who had been humbled by the serial defeats and loss of territory were appalled. Groups began meeting clandestinely to agitate for reforming the army and navy and indeed the government itself. The immediate goal would be to restore the constitution of 1876. The secret meetings, mostly attended and sparked by junior officers, resulted in the founding of several underground organizations. They went under such names as the Committee for Unity and Progress (CUP), but they were referred to—and referred to themselves as—"the Young Turks."

Mustafa from Salonica was an early recruit.

TRAINING FOR A LARGER FUTURE

When Mustafa entered the military preparatory school, he was just plain "Mustafa," but he graduated as "Mustafa Kemal." In another example of the Turkish clinging to past traditions, surnames were reserved for the educated and the high-born. However, Mustafa's mathematics teacher was also named "Mustafa." Because of the young student's flair for math and eagerness to learn more, the two often exchanged his lessons in writing. But after weeks of confusion, the teacher decided the student must have a different name. He had been reading a patriotic poet, Kemal, and greatly admired his poetry. "My boy," he wrote Mustafa. "You and I cannot have the same name. From now on, you will be called 'Mustafa Kemal.'" Mustafa liked the new name and carried it the rest of his life.

Mustafa was making a name for himself in another way. Because of his skill in mathematics, he quickly rose to the top of his class. When he completed the military prep school, he stood fourth in his class. He then moved on to the military high school in Manastir, where he spent another three years. He ranked second when he graduated in 1898. This academic record took him to the War College, which prepared cadets for command positions.

After admittedly frittering away his first year "drinking and wenching," as one report had it, Mustafa buckled down to his studies. In that first year, he stood twenty-seventh in a class of 700; by the second year he was eleventh, and he graduated eighth. Mustafa also continued attending meetings of the Young Turks. He was commissioned an infantry lieutenant and achieved another goal: appointment to the Staff College, which groomed young officers for places in the High Command.

When time came for the new captains to receive assignments, Kemal, as he now called himself, hoped for a posting in Macedonia, near his home in Salonika. Meanwhile, he and other young officers rented a flat in Constantinople (now Istanbul), where they could discuss politics and where they published a revolutionary newspaper. Discovered by the sultan's secret police, all were arrested and jailed. Kemal spent two days in solitary confinement, then nearly a month confined in the officers' barracks. When Kemal was freed, he still hoped for Macedonia. Instead, he was "exiled" to a cavalry unit in Syria. Consequently he played only a minor role in the Young Turk rebellion of 1908.

Behind a blaring brass band, the Young Turks marched into Constantinople in 1913 and took over the government.

THE RISE OF THE YOUNG TURKS

In July 1908, the uprising that everyone had come to expect was ignited not by the Young Turks but by two European monarchs hundreds of miles away. The governments of Great Britain and Russia had become concerned that the over-throw of Ottoman rule would be a threat to Europe's uneasy peace. It would strengthen the Austro-Hungarian Hapsburg Empire and its ally Germany, and destabilize Ottoman territories in southeastern Europe.

British King Edward VII and his cousin Tsar Nicholas II of Russia met in Revel (now Tallinn, capital of Estonia) and produced a proposal to head off the incipient problem. They suggested that Macedonia become an independent state with a ruler whom the five "Great Powers" would choose, just as they had installed a Bavarian prince as king of Greece after the Greco-Turkish War of 1832. The new head of state would be an Ottoman subject, but would be advised and assisted by a cadre of Europeans, who would be paid from the Macedonian treasury. France immediately agreed, but not surprisingly Austria-Hungary and Germany balked. The proposal died.

The Committee of Unity and Progress or CUP (as the Young Turks called their organization) objected. Apart from restoring the constitution, a major Young Turk objective was to preserve the boundaries of the empire. The military had been embarrassed by the nibbling away of Greece, Bosnia-Herzegovina, and Albania, and by the ongoing contest with Serbia.

Although the Ottomans eventually yielded the North African territory, Mustafa Kemal emerged with a burnished reputation for having withstood a strangling Italian siege of the important port of Tobruk.

The dissidents sent a manifesto to the consuls of the Great Powers in Salonika. It claimed that the CUP alone could bring peace to the region, and the rest of Europe should keep its hands off. One CUP leader took 200 men into the hills of Macedonia to fight a guerrilla war. Muslim Albanians in Kosovo passed a resolution demanding a restored constitution. Other provinces followed suit. After several assassinations and kidnappings, the sultan dismissed the grand vizier, the equivalent of prime minister.

A new cabinet announced that the 1876 constitution was now in force and called for parliamentary elections. Acceding to the Young Turks' urgent demands, the sultan issued a directive ordering that the Turkish military "must be improved," especially the weapons and training. The Young Turks had won, and they effectively gained control over the government as well as the military.

Kemal had remained on the sidelines throughout, serving quietly on the staff of the Third Army command in Syria. Ever since military high school, he had engaged in a silent competition with another cadet with a single name, Enver, whose academic prowess had placed him two years ahead of Kemal, despite their identical ages. Enver, already a major, was one of three top leaders of the uprising, once even forced into exile to elude the secret police. After the successful coup, Enver assumed a prominent role in the new government. Indeed, even before the coup succeeded, he had independently proclaimed restoration of the constitution in his Second Army territory. Then Kemal was dispatched across the Mediterranean to Cyrenaica (now Libya) in North Africa, where Italy had pounced in the hope of carving out a North African colony from Ottoman territory.

Kemal spent two years in the desert. Although the Ottomans eventually yielded the territory, Kemal emerged with a burnished reputation for having withstood a strangling Italian siege of the important port of Tobruk. When Kemal returned, he and Enver resumed their rivalry. Both men developed plans to upgrade the Turkish military. Enver admired Germany's growing military power. He imported German officers and gave them ranking positions in the Turkish army, and he insisted that the army be schooled in German military methods and outfitted with German weapons.

Enver strongly supported German construction of a Berlin-to-Baghdad railway across Ottoman territory, believing it would benefit the movement of Ottoman troops within the empire. Kemal opposed it. While also admiring German methods, he felt that Turkey, now reduced to a mere toehold in Europe but retaining a far-flung empire in Asia and Africa, should not align itself so closely with one European country when the great powers were obviously choosing sides for a showdown.

Kemal was not alone in opposing Enver's policies. The Young Turk movement was riddled with factionalism, and it temporarily lost power. In November 1913, Kemal was sent to Sofia, Bulgaria, as a military attaché. He welcomed the posting. The Balkan states had risen up against Ottoman rule. The Young Turks simply washed their hands of the issue, granting Albania independence and letting the others divide the remaining territory among themselves. Bulgaria emerged the strongest survivor, its German-trained army making it the "Prussia of the Balkans." Whereupon the others ganged up on and defeated Bulgaria in the Second Balkan War, which became the prelude to the "Great War" to follow.

"I'M ORDERING YOU TO DIE!"

The "guns of August" boomed across Europe that hot, lazy summer of 1914. Germany attacked France through Belgium. Austria-Hungary turned on Serbia. Britain supported France and dispatched an expeditionary force across the English Channel. Russia declared war on both Germany and Austria-Hungary and mobilized huge numbers of troops at its borders.

In Istanbul, the no-longer-so-young Turks who again controlled the government watched nervously. At first, they declared themselves neutral, but Enver, now given the honorific title "Enver Pasha," had become war minister at the age of thirty-four, and he revealed a secret pact with Germany. The two countries would come to each other's aid in the event of war, and German officers would command Turkish forces.

After Germany agreed to loan the cash-short Ottoman government five million gold liras, Turkish warships commanded by a German admiral launched a surprise bombardment on Russian ports in the Black Sea and sank a number of Russian vessels. Russia declared war on Turkey, and Turkey officially joined the Central Powers—Germany, Austria-Hungary, and later Bulgaria.

Germany dispatched one of its foremost generals, Otto Liman von Sanders, to Istanbul to whip the Turkish forces into fighting shape. Kemal returned from Sofia and was given command of the 19th Division at Gallipoli, the small peninsula below Con-

Atatürk's longtime rival, General Enver Pasha, center, led the Young Turk coup and engineered a military alliance with Germany.
©Photo12 / The Image Works

stantinople. His position was to defend the Dardanelles, the straits linking the Mediterranean and Black Seas, and dividing European and Asian Turkey. Critical to both sides, the waterways provided the Allies with a supply route to Russian Black Sea ports.

Turkey's declaration of war closed the waterways to Allied shipping. Prodded by Winston Churchill, Britain's first lord of the admiralty, the Allies decided to open them by force. In March 1915, the British and French navies attempted to blast their way through the waterways. A massive fleet of sixty warships led by the new battleship *Queen Elizabeth* launched enormous firepower on the Turkish installations. A small landing party of Royal Marines was sent in to capture the shore batteries. The effort failed to dent the Turkish defenses; nor did they silence the coastal artillery. The British fleet tried again the next day and continued its barrage for four consecutive days before pulling back to try a ground invasion instead. It would land in force at Gallipoli virtually under Kemal's nose.

On April 25, 1915, colonial troops from Australia and New Zealand—the "Anzacs"—began swarming ashore at Ari Burna, known thereafter as Anzac Cove. From the heights above, Kemal and Liman von Sanders watched them come. Kemal had positioned his men in protected niches in the rugged hillsides that rose abruptly from the beach. As the Anzacs debarked from the troop transports to the landing boats, rifle and machine-gun fire raked the beach. Artillery in the heights bombarded the transports and landing craft. The normally blue waters of the Dardanelles turned red with blood. Men attempting to enter the landing boats had to step over the floating corpses of their comrades.

By nightfall, the Anzacs had lost nearly one-third of their men, and the landing party was pinned down on the beach by the withering fire. The stated objectives were to storm the heights, control the waterway, and advance toward Constantinople. They were unable to advance more than a few yards. The struggle went on for days with the invaders unable to gain higher ground, Kemal's 19th Division repeatedly beating back each attempt.

The normally blue waters of the Dardanelles turned red with blood. Men attempting to enter the landing boats had to step over the floating corpses of their comrades.

After a lull in the fighting, both sides regrouped to treat the wounded and bury the dead. Liman von Sanders was technically in command of the battle, but he wisely left many tactical decisions to Kemal, who knew the defenders and the territory. War minister Enver Pasha likewise kept his distance and promoted Kemal to brigadier general with command of a corps.

From Kemal's vantage point, he could see that the battle was far from over. Additional transports were bringing fresh troops and offloading great quantities of weapons and ammunition. Kemal recognized that further attempts to storm the heights were coming, and he sought to prepare his weary troops. The speech Kemal delivered still rings through military history, "Men! I do not order you to attack! I order you to die! By the time we are dead, other units and commanders will have come up to take our place!"

On August 6, 1915, a new wave of Anzacs came ashore to be met by inspired Turks willing to die. And die they did. Turkish casualties at Gallipoli totaled 55,000 dead, 100,000 wounded, 25,000 dead of disease. Anzac casualties reached 205,000 and the French 47,000, many due to illness and heat prostration. Then the Allies called off the attack and began withdrawing troops. The last of 480,000 Anzacs pulled out on January 12, 1916.

Kemal emerged covered with glory. His biographer, Andrew Mango, declared, "Gallipoli was the foundation of Mustafa Kemal's career."

EXIT STAGE LEFT, TEMPORARILY

After Kemal's heroism at Gallipoli, he was dispatched to the Caucasus, the mountainous region shared by Russia and Turkey, where a German-influenced and Enver-commanded effort was underway to increase pressure on Russia. When the revolutionary Bolshevik government removed Moscow from the war, he was transferred to Syria, where "Lawrence of Arabia" and an aroused Arab force backed by the British army had reached the gates of Damascus. Kemal eventually became commander of the whole Ottoman army. Although he was outnumbered and underequipped, he stubbornly held out until the armistice of November 1918.

Kemal returned to Constantinople on November 13. The government had fled. Enver escaped to Germany. (Later he went to Russia, where he was killed fighting for the White Russian Tsarist forces against the Reds.) By now a general, Kemal was one of the few senior officers still standing. He set about reorganizing and revamping the army.

The Allies still occupied much of the old Ottoman territory, and they showed no signs of leaving. Britain had completely taken over Constantinople. Greece had dug in at Izmir, formerly Smyrna, where there was a large and prosperous Greek colony. France and Italy maintained forces in Macedonia and Thrace. Then, in July 1920, the Allies produced the Treaty of Sèvres, ending the war with Turkey on harsh terms.

President Atatürk revolutionized the Turkish medieval dress code and set an example with white shirt and tie. Kemal (Mustapha) Atatürk (1881–1938) c.1925–30 (w/c on paper), French School, (20th century) / Private Collection / Archives Charmet / The Bridgeman Art Library International

France and Britain took control of large chunks of Arab-populated, Ottoman-ruled territory, carving out the states of Syria, Lebanon, Palestine, Jordan, Kuwait, and Iraq as "protectorates" under League of Nations mandate. Greece received Smyrna in Asia Minor and parts of Macedonia and Thrace, as British Prime Minister David Lloyd George had promised to lure Greece to the Allied cause.

When Sultan Muhammad VI accepted the treaty, Turks were outraged, no one more than Kemal. He surreptitiously left for Ankara to join a nascent Turkish National Movement protesting the treaty terms. He soon took over the leadership, began organizing an army, and formed a rival government with Ankara as capital and himself as leader. The sultan charged him with treason and sentenced him to death. But Turks and, critically, army veterans, rallied to him. Greece, backed initially by the other Allies, sent thousands more troops to Turkey to consolidate its winnings. Greek troops came within 50 miles (80 km) of Ankara when Kemal took personal command and rallied the troops. "Armies!" he exhorted his patchwork force in urging them to drive out the invading Greeks. "Your first goal is the Mediterranean! Forward!"

By July 1922, the Greeks had indeed been pushed to the sea and called for an armistice. The Treaty of Sèvres was scrapped and replaced by a Treaty of Lausanne, which restored most of the forfeited lands, including Smyrna, to Turkish sovereignty. The treaty also recognized Turkey as an independent and sovereign republic with Kemal as its first president, and arranged an exchange of Greek and Turkish populations, with 1.5 million Greeks repatriated to Greece and 800,000 Turks to Turkey.

Kemal was elected four times—in 1923, 1927, 1931, and 1935. In fourteen years of rule, he changed Turkish society from top to bottom. He abolished the sultanate, sending the sultan to refuge on a British warship, and the caliphate, rejecting Islam as the state religion. Public schools replaced religious ones. He named Ankara capital instead of Constantinople, whose name he changed to Istanbul. The Latin alphabet became the official written alphabet, replacing Arabic script; all citizens younger than forty were compelled to learn it.

Kemal ordered all Turks to adopt a surname, and chose Atatürk —"Father of the Turks"—for his own. He forbade polygamy, abolished the religious orders, and gave women full voting rights.

And Kemal changed the way Turks dressed. He prohibited men from wearing the traditional fez, women from veils, and (successfully) urged all Turks to adopt Western clothes. When he was inaugurated for his fourth term in 1935, he wore a plain business suit with a white shirt and carefully knotted necktie, along with a soft felt fedora. In modern Turkey, no schoolboy would be forced to wear ballooning white trousers to school.

CHAPTER EIGHTEEN

HO CHI MINH, 1890–1969: A KITCHEN HAND LEADS A REVOLUTION

In 1919, a nationalistic young Vietnamese appealed to U.S. President Woodrow Wilson to help his country, and then worked for fifty years to make it come true.

The young kitchen hand from Indochina certainly wasn't much to look at. Nguyen Tat Tranh was short, slight, and slim almost to the point of emaciation. His almond eyes were set in a narrow, pinched face. He spoke in a thin, quavering whisper—when he did speak. He was so timid that in one Paris group he was known as "the mute from Montmartre." Although he had studied French and lived in Paris for three years, he considered his command of the language shaky. For that reason he enlisted a more fluent friend to help with a most important letter.

In June 1919, the leaders of the Big Four powers who had won the Great War of 1914–1918 had gathered at Versailles Palace to draft a treaty to bring peace to Europe and indeed the world after four harrowing and bloody years of conflict. The conference had the additional noble aim of constructing a new world structure where war could never happen again. The young man had haunted Paris libraries and bookstalls, devouring newspapers and journals to brush up his French to read about the negotiations. U.S. President Woodrow Wilson played a leading role, emphasizing the "Fourteen Points" that he had outlined to Congress as the principles the new treaty must reflect.

Nguyen Tat Tranh had read Wilson's words avidly, especially those calling for "self-determination of peoples." These were words close to his heart. Having

World leaders assembled at the Palace of Versailles in 1919 to draft a peace treaty ending World War I. U.S. President Woodrow Wilson, to whom young Ho Chi Minh directed an appeal on behalf of Indochina, sits at center. The Treaty of Versailles, 1919 (oil on canvas), Orpen, Sir William (1878–1931) / Private Collection / The Bridgeman Art Library International

grown up under French colonial administration, where his countrymen had no voice and decisions were made by foreigners, "self-determination" and "independence" were consuming passions. He hoped the principles would apply not just to Europeans but to the whole world, including his people and his country. And he wanted to write President Wilson to tell him so.

His Indochinese friend, Phan Van Truong, helped him write the letter in French. "All subject peoples are filled with hope by the prospect that an era of right and justice is opening to them," he wrote. For his own country, he asked for a lifting of the colonial yoke, to be replaced with a constitutional government and the traditional freedoms associated with self-government—speech, press, assembly, and religion. He signed the letter "Nguyen Ai Quoc" ("Nguyen the Patriot)". Then he addressed the letter to President Wilson and boarded a bus to Versailles.

The unprepossessing young man without official credentials was politely but firmly refused entry, so he handed the letter to a guard. Then he took a copy to Paris's Socialist-leaning newspaper, *L'Humanité*. A few days later, he received a courteous, thank-you-for-writing letter from Colonel Edward House, Wilson's top adviser. House assured him that the letter would be brought to the president's attention.

In 1945, he addressed a similar appeal stressing the same principles on the eve of the conference founding the United Nations. This time he signed with a different name, which would have a powerful and lasting impact on history. Ho Chi Minh.

A MAN OF MANY SIGNATURES

Ho Chi Minh was born in the small village of Hoang Tru in central Vietnam on May 19, 1890, at a time when French colonial Indochina consisted of Cambodia, Laos, and Vietnam. Vietnam itself was divided historically into Tonkin, around Hanoi and the Red River delta in the North, Cochin China around Saigon and the Mekong Delta in the South, and Annam, where Ho was born, in the middle—a stringbean-shaped territory centered on the ancient imperial capital, Hue, and wedged between the rugged Annamese mountain chain and the South China Sea. Despite its poor and rocky soil, Annam was considered the richest, most productive, and—thanks to its university—most learned of the three.

Ho's father, Nguyen Sinh Sac, was one of the scholars who gave Annam its intellectual reputation. He was revered in his community for the depths of his knowledge and his willingness to use it in helping his neighbors. He had studied diligently from boyhood for the civil service examinations, receiving first the *tu*

May 19, 1890
Ho Chi Minh is born Nguyen Sinh Cung in Hoang Tru, Annam, Vietnam.

1901
Renamed Nguyen Tat Tranh.
June 5, 1911
Ships out as an assistant cook on the ocean liner *Amiral Latouche-Trevellis*, bound for Marseille.
1912
Visits the United States and lives in New York and Boston for seven months.
1913
Moves to London. Works as a cook.

1917
Moves to Paris. Works as a kitchen hand and photo retoucher.
November 11, 1918
Armistice declared, ending World War I.
June 18, 1919
Goes to the Versailles treaty conference to urge U.S. President Woodrow Wilson to apply Wilson's ideals of freedom to Indochina. Fails to see Wilson. Signs his petition "Nguyen Ai Quoc" ("Nguyen the Patriot").
Autumn 1919
Becomes a member of the French Socialist Party (FSP).
December 1920
At Tours Congress, FSP splits into two factions. Sides with radical faction and joins the French Communist Party.

1923
Recruited by Comintern, the communist international revolutionary movement, and moves to Moscow. Visits Asian countries to establish local communist parties.
1924
Accompanies Mikhail Borodin, a Comintern agent, to China, working with Chiang Kai-shek to revolutionize China.
1927
Flees China when Chiang turns against the Communists.

1930
Founds the Indochinese Communist Party in Hong Kong.
1931
Arrested in Hong Kong, jailed for two years.
1932
Returns to Moscow. Treated for tuberculosis.

September 1, 1939
Germany invades Poland. World War II begins.
June 22, 1940
France surrenders to Germany.
September 1940
Japan occupies Indochina.
January 1941
Crosses the Chinese border into Vietnam, marking his first return in thirty years. Establishes the League for Vietnamese Independence, known as the Viet Minh. Adopts new name, Ho Chi Minh.
December 7, 1941
Japanese planes attack Pearl Harbor. United States declares war on Japan, Germany, and Italy.

June 6, 1944
Allied troops land in France and push toward Germany.
September 2, 1945
After Japan signs a peace treaty with the United States, Ho proclaims Vietnamese independence. Becomes president of the new Republic of Vietnam.
December 1946
Goes to Fontainebleau, France, in an effort to make peace with the French. Negotiations are fruitless; war breaks out between the Viet Minh and the French.

May 8, 1954
French forces are besieged at Dien Bien Phu. France surrenders.
July 1954
Geneva conference declares an end to hostilities; Vietnam is divided at the 17th Parallel. Ho becomes president of North Vietnam at Hanoi. Ngo Dinh Diem becomes president of South Vietnam.
April 1955
U.S. and South Vietnamese armies continue the war with North Vietnam and the guerrillas, known as the Viet Cong.

January 31, 1968
Vietnamese New Year (Tet) offensive by North Vietnam begins with the capture of Hue. After twenty-six days of fighting, Hue is recaptured by the United States. Public opinion turns against war.
September 2, 1969
Ho dies of heart failure in Hanoi at age seventy-nine.

tai ("cultivated talent"), the first level of achievement in the Confucian learning system, akin to a bachelor's degree in the United States. He then went on to the *cu nhan* similar to a U.S. master's degree, and then to a doctorate, the *pho bang*. The awards increased his already lofty local prestige. No one in Hoang Tru had ever earned a pho bang before. The honor allowed the humble village to term itself a *dat van vat, chon thi tu,* ("a civilized spot, a literary location"). The grateful population built Sac a three-room house for his family, plus a small annex for a study. He also received 3 acres (12,000 m²) of rice land and a small garden.

At ten, Ho received his grownup name: Nguyen Tat Tranh ("He who will succeed").

The pho bang also opened the way for a comfortable position in the colonial administration, which would have meant a small stipend. Sac was offered a post in Hue supervising the tu-tai exam. The idealistic Sac turned down the offer, ostensibly because his wife, Loan, was ill, but actually because he considered all government posts exploitative. Sac chose to remain in the village, where he opened a small school and taught classics for a modest income. Loan tended the small rice fields, as was the Vietnamese wifely custom. When their son was born they gave him the "milk name" Nguyen Sinh Cung. Vietnamese parents traditionally chose a name at birth, then could change it at adolescence to reflect their aspirations. Nguyen Sinh Cung was the first of many names Ho would use in his lifetime.

Cung quickly demonstrated curiosity and flair for learning. He could recognize and trace Chinese characters at age five, which were necessary for studying Confucius. But he still found time to fish, run through the fields, fly kites, and especially listen to grownups' tales of patriotic exploits by Annamese heroes. He continued to study in his father's small school. At ten, he received his grownup name: Nguyen Tat Tranh ("He who will succeed").

Sac did indeed have high aspirations for his son, not measured in money or status. He chafed under French colonial rule, which he saw as trampling the Vietnamese peasantry under their boots while plundering the country's riches. Sac set a lofty example. When the village fathers proposed an elaborate ceremony to celebrate his pho bang, he objected. Use the money to feed the poor, he told the party planners.

While Sac detested his French overlords, he recognized the importance of learning their language. "If you wish to defeat the French, you must understand them," he quoted a friend. "To understand them, you must first understand the French language." Sac himself had never fully mastered French, but he insisted that his son become fluent. He convinced Tranh, as Ho was now called, that he must go to France, never mind the wherewithal. When Tranh told a young friend about his plan and urged him to join, the other shook his head. "Where will we get the money?" he asked. Tranh held up his hands, turning them back and forth. "Here is our money," he said. They would work their way across the ocean.

GETTING A GLOBAL EDUCATION

At seventeen, Tranh left home for Saigon, the now mush-rooming city in Cochin China to the south. The French colonialists and Chinese entrepreneurs had created a boomtown atmosphere in what had been a minor trading post on the Saigon River. The Mekong Delta had been drained and converted into rice plantations; rice mills had been built around the city and Cochin China had become the third largest rice exporter in the world. What had once been forests and brush was planted with rubber-tree seedlings imported from Brazil. The little riverport had grown to a major shipping facility for oceangoing vessels. Young men were flocking to the city's jobs in factories and wharves. With a quarter of a million people, Saigon was rapidly overtaking Hanoi as the most populous city in Vietnam.

Most of the newcomers, including Tranh, were jammed into squalid, rat-infested slums along the river, close to the jobs. Many were living five or six to a room, unable to do better on their meager wages. The experience solidified Tranh's resolve that his country must be relieved of outside exploitation. He would go to France, master the language, and then bring freedom to his people as his father had counseled.

Sac, now an itinerant teacher, had followed his son to Saigon. The two worked out a plan. Two steamship companies operated from Saigon. One, the Char-

Ho Chi Minh, then calling himself Nguyen Ai Quoc, sat for this portrait in Moscow as a Comintern official in 1924. AFP/Getty Images

geurs-Reunis, advertised for young Vietnamese as waiters and kitchen helpers on voyages to Singapore, Colombo, Port Said, Marseille, and Bordeaux. The *Amiral Latouche-Trevellis* had recently docked at Tourane (as the French had renamed Da Nang after colonizing it in 1858) near his home in Annam. Sac had made friends with its officers. He arranged a job interview with the captain. On July 2, 1911, a twenty-one year old calling himself simply "Ba," a familiar term for "third-born," appeared at the pier and presented himself to Captain Louis Edouard Maisen. Although Ba protested he could "do anything," Captain Maisen saw the young man as too slight and frail for the seagoing voyage. The captain finally agreed to hire him as an assistant cook. The next day, Tranh was washing dishes and pans, mopping the galley floor, preparing vegetables, and shoveling coal. On June 5, the *Amiral Latouche-Trevellis* pushed off for its next port of call, Singapore, en route to Marseille.

Ho Chi Minh was particularly impressed by the United States' concern for the rights of man (as he had been about the French Revolution gospel of "liberty, fraternity, equality"), and he wanted to personally see whether it might be a model for a free Vietnam.

The ship took four weeks to reach Marseille. It was not precisely a pleasure cruise. The ship tossed about in "waves as big as mountains," Ho was to write later, and once he was almost washed overboard. Still, he wrote mockingly to a friend, "the hero goes joyfully through his day doing what he pleases, polishing the brass and the washroom and emptying the buckets of human waste." The work apparently was not so onerous as to make him jump ship.

Tranh enjoyed a few days in Marseille, spending his pittance wages and observing that poverty existed in France as well as Vietnam, and that "the French in France are better and more polite than those in Indochina." Ordering a cup of coffee at a café, he was for the first time in his life addressed as "Monsieur." He made another round-trip voyage between Saigon and Marseille, and briefly worked as a gardener while the ship was in drydock. He then shipped out again, visiting ports in Africa and Asia until he wound up in the United States.

Tranh's reading about U.S. democracy had always fascinated him. He was particularly impressed by the United States' concern for the rights of man (as he had been about the French Revolution gospel of "liberty, fraternity, equality"), and he wanted to personally see whether it might be a model for a free Vietnam. How he spent his seven-month stay in the United States, however, is cloudy. He apparently worked briefly as a laborer, by one account earning the princely sum of $40 a month. He wrote later that he had attended black activist group meetings in Harlem and that he had served as a cook's helper in the Parker House in Boston.

In 1913, Tranh shipped out again, for England, hoping to master English and to meet Asian immigrants and working-class Britons. There he worked at the Carlton Hotel for the famous chef Auguste Escoffier. Escoffier took a liking to the young man who cleaned up the kitchen but protested that the discarded scraps of food could feed the poor. "Young man, listen to me," the chef said. "Leave your revolutionary ideas aside for a moment, and I will teach you the art of cooking." He took Tranh to the cake section and made him an apprentice baker at higher wages. But neither cooking nor money attracted Tranh. He went back to France and his rendezvous with Woodrow Wilson.

WORKERS OF THE WORLD, UNITE!

Tranh's letter may not have attracted attention from Wilson and the others at Versailles, but its publication in *L'Humanité* certainly echoed in Paris's tumultuous radical community. A few days after the letter appeared, the French Socialist Party (FSP) invited Tranh to a party meeting. A vintage photograph shows "Nguyen the Patriot," with his hair neatly combed and wearing a dusty-looking jacket, surrounded by pompous-looking, middle-aged Frenchmen with bristling mustaches. Not surprisingly, he was very nervous and sat silently (earning the "mute from Montmartre" sobriquet). Asked to speak about his country's anticolonial grievances, he stammered and whispered so rapidly in his broken French that few understood him. Nonetheless he received a warm round of applause and was asked to attend future meetings.

Within a few weeks and by now less timid, Tranh became the party's leading voice on colonial exploitation and the woes of Asian workers in France. He was named to the party board and attended the raucous Congress of Tours of 1921 where the party split into a militant, Moscow-oriented Communist wing and a smaller faction

Slender, tubercular, and in ill-fitting clothes, young Nguyen Ai Quoc addressed the 1920 French Socialist Party Congress, in which the Socialists split into Socialist and Communist parties. He joined the Communist wing. The Tours Congress, Ho Chi Minh (1890-1969) from 'L'Humanite', December 1920 (b/w photo), French Photographer, (20th century) / Bibliotheque Nationale, Paris, France / Archives Charmet / The Bridgeman Art Library International

of more moderate Socialists under the redoubtable Léon Blum, who was to become French premier in the Popular Front government of the 1930s. He joined the Parti Communiste Francais, the French Communist Party, even though his sympathies lay with Blum's group, who was moderate like himself. Later he explained that he did not consider himself a Marxist, but felt his nationalist aims were more likely to be attained with the strength of the Soviet Union behind them.

Tranh was soon employed by the Comintern, the Soviet-directed international network seeking to accelerate the spread of Communism worldwide, and was called to Moscow. There he met Vladimir Lenin, Leon Trotsky, and other Communist notables. He became the Comintern's point man for Asia, performing missionary work with Communist cells throughout the Far East. In 1925, now using the name

Nguyen Ai Quoc, he went to Canton, China (now Guangzhou), where activists led by the dedicated Mikhail Borodin were collaborating with Chiang Kai-shek against the warlords, while also endeavoring to found a central government based on Leninist principles. Quoc remained until 1927, when Chiang abruptly turned on his allies and established a national government built on his Kuomintang nationalist party.

Quoc fled to Moscow where he was hospitalized with tuberculosis for nearly a year. He returned to Paris for additional treatment, headed back to China, and after another year was arrested as a subversive by British agents in Hong Kong. He spent two years in a Hong Kong jail before going back to Moscow, China, and finally Paris.

Quoc was still agitating in the 1930s for a free and independent Vietnam, although by 1940 he had not set foot in the country for nearly thirty years.

THE TIGER AND THE WOLF

In May 1940, German armies swept overwhelmingly into France. Within six weeks, the French government surrendered. Germany's ally Japan saw an opportunity and sent troops into Indochina to snatch its precious resources of rice, rubber, tin, and timber, all important to the Japanese war machine. Vietnam also gave Japan a stepping stone to the Dutch East Indies with its even greater storehouse of precious oil and metals. Tokyo tried to convince the European colonies that Japanese hegemony would benefit all of them. Its goal, Japanese propaganda insisted, was "Asia for the Asians."

Quoc, a longtime Japanese antagonist, was not buying it. In the 1920s, when a rapidly modernizing Japan looked like the rising political and economic power in the Pacific, its authoritarian government was held up as a model for independence movements across Asia. It was suggested that Quoc might want to visit Tokyo and copy Japanese tactics. In 1940, he gave the same warning about Japanese motives as in 1923, "We must not push the tiger out the front door and allow the wolf in at the back."

But Quoc did see the Japanese invasion of Indochina and the beginning of World War II as an opportunity for his cause. He slipped across the Vietnamese

General Vo Nguyen Giap led the North Vietnamese military against the French and Americans. Time & Life Pictures/Getty Images

border, avoiding security problems by posing as a Chinese journalist. He took the name "Ho Chi Minh" ("He who enlightens"). A few at a time, he infiltrated young Communists into the rugged jungle terrain along the Chinese–Vietnamese northern border and there (with help later from the United States) established small pockets of guerrilla fighters and training bases that eventually turned out forty fighters every ten days.

Ho considered himself a political operative, not a guerrilla fighter, but he led several successful raids against Vichy French and Japanese positions. Then he delegated military leadership to a fellow Communist who was to become a legend, Vo Nguyen Giap, and put his own persuasive political skills to work. He recognized that not only peasants and workers—and Communists—had been oppressed under the colonial regime, but landlords, business owners, professionals, and religious groups.

Ho forged an alliance with more middle-class and Buddhist religious groups combating the foreigners. The united front was called the Viet Minh. Ho stressed that the united front was not Communist even though he was its leader. By late 1943, the Viet Minh controlled one-third of the villages in Vietnam's northern reaches, and a year later, held one-fourth of the country. A provisional government was formed in opposition to the French puppet regime under Emperor Bao Dai. Ho Chi Minh was its chairman.

Ho still believed that the United States, with its democratic tradition, would stand up for Vietnamese independence, and he was partly right. In 1943, President Franklin D. Roosevelt wrote to his secretary of state, Cordell Hull, opposing the restoration of the French regime in Indochina. "The French have had the country for a hundred years," the president wrote, "and the people are worse off than they were at the beginning. France has milked them for a century. The people of Indochina are entitled to something better than that." Ho's heart jumped. But Roosevelt couldn't go public; he needed to keep imperial Britain and France focused on the war. He handed off the problem to the United Nations. And then he died.

World War II ended in Europe in May 1945, in Asia in August, after the nuclear bombing of Hiroshima and Nagasaki. On September 2, 1945, Ho, ill with malaria and dysentery and described by one American as "a faded yellow skin containing a bag of bones," dressed himself in the rubber thongs, black work clothes, and conical hat of the Vietnamese peasant, mounted a platform in Hanoi and proclaimed Vietnamese independence with words he learned in the library:

"We hold truths that all men are created equal, that they are endowed by their Creator with certain inalienable rights. Among these are life, liberty, and the pursuit of happiness."

Then he went on to give credit to the United States' founding fathers:

"This immortal statement is extracted from the Declaration of Independence of the United States of America in 1776. Understood in the broader sense, this means: All have the right to be happy and free. These are undeniable truths."

It was the moment the former kitchen hand had been working toward since his bus trip to Versailles twenty-six years before.

It wasn't that easy, of course. The French returned with troops in 1946, the Viet Minh resistance returned to the countryside, and eight years of bitter fighting continued until the French unwisely chose to make a stand at the strongpoint of Dien Bien Phu, where they were besieged until they finally gave up on May 8, 1954. A four-power conference at Geneva divided the country in two, with Ho presiding over North Vietnam from Hanoi and South Vietnam with a leader handpicked by the Americans, Ngo Dinh Diem. But the war continued, with increasing American involvement until President Richard Nixon declared an end to the U.S. role in 1973 after 58,000 U.S. deaths. The last Americans left Saigon in 1975, which had been renamed "Ho Chi Minh City" in honor of the "mute from Montmartre" who was still speaking up for his country when he died of heart failure in 1969.

CHAPTER NINETEEN

CHARLES DE GAULLE, 1890–1970: A POW'S FIVE ESCAPE ATTEMPTS

Captured and imprisoned, Charles de Gaulle had only one thought: Escape. In all his attempts, he demonstrated courage, loyalty to France, and refusal to quit— qualities that would earn him a hero's halo and, eventually, the presidency of France.

Charles de Gaulle was not easy to hide, or to disguise. He stood six feet, five inches (196 cm), and had an unmistakably haughty bearing and a prominent nose like the snout of a camel. No matter. He was also indomitable. Surrender was not a word in his nature. As a French prisoner of war, captured wounded and unconscious by the German army in 1916, Captain de Gaulle was determined to make his way back to the French lines and continue fighting. Thus, one day in September 1916, he concocted an elaborate prison escape plot that would have done credit to James Bond or Alexandre Dumas.

De Gaulle was being held in Germany's maximum-security prison, a Bavarian fortress named Fort IX at Ingolstadt on the Danube River, 100 miles (160 km) north of Munich. Fort IX featured walls 60 feet (18 m) high and was surrounded by a 10-foot-deep (3 m) moat. De Gaulle saw that as a challenge, not a problem. He teamed up with another officer-prisoner, Captain Ducret, whose first name was lost to history.

De Gaulle discovered that the prison hospital was an annex to the main hospital outside Fort IX's walls. In the dank prison atmosphere de Gaulle had developed chilblains on his feet, which are similar to the blisters of trench foot. De Gaulle's mother sent him an ointment to treat them. But instead of smearing the ointment on his blistered feet, de Gaulle swallowed it, producing unmistakable symptoms of

Six feet five inches tall (196 cm), Captain Charles De Gaulle was nicknamed "the Great Asparagus Stalk."
© akg-images / Alamy

advanced jaundice. The prison doctor took one look at de Gaulle's yellowing eyes, blotched skin, and cloudy urine, and ordered him to the hospital forthwith.

Ducret, meanwhile, blackmailed a German officer to procure a German helmet and a map and, finally, to contribute his trousers. Ducret dressed as a German officer bringing a patient to the hospital for care. Then the two simply walked out the main door and headed for the Swiss frontier at Schaffhausen, 190 miles (300 km) away. Nine days later and in a driving rain, they were recaptured, soaked and unrepentant, some 60 miles (100 km) short of their goal. They were handcuffed and hustled back to Fort IX.

That was not de Gaulle's first attempt at escape, nor would it be his last. Over two years, he tried—and failed—five times. In all of de Gaulle's attempts, he demonstrated qualities of courage, loyalty to France, and refusal to quit that would eventually earn him a hero's halo and carry him to the presidency of France.

RAISED IN FAITH AND PATRIOTISM

One of five children, Charles de Gaulle was born November 22, 1890, in Lille, northern France. His was a religious family that honored patriotism, tradition, and duty above all else. Henri de Gaulle, his father, had sought a military career, but he was rejected for St. Cyr, the French equivalent of the U.S. Military Academy at West Point, and he became a teacher. Henri enrolled Charles in Jesuit schools and when the republican government banned the Jesuits, sent the boy to Belgium to continue his education. The young boy was imbued with patriotic and military fervor. Once, when he was seven years old and playing toy soldiers, his brother Xavier wanted his soldiers to represent France. "Never!" shouted Charles. "*I* am France!"

It was inevitable that de Gaulle would try for the military. He studied two years in a prep school to ready himself for St. Cyr, and then enlisted for a year in the infantry because he was told applicants from the ranks received priority in appointments to the academy. At St. Cyr, de Gaulle was teased mercilessly about his height and his great nose and was nicknamed *L'asperge grande* ("great asparagus stalk"). Graduating thirteenth in a class of 211, de Gaulle chose reassignment to the infantry over an elite unit or a plum staff job. He was assigned to the 33rd Infantry Regiment as a lieutenant in 1913. The regiment was commanded by Colonel Henri-Philippe Petain. De Gaulle became a Petain protégé, with good and bad effects on both in the years ahead.

November 22, 1890
Charles de Gaulle is born in Lille, France, son of Henri de Gaulle, a teacher.

September 1909
Appointed to Ecole Militaire in St. Cyr.
June 1913
Graduates from St. Cyr, commissioned lieutenant in the 33rd Infantry Regiment.
August 4, 1914
Germany invades Belgium, World War I begins.
August 8, 1914
Wounded in the Battle of Dinant Bridge and hospitalized for seven weeks.

February 1915
Promoted to captain.
February 21, 1916
Battle of Verdun begins.
March 1916
Wounded and captured while defending Fort Douaumont. Evacuated to a German field hospital.
May 1916
Makes the first of five failed attempts to escape from prison.
November 11, 1918
Armistice ends World War I. France and Allies are victors.

1921
Assigned as military adviser to new Polish government with rank of colonel. Remains three years.
1925–1939
Holds staff positions in the French army. Writes controversial articles demanding that the infantry-based French army mechanize.

September 1, 1939
Germany invades Poland, a French ally. World War II begins.
May 10, 1940
Germany invades the Low Countries and France.
May 15, 1940
Named under secretary of national defense in the war cabinet.
June 18, 1940
France surrenders to Germany. De Gaulle escapes to London and broadcasts an appeal to French citizens to join him in a Free French resistance.

June 6, 1944
Allied D-Day landings in Normandy, France.
June 14, 1944
Arrives in France with first Free French troops.
August 25, 1944
Leads triumphant Free French in the Allied liberation of Paris.
October 1945
Unanimously elected the president of France's first provisional government.
January 1946
Resigns in disapproval of new the French constitution. Retires to write his memoirs.

May 13, 1958
Widespread rioting and demonstrations in Algeria, which the government is unable to stop.
June 1, 1958
National Assembly names de Gaulle as the only one who can stop the crisis and names him premier with wide emergency powers.
September 1958
France adopts a new constitution and establishes the Fifth Republic. Grants independence to Algeria and other French colonies.
December 1958
DeGaulle elected president.

May 1968
Violent student demonstrations and a general strike shake the de Gaulle government.
April 1969
Resigns the presidency and retires again after losing a reform referendum.
November 9, 1970
Dies of a heart attack at his country estate, Colombey-les-Deux-Eglises.

Lieutenant de Gaulle and the 33rd were plunged into World War I almost from the very first day. Germany declared war on France and sent troops into Belgium on August 4, 1914. The 33rd was ordered forward 50 miles (80 km) to the Belgian frontier, to take position at a bridge on the Meuse River. German troops already occupied the fortified citadel of Dinant, on the opposite bank. At daybreak, just as the exhausted troops arrived after a 50-mile (80 km) forced march, German artillery opened a barrage, and machine gunners stationed in the citadel began picking off the huddling troops. De Gaulle was told to storm the bridge to prevent the Germans from crossing. While considering the move foolhardy, the young officer waved his sword and led his men forward. Just as the platoon reached the bridge, machine-gun fire sprayed the oncoming French. De Gaulle went down, his knee shattered by bullets. His platoon sergeant fell dead on top of him. When the fighting died down, de Gaulle was evacuated to a field hospital.

De Gaulle spent the next seven weeks in hospital having his knee rebuilt. When he returned in mid-October, the Battle of the Marne had been fought and the war had begun to settle into the grim, tedious, trench-warfare slog that continued for four years. The gung-ho de Gaulle was angered that his superiors liked it that way. They preferred quiet evenings with no rocking of the boat, and they celebrated with champagne dinners.

When de Gaulle discovered that German troops had infiltrated the French trenches and suggested an innovative way to flush them out, he was refused permission. Such action "might cause a conflagration," he was told. When de Gaulle's platoon received two new mortars, he was cautioned not to fire them at the enemy. Mortar fire might bring provoke retaliatory German artillery fire, which might ignite the whole front. De Gaulle rebelliously fired anyway. The next day, his company was sent to the rear and replaced by one with more obedient officers.

In December 1914, de Gaulle was named regimental adjutant, reporting directly to the commanding officer. In February 1915, his temporary promotion to captain was made permanent. In a month of savage fighting that cost the 33rd nineteen officers, de Gaulle was wounded again. A seemingly minor shrapnel wound became infected, and he was hospitalized until June. By then his regiment had moved forward to the front lines in Flanders. From June 1915 until January 1916, Captain de Gaulle was involved in almost daily battle, usually fought for only a few hundred yards of chewed-up earth. Then came Verdun.

ILS NE PASSERONT PAS! ("THEY SHALL NOT PASS!")

On Christmas Day 1915, German Chief of Staff Erich von Falkenhayn wrote a letter to Kaiser Wilhelm II, the German emperor. Von Falkenhayn was frustrated by the deadlocks on both Eastern and Western fronts and with bloody expenditure of men and munitions for negligible gains. He envisioned a new German strategy that would break the stalemate and bring a German victory.

Instead of fighting on both fronts, von Falkenhayn suggested that Germany softpedal the Eastern fighting because he believed (correctly, as it turned out) that Russia was on the brink of revolution anyway and would soon collapse. Von Falkenhayn said that Germany should concentrate the bulk of its resources and efforts in France. He proposed an offensive to "bleed France white." He would throw in more troops than France could match and cause far more casualties than France could tolerate, and he would continue the onslaught until France fell to its knees and was compelled to surrender. Britain would then surely follow, and a failing Russia, lacking allies and at the total mercy of the German army, would capitulate, ending the war.

The Battle of Verdun was perhaps the most titanic, most savage, and bloodiest battle in world history. It raged for seven months and claimed the lives of 700,000 men—the greatest single-battle carnage that has ever been recorded.

The kaiser assented, and on February 21, 1916; 1,400 German guns, from 75 millimeters to Big Berthas, firing 100,000 rounds an hour, launched an around-the-clock bombardment that "shook the earth for miles" at the French bastion of Verdun.

In the Franco-Prussian War of 1870–71, Verdun had held out against the invading Prussian army until the very last. Its defenders did not give in until the French government itself raised the white flag of surrender. Verdun was not actually a fort but a series of forts grouped around the town of Verdun in northeastern France. The defenses had been upgraded since 1871, but they were still antiquated by 1916 standards. France had stationed only green troops there, using it mainly for training purposes.

Nevertheless von Falkenhayn concluded (again correctly) that Verdun's importance was not military, but symbolic. It was the very emblem of French resistance. France would be obliged to defend it, no matter the cost. Losing Verdun would be a crippling blow to French morale from which the country would never recover. Germany's massive offense would be expensive for Germany, too, but Germany had greater resources. It had more up-to-date and stronger weapons and, by transferring some units from the Eastern front, it could muster greater manpower.

The French saw exactly the same picture, if in reverse. The French acknowledged a German advantage in weapons and men, but they enjoyed a kind of home-court advantage. At Verdun, France would be playing defense and on its own soil. French troops would be inspired to protect their homes and farms. The French public would rally around the flag and, just as von Falkenhayn had predicted, demand that Verdun be held, despite the price. The symbol must be preserved.

De Gaulle's old mentor, Henri-Philippe Petain, now a marshal of France, was given the task of preserving it. Petain had jeopardized his career and been repeatedly passed over for promotion because of his flagrant opposition to the high command guiding philosophy of "Attack, attack, attack, always attack." Petain insisted that strength lay in concentrating on masses of heavy guns and dug-in positions, and letting an enemy wear itself out attempting to break through. To carry that out at Verdun, he coined a slogan that still rings through history: "*Ils ne passeront pas!*" ("They shall not pass!").

Thus began what most military historians agree was the most titanic, most savage, and the bloodiest battle in world history. It continued for seven sanguinary and indecisive months and claimed the lives of 700,000 men—the greatest single-battle carnage ever recorded. Von Falkenhayn called it off (and was replaced as chief of staff) in November 1916. Verdun was still in French hands, and both sides were still in virtually the same muddy positions they had occupied the previous February.

And it was fought almost completely without Charles de Gaulle.

French soldiers unload trucks near the Verdun battlefield in 1916. The fighting at Verdun lasted for seven months and cost 700,000 lives—the greatest single-battlecarnage ever recorded. AFP / Getty Images

ESCAPE ATTEMPTS

A small fort and village named Douaumont squatted on a fortified height squarely in the middle of the Verdun complex. Though small and unprepossessing, the fort was considered a key to the whole defensive barrier. It, too, stood for French resistance and must not be yielded without a fight. The 33rd Infantry Regiment was given that difficult assignment. On March 2, the regiment dug in around the

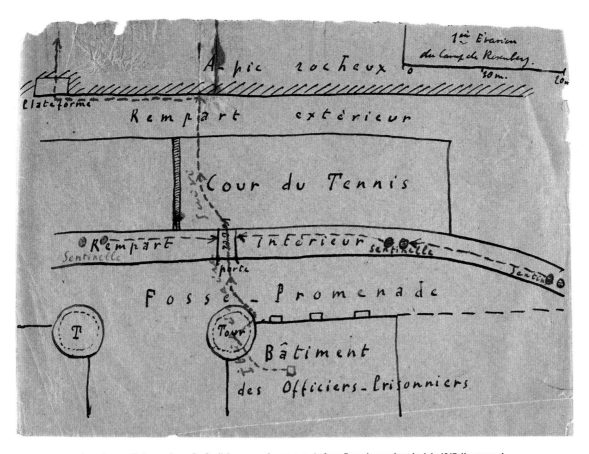

A crude, penciled map shows De Gaulle's proposed escape route from Rosenborg prison in July 1917. He escaped the prison but was captured at a nearby railway station. Map of Captain Charles de Gaulle's first escape from the Rosenberg Fort, July 1917 (pencil on paper), Gaulle, Charles de (1890–1970) / Archives de Gaulle, Paris, France / Giraudon / The Bridgeman Art Library

church in Douaumont village. At dawn, a bombardment began. "It was like an earthquake," one survivor recalled. After six hours of nonstop fusillade, German infantry piled out of their trenches and attacked the 33rd position.

It was a savage struggle. Men fought hand to hand with drawn bayonets and rifle butts, hurling grenades, and firing at close range. The German thrust split the French defenders in two, isolating one group from the other. Captain de Gaulle, not sure where the rest of the unit could be found, was leading a handful of men through a trench trying to join the others when the party stumbled into a German detachment huddled in a shell hole. In the resulting melee, de Gaulle was bayoneted through the thigh. As he tried to stand, he was blinded and knocked down by a grenade bursting directly in front of him. He passed out. The others in his party left him for dead. Petain wrote a glowing tribute to the brave, fallen officer.

But when de Gaulle regained consciousness, he found himself in a German military hospital in Mainz. Along with other wounded, de Gaulle had been evacuated by German stretcher-bearers. He remained there ten days while the wound was treated, then went to a series of prison hospitals before reaching a prisoner-of-war installation at Neisse, far from the Western front. Assessing his plight, de Gaulle harbored only one thought: He must get back to the fighting. He must escape.

His first attempt didn't take him very far. Neisse was situated near the headwaters of the Danube River. Most of the French prisoners shared de Gaulle's desire to escape; in fact, he was to say later, no one in the camp thought of anything else. Escape plots were being hatched all over the prison. De Gaulle assembled a small knot of would-be escapees and outlined a rather far-fetched plan. The prison was lightly guarded. They would overcome the guards, exit the prison, steal a boat, and sail down the Danube to the Black Sea, where they would join their allies, the Russians. The plan was too disorganized to succeed, and it was quickly discovered. The plotters were rounded up and sent off to a more restrictive and remote prison in Lithuania.

There de Gaulle fell in with Lieutenant Colonel Tardiu, a French officer of Indochinese background whose first name was lost to history, but who talked back to his captors so insolently that he had accumulated more than 100 hours of detention by the time he was freed in 1945. Tardiu's head was full of ever more creative escape plans, some of them fanciful. De Gaulle was a willing listener. The two recruited a third officer-prisoner, a tunneling expert who proposed they dig their way out of the camp. The tunnel had progressed only a few dozen feet, and de Gaulle was still digging when they were discovered and sent off to Ingolstadt. Maximum-security Fort IX had become the holding pen for incorrigible serial escapees.

TRY, TRY AGAIN

But "La Grande Charles" was not finished yet. The hospital masquerade and dash through the rain toward Schaffhausen was next. When that attempt was thwarted, the three bedraggled fugitives were incarcerated again, and, according to one account, "suitable punishment meted out."

Captain Charles de Gaulle, seated at right with crossed arms, among prisoners at the camp of Sczuczyn, Lithuania, May to September 1916 (b/w photo), French Photographer, (20th century) / Archives de Gaulle, Paris, France, Giraudon / The Bridgeman Art Library International

But then a seemingly chastened de Gaulle appeared to adopt a policy of "If you can't beat 'em, join 'em." He threw himself into praiseworthy prison activities. He began serious study of German, worked in the prison library, and delivered a series of lectures to fellow inmates that he later incorporated into a book. He made friends with an imprisoned Russian officer, Mikhayl Tukhachevsky, a dedicated Marxist who afterward became a marshal of the Soviet Union and was executed in the Stalinist purges of the 1930s. De Gaulle taught the Russian French and Tukhachevsky taught de Gaulle Russian, and they maintained correspondence after the war.

But escape never left de Gaulle's mind. He was only biding his time and hatching new plots. For some unfathomable reason, prisoners were permitted newspapers with uncensored war news, so de Gaulle could follow the course of the war, learning about the United States' entry into the war and the upheavals in Russia. He read disparaging articles about the Allies' "inhumane" use of "tanks," which was a totally new weapon to him. De Gaulle could immediately imagine their impact on twentieth-century warfare, and he would make tanks the centerpiece of his postwar campaign to mechanize the French army in the 1930s. De Gaulle felt even more pressed to return to France and participate in a war that was passing him by. He capitalized on his seven months of nice-guy behavior;

now supposedly a model prisoner, he applied for transfer to a less restrictive environment. De Gaulle and three other well-behaved officers were transferred to the minimum-security prison at Rosenberg, in Franconia. Within four months, all of them had escaped.

Again, the plotters headed for Schaffhausen, and again were arrested en route. Back they went to Rosenberg where de Gaulle and a fellow prisoner sawed through the bars of their cell windows and lowered themselves down the steep cliff on which the fortress stood. There they switched to civilian clothes and donned false mustaches and spectacles. None of these disguises succeeded. De Gaulle was still six feet, five inches (196 cm) tall, and no false facial hair nor civilian clothes could conceal his great height. As soon as the men reached the local railway station and sought to buy tickets for the Dutch frontier, they were arrested.

De Gaulle went back to maximum-security Fort IX at Ingolstadt and was immediately clapped into solitary confinement. He spent two months in a tiny cell. He emerged imperturbable but was held at Fort IX until April 1918. A scandal toppled the prison administration, and the prison was closed, whereupon de Gaulle was switched to another maximum-security prison, Wülzburg in central Bavaria.

And whereupon, never-say-die, de Gaulle tried to escape again. This time he reprised his earlier James Bond scenario. He managed to steal a German uniform, which a fellow French prisoner wore while escorting him to the prison gate. The French chaplain accompanied them. De Gaulle headed for Nuremberg, hoping to buy a rail ticket for Frankfurt, but after a day and a night was spotted and arrested. As soon as de Gaulle was sent back, he tried again. This time he tried to mask his height by curling up under soiled bedclothes in a laundry cart. He reached the rail station successfully and even purchased a ticket and boarded a train before he was felled by a bout of gastric influenza. He was returned to the prison hospital and remained in one prison or another as the war wound down and armistice was declared on November 11, 1918.

Despite de Gaulle's many tries, he never managed to break out of prison, and he missed most of the war he had been preparing for since his schoolboy days. But there was another war to be fought, and in 1940 his unshakeable courage, persistent effort, and stubborn refusal to accept defeat made General Charles de Gaulle the rallying point for the Free French army and government-in-exile in World War II, and eventually anointed him president of the Fifth Republic.

CHAPTER TWENTY

ROSA PARKS, 1913–2005:
THE BUS RIDE THAT CHANGED HISTORY

Rosa Parks was tired—tired from a hard day's work and from enduring forty-two years of racial oppression. When a bus driver demanded that she give up her seat to a white man, Rosa chose to make a stand by remaining seated.

It was well after midnight when Rosa McCauley awoke in a cold sweat. Despite the stifling heat and the fact that she was fully dressed, the little girl shivered uncontrollably. A nightmare had disturbed her uneasy sleep. The six-year old had good reason to worry. It was 1919 and rumors of a planned raid by the Knights of the Ku Klux Klan had been spreading through the black community of Pine Level, Alabama, all week long. Sometimes the Klan rode through the town on horses, their pointed hoods perched like grotesque crowns atop their covered faces. Other times they marched by on foot, the hems of their makeshift white robes stained green and brown from traipsing through muddy fields. They came under cover of night. Like vampires, Klansmen hid from daylight.

Rosa's pretty face clouded with fear imagining those terrible figures in their white hooded robes descending on her home. In her mind's eye, the Klansmen took on mythic proportions. They loomed 7 feet (2 m) tall, held their burning torches aloft with long, spindly, fingers, and glared from their makeshift eye holes with pupils as red as hot pokers.

Rosa, who lived with her mother, grandparents, and younger brother, had seen the Klan from afar. Sometimes a dozen strong, the Klan was a terrifying sight to behold, especially for a young child. The McCauleys, like all African-American families in the area, were painfully aware of the constant threat the

Rosa Parks holds a program from the Rosa Parks Elementary School dedication in San Francisco in 1997. Parks, who died in 2005, helped spark the Civil Rights movement by her refusal to give up her seat on a public bus to a white passenger in 1955. Associated Press

Klan posed. Rosa's family members regularly slept in their street clothes in case they had to flee their home in the middle of the night.

Alert, the petite child sat up in bed, listening for foreign sounds outside her window. The crickets that usually lulled her to sleep with their rhythmic chorus now seemed to be chirping off key, almost as if they were sending her an ominous message. Rosa was too frightened to sleep. She climbed out of bed and crept barefoot into the living room where her grandfather, Sylvester Edwards, sat in a wooden rocking chair, with a double-barreled shogun at his side. He spent most nights in that well-worn chair, a vigilant sentinel prepared to defend his home and family from the white men hiding beneath the white sheets. Once, Edwards stood on his front porch, shotgun at the ready, as the Klan marched through the neighborhood.

A former slave, Edwards was a proud man who held his head high and considered himself equal to any white man. Of mixed heritage, he was exceptionally light-skinned and frequently passed for white. For sport, he would sometimes address white men as if he were a peer. The men invariably became annoyed when they realized the light-skinned gentleman was actually African-American. Ironically, Edwards was denied membership into a local black civic organization because he looked "too white."

Rosa Parks knew that the Klan could kill her family and burn her home to the ground without a moment's notice.

The sight of her grandfather and his shotgun calmed Rosa's nerves. He patted her head and assured her he would protect them, or die trying. "I'll take them out as they come through that door," he promised. Rosa vowed to help fight the intruders when the time came. Edwards beamed at the young girl. She should go back to sleep and get some rest, he said. But Rosa knew she would be unable to sleep in her own bed. She felt safer with her grandfather nearby. Like a cat, she curled up on a rug at his feet, ever-ready to pounce into action if needed.

The daylight brought safety. The Klan had not struck. Over breakfast, Rosa's fear gave way to anger. She hated the men who terrorized her people, who murdered and went unpunished. Her grandfather said they were cowards, hiding

February 4, 1913
Rosa McCauley is born in Tuskegee, Alabama, to James McCauley,
a carpenter, and Leona Edwards, a teacher.

1929
Leaves high school to care for her ailing mother and grandmother.
December 18, 1932
Marries Raymond Parks, a barber, in Alabama.
1934
Completes her high school education, earning a diploma,
at age twenty-one.

December 1943
Joins the Montgomery, Alabama, chapter of the National Association for the
Advancement of Colored People (NAACP) and is elected secretary.
December 1, 1955
Arrested for refusing to give up her seat on a bus to a white passenger.
Tried and found guilty for violating the Chapter 6, Section 11 segregation
law of the Montgomery city code. The NAACP and other community groups
organize a boycott of the Montgomery buses.
December 20, 1956
The Montgomery bus boycott ends after 381 days.
December 21, 1956
Parks boards a newly integrated Montgomery city bus.

1957
Moves to Detroit, Michigan, with her husband.
1965
Hired as a secretary for African-American U.S. Representative
John Conyers.
1977
Husband, Raymond Parks, dies.

February 1986
Cofounds the Rosa and Raymond Parks Institute for Self Development,
to introduce young people to important civil rights issues.
1992
Publishes her autobiography *Rosa Parks: My Story*.
October 16, 1995
Speaks at the Million Man March in Washington, D.C.

September 1996
Receives the Presidential Medal of Freedom from President Bill Clinton.
July 1999
Receives the Congressional Gold Medal.
October 24, 2005
Dies in her apartment in Detroit at the age of ninety-two.

The virulent Ku Klux Klan instilled fear and anger in the hearts of African Americans. The organization is seen here marching in Washington, D.C. National Photo Company Collection, Prints & Photographs Division, Library of Congress, LC-USZ62-59666

their identities under bed sheets and attacking unarmed families in the dead of night. Rosa agreed. Brazenly, she admitted to her grandfather that she wished he had shot one of the Klansmen in the night. She knew it was wrong to kill, but she also knew that the Klan could kill her family and burn her home to the ground without a moment's notice. The Klan enjoyed the fear it aroused in her community, relished the sight of its victims crying as they cleared the charred remains of crosses set afire in their yards in the dead of night.

A CLIMATE OF FEAR AND INTIMIDATION

Weeks earlier, a young African-American man, barely out of his teens, had been found murdered in the woods nearby. Everyone suspected the Klan had killed him, just as it had taken the lives of so many other young black men. There was no homicide investigation; the victim's death went unavenged. The black community knew better than to question the sheriff about the crime. To speak out was to attract the attention of the Klan and put oneself in harm's way. It was better to remain silent and under the radar.

Nearly fifty years earlier, slavery had been abolished. Technically, blacks were free. The reality was that in Pine Level, and in most of the South, African-Americans were routinely oppressed and treated as pariahs who did not deserve the citizenship they were granted after the Civil War.

The Ku Klux Klan ran rampant through the South, creating an atmosphere of fear in the black community. It set fire to the churches and brutalized the citizens. In Alabama alone, the Klan lynched more than 200 African-Americans between the years of 1885 and 1918. It was well known that many of the local law enforcement officials and the town's wealthiest businessmen were card-carrying Klansmen. A black person looking for justice had nowhere to turn.

Sylvester Edwards instilled in Rosa a sense of pride and self-respect. She was taught that she was as good as any white child, if not better. It was a lesson that would serve her well in later years.

A LEGENDARY BUS RIDE

Rosa grew into a fine, independent young woman. She moved to Montgomery, and in 1932, she met and married Raymond Parks, a barber and active member of the National Association for the Advancement of Colored People (NAACP). The new Mrs. Parks joined the organization as well, and the couple worked to raise money to fund the defense of the "Scottsboro Boys," a group of African-American men falsely accused of raping two white women on a train.

Parks gained a reputation as an upstanding hard worker and a devoted advocate for civil rights. She eventually was elected secretary of the Montgomery branch of the NAACP. (When Martin Luther King accepted a position on the executive committee of the Montgomery NAACP, his letter of appointment came from Rosa Parks.) As a teenager, Parks had dropped out of high school to care for her ailing mother and grandmother. Her husband encouraged her to return to school. At twenty-one, Parks received her high school diploma from Alabama State Teachers College High School.

In 1955, Parks was working as a seamstress for the Montgomery Fair Department store. She worked long hours hunched over a table making alterations to the mass-produced garments sold in the store. December was an especially busy month as customers flocked to the store to do their Christmas shopping. On December 1, 1955, Parks had put in a long day at work. As she headed home, her feet hurt, and her back strained from the weight of the several packages she carried.

Around 6 p.m. she boarded the bus at Cleveland Avenue. Parks was exhausted and relieved to discover that the front of the bus—the section reserved for white people only—was empty. This meant Parks could proceed directly to a seat in the "colored" section at the rear of the bus. Had the white section been occupied with even one passenger, Parks would have been required to pay her fare at the front of the bus, exit, and then reenter through the door at the back.

This affront was just one of the many black Americans had to endure under the racist Jim Crow laws. Quite often, black passengers were left stranded by bus drivers who departed before they had time to reenter through the rear door. A year earlier, Parks had been ordered to exit the bus and reenter through the rear door. As she turned to leave, she dropped her purse, and the contents spilled onto the floor. She took too long to collect her things, and bus driver James Blake sped off seconds after Parks exited the front door, leaving her stranded in the rain.

On this dry but chilly Thursday evening, Parks sank wearily into her seat in the section marked "For Colored People." She stared out the window and replayed the events of a meeting she had attended earlier that week addressing the horrific murder in Mississippi of Emmett Till, a fourteen-year-old African-American boy who was lynched and beaten by two white men for allegedly whistling at a white woman. Till's killers were exonerated by an all-white jury.

As Parks thought of Till, the bus made its way through the downtown area, picking up more passengers along the way. Soon all the seats were taken. Several white men boarded at the bus stop in front of the Empire Theatre. There were no seats left to accommodate these new passengers. The bus driver stood and approached the back of the bus. Parks realized then that driver was James Blake, the same man who had left her stranded in the rain the previous year. He waved in Parks' direction. "Y'all better make it light on yourselves and let me have those seats," Blake demanded.

According to the law, the African-American riders were legally entitled to retain their seats in the "Colored" section. However, they had learned long ago that the law was not likely to be enforced on their behalf. Justice was far from color-blind in Montgomery, Alabama. Reluctantly, three of the black passengers relinquished their seats to the white passengers. The fourth, Parks, remained seated. She was tired of being pushed around because of the color of her skin, and fed up by a lifetime of oppression. Blake wanted her to stand. She refused.

"If you don't stand up," he told her, "I'm going to have to call the police and have you arrested." Parks was resolute. The demure forty-two-year old held her head high and said, "You may do that." Parks would later admit that she "felt a determination cover my body like a quilt on a winter night."

Rosa Parks's arrest for refusing to relinquish her seat to a white passenger sparked the legendary 381-day bus boycott in Montgomery, Alabama.
New York World-Telegram & Sun Collection, Prints & Photographs Division, Library of Congress, LC-USZ62-109643

Parks was arrested, taken to police headquarters, fingerprinted, and fined $14. After paying the fine, she was released. Had the matter ended there, Parks would most likely have lived her life in relative obscurity. Parks had not been the first African-American to be arrested for failing to give up a seat to a white passenger, but she helped ignite a civil rights movement that led to dissolution of Jim Crow laws in the South.

A BOYCOTT SHAKES MONTGOMERY

The NAACP had long wanted to take a test case to court to challenge the legality of segregation in public facilities. With Parks' sterling character and demure yet proud stature, she presented the organization with a perfect poster child.

However, the attorneys for the NAACP wanted to make sure Parks was committed to seeing the case through to the end. Parks told them she needed to consult with her husband before making a decision. Raymond Parks was concerned for his wife's safety and pleaded with her to walk away from the case. "The white folks will kill you, Rosa," he told her.

Parks knew that she would be exposing herself to potential retribution and attacks from Montgomery's segregationists. Still, she wasn't one to give up without a fight. She had inherited her grandfather's feisty nature—and his sense of justice. After mulling it over, she told the NAACP she was ready to move forward. "If you think it will mean something to Montgomery and do some good, I'll be happy to go along with it," she said. Found guilty of violating the Montgomery City segregation code, Parks appealed the verdict.

While the lawyers prepared their test case, the NAACP and the Women's Political Council, a group made up of community members and congregants of local churches, joined together to organize a boycott of the Montgomery Bus Company. Thousands of pamphlets were distributed throughout the black communities in Montgomery, urging citizens to "stay off the buses in protest of the arrest and trial." The Montgomery Improvement Association (MIA) was founded to handle and lead a continuing bus boycott. Dr. Martin Luther King Jr., then a young, relatively unknown preacher, was chosen to head the newly formed MIA.

The boycott began on December 4, 1955, and it lasted for 381 days. On the first day of the boycott, 40,000 black commuters shunned public transportation, choosing instead to walk or carpool to their destinations. For more than a year, these dedicated citizens made the enormous personal sacrifice of walking miles to work and school. Despite blisters, inclement weather, exhaustion, harassment from local police officers, threats of violence, and the bombings of black churches by rabid segregationists, the black commuters kept up the boycott.

The vast majority of passengers who used public transportation were African-American. Without their business, the Montgomery Bus Company teetered on the edge of bankruptcy. The bus boycott struck a huge blow against segregation.

ROSA PARKS FINDS HER VOICE

In February 1956, the MIA filed a class action suit challenging the segregation policy on public buses. Because Parks' case was a criminal, not a civil one, she was not named as a defendant. (A criminal case must wind its way through a number of state courts before a federal appeal can be made.) The court ruled that segregation was illegal. The Supreme Court later upheld the ruling, declaring segregation of public buses unconstitutional. Alabama was ordered to desegregate its public buses. MIA officially ended the boycott that December.

Four days before Christmas—just over a year after Parks was arrested for refusing to relinquish her seat to a white passenger—she boarded a newly integrated Montgomery bus. Parks chose a seat up front. Looking back on her actions on that fateful day she remarked:

"I did not want to be mistreated, I did not want to be deprived of a seat that I had paid for. It was just time... there was opportunity for me to take a stand to

In 1956, Rosa Parks boarded a newly integrated city bus in Montgomery. She chose a window seat at the front of the vehicle. New York World-Telegram & the Sun Newspaper Photograph Collection, Prints & Photographs Division, Library of Congress, LC-USZ62-111235

express the way I felt about being treated in that manner. I had not planned to get arrested. I had plenty to do without having to end up in jail. But when I had to face that decision, I didn't hesitate to do so because I felt that we had endured that too long. The more we gave in, the more we complied with that kind of treatment, the more oppressive it became."

Parks spent the remainder of her life working as a civil rights activist, encouraging African-American voter registration and fighting oppression worldwide. In 1985, she joined the Free South Africa Movement, walking the picket lines in Washington, D.C. A year later, she opened the Rosa and Raymond Parks Institute for Self Development, an organization that offers guidance and inspiration to black youth.

Known as the "Mother of the Modern Civil Rights Movement," Parks received numerous awards, including the Presidential Medal of Freedom, the Congressional Gold medal, and the Humanitarian Award. Parks died on October 24, 2005. The American Transportation Association designated December 1 "Rosa Parks Day" in her honor.

CHAPTER TWENTY-ONE

JOHN F. KENNEDY, 1917–1963: "EVERYBODY INTO THE WATER!"

**"How did you become a hero?" John F. Kennedy was once asked.
"It was simple," he replied. "They sank my boat."
Kennedy's courage and leadership in rescuing his crew helped propel
him to the presidency of the United States.**

The night of August 1, 1943, was pitch-black and moonless as fifteen U.S. motor torpedo boats pushed off into the silent waters off Guadalcanal Island in the South Pacific. It was so dark, an Australian coastwatcher said, he could see nothing but the illuminated hands of his wristwatch.

Navigating mainly by compass, shadowy landmarks, follow-the-leader, and sheer guesswork, the tiny flotilla headed toward the infamous "Slot" of New Georgia Sound. The passageway was the main route for Japanese convoys attempting to resupply and reinforce their beleaguered troops in the bitterly contested Solomon Islands. Naval intelligence had discovered that the "Tokyo Express" had scheduled a resupply run that dark night. The boats, designated by the navy as "patrol torpedo boats," or PT boats, were given the mission to intercept the destroyer-escorted convoy. Each of the wooden 80-foot (24 m) boats carried a crew of twelve and four torpedoes for the task.

The PTs were deployed into four divisions, each assigned an area to patrol. Leading the way as senior officer and commanding Division B was Lieutenant Henry Brantingham, a spit-and-polish Annapolis graduate and veteran destroyer officer. Brantingham skippered PT-159. The others followed him to their assigned stations. The last in line was PT-109, captained by a young, slim, sandy-haired

A young Lieutenant junior grade (j.g.) John F. Kennedy, his rank signified by the half stripe on his sleeve, poses in full uniform in 1942 and was soon headed for his first command in the South Pacific. Photograph in the John F. Kennedy Presidential Library and Museum, Boston.

Harvard graduate and lieutenant junior grade (j.g.) exercising his first command. His name was John Fitzgerald Kennedy.

In the darkness, the little vessels quickly lost touch with each other. Only four PTs were equipped with radar, and it was a primitive form at that. Boat commanders were told to observe radio silence, and after reaching their patrol area, cut their engines and cruise quietly to minimize noise and wake. After about an hour, Brantingham saw green blips on his radar screen. He assumed they were low-lying supply barges, and he moved closer. As Brantingham approached, however, he was welcomed by heavy gunfire and recognized that the blips represented destroyers, not barges. Moving into range, he fired two torpedoes. To his horror, one torpedo burst in the tube and lighted up the sky, revealing his position. He told PT-157 to move up and fire. All four of 157's torpedoes misfired, whereupon the two boats headed for home.

None of this information reached PT-109. Kennedy saw fiery flashes across the water, but he assumed they came from shore batteries. He heard staticky transmissions that seemed to say "Have fired fish" (torpedoes) and "Better get out of there," but he had no clue to their origin. Kennedy could not know, either, that the PTs of Division C and R had fired their torpedoes, too, without a single hit. After midnight, PT-162 maneuvered alongside, and Lieutenant j.g. John Lowrey asked Kennedy if he had heard further orders. Kennedy said no. The two young skippers decided to break radio silence and asked the home base at Rendova harbor for instructions. They were told to continue patrolling.

About 1:30 a.m., PT-109 was idling quietly amid an almost unearthly stillness. Two crewmen were sleeping on the deck. Ensign George Ross, nicknamed "Barney" for the prizefighter, had hitched a ride because his own PT had been disabled by dive bombers. He lay alongside the forward gun, sometimes slithering back to the cockpit to chat in low tones with Kennedy at the wheel by the deckhouse. Others were sleepily manning their battle stations.

Suddenly the hush was broken by the roar of ships' engines nearby and rapidly coming closer. Before Kennedy could bring the starboard engine up to full power and start the other two, he heard the lookout's cry of "Ship at two o'clock" followed by a huge roar and a crunching, crashing sound. A split-second later, Kennedy was hurled against the deck house. A moment after that he was shouting, "Everybody into the water!" and in one more moment was himself thrashing about in the warm waters of Blackett Strait, which was now

May 29, 1917
John Fitzgerald Kennedy is born in Brookline, Massachusetts,
the second son of Joseph Patrick and Rose Fitzgerald Kennedy.

September 1931
Enters the Choate School in Wallingford, Connecticut and graduates in 1935.
September 1937
Father, Joseph P. Kennedy, is named the U.S. ambassador to Great Britain.
September 1, 1939
Germany invades Poland. European War breaks out.

June 1940
Graduates from Harvard College cum laude with a
bachelor of science degree.
July 1940
His Harvard thesis, *Appeasement in Munich*, is published as
Why England Slept.
September 1941
Sworn in as an ensign in the U.S. Naval Reserve.
December 7, 1941
Japanese aircraft attack Pearl Harbor. United States declares war
on Japan, Germany, and Italy.

March 1943
Lieutenant Junior Grade (J.G.) Kennedy assumes command of
PT boat 109 in the Solomon Islands.
August 2, 1943
PT-109 is rammed and sunk by a Japanese destroyer, killing two crewmen
and wounding two others. Kennedy and his crew are marooned for seven
days before being rescued.
June 11, 1944
Awarded the Navy and Marine Corps Medal and a Purple Heart for
his bravery on PT-109.
August 12, 1944
Brother Joseph P. Kennedy Jr. is killed on a mission over France.

March 1, 1945
Honorably discharged with the rank of full lieutenant.
May 8, 1945
V-E Day: War ends in Europe.
August 14, 1945
V-J Day: Japan surrenders in the Pacific.
September 2, 1945
The Japanese sign the final article of surrender aboard the USS *Missouri*.

November 6, 1946
Elected to the U.S. House of Representatives from the 11th Congressional
District, Massachusetts. Reelected in 1948 and 1950.
November 1952
Elected to the U.S. Senate from Massachusetts, defeating
Henry Cabot Lodge Jr.
November 6, 1960
Elected the president of the United States, defeating Richard Nixon.

January 20, 1961
Sworn in as the thirty-fifth president of the United States.
November 22, 1963
John F. Kennedy is assassinated in Dallas, Texas.

engulfed in gasoline-fueled flames. Kennedy spent thirty hours in the water, and he performed feats in the next days that would earn him the Navy Cross and a place in history.

LEARNING THE ROPES IN EIGHT WEEKS

"Jack" Kennedy was one of nine children of Joseph Kennedy, a prominent New Deal Democrat and Wall Street buccaneer who had served as the first chairman of the Securities and Exchange Commission and then as U.S. ambassador to Great Britain. After graduating with honors from Harvard College, Jack Kennedy lived in London, where the twenty-two year old met such notables as Winston Churchill, Noël Coward, and Anthony Eden and published his Harvard thesis about political events leading to war. *Why England Slept* became a bestseller.

After London, the young man concluded that the United States would soon be at war with Hitler's Germany. He volunteered for the army but was rejected because of a lower back sprain suffered in junior-varsity football at Harvard. Kennedy performed strengthening exercises and tried the navy. The Kennedys owned a summer home on Cape Cod, and Jack had been sailing since he was eight. Kennedy passed a fitness test, and was he commissioned an ensign in the Naval Reserve. First assigned to a Washington office, he was at a professional football game when the Japanese attacked Pearl Harbor. Kennedy immediately applied for active sea duty. Instead he was assigned to a series of "boring" desk jobs before being sent to the Naval Reserve Officers' Training School at Northwestern University.

Winter 1942 was a dismal period for the U.S. cause. The United States had lost most of its Pacific fleet at Pearl Harbor, allowing the Japanese to capture Guam and other U.S. outposts in the Pacific, roll over the United States–held Philippines, take Britain's stronghold at Singapore and the resource-rich Dutch East Indies, threaten Australia, and virtually turn the Pacific into a Japanese lake. Then a squadron of small, fast vessels performing deeds of daring and surprise captured the U.S. imagination. Motor Torpedo Boat Squadron 3 under Lieutenant John D. Bulkeley swooped into Manila Harbor under Japanese noses and plucked General Douglas MacArthur, his family, and top officers off Corregidor Island and whisked them to Australia, where MacArthur was to become supreme commander in the southwest Pacific. The squadron also sneaked into the Japanese naval base at Subic Bay and sank an auxiliary cruiser. Bulkeley became a hero and received the Medal of Honor. His PT boats' exploits were chronicled in the bestselling *They Were Expendable.*

Young naval officers, including Kennedy, immediately aspired to the PT boat service. When Bulkeley came to Northwestern University on a recruiting mission, Kennedy immediately stepped forward. Bulkeley called for athletic young men with good academic records who were experienced in handling small boats. Kennedy had graduated cum laude, was a varsity swimmer, and had won medals in a Star-class racing sloop on Long Island Sound. He qualified on all counts. Still many other young officers were vying for the slots.

Kennedy was not too proud to have his father pull a few strings and jumped to the head of the line. Then, after Kennedy completed an eight-week training course in PT boats on Narragansett Bay and received an order to remain there as an instructor, to be followed by assignment to a squadron in Panama, his father used his connections. Instead of heading to Panama, Kennedy was pulled out and sent to the Solomon Islands in March 1943 as an officer replacement.

Kennedy had achieved the active duty he wanted. But no training had prepared him for plunging into a flaming sea, in command of a boat turned into matchsticks, and leading twelve other young men, two of them seriously wounded, two missing, and all of them very, very scared.

HEAVENLY MIST

The four Japanese destroyers forming the "Tokyo Express" on August 1 were bound for Vila on Kolombangara Island, which was a staging post for Japanese forces protecting a key strategic air base. They stood about a hundred yards (91.4 m) off shore while troops scrambled down landing nets and the crew tossed supplies into waiting, shallow-draft barges. Food, blankets, clothing, ammunition, weapons, were hurriedly dropped over the sides. The crews moved fast because the torpedo attack would surely alert other U.S. vessels. The coming daylight would also make the stationary destroyers sitting ducks for aircraft.

"Hurry, hurry!" implored Commander Kohei Hanami, captain of the destroyer *Amarigi* ("Heavenly Mist"). *Amarigi* was to be the last ship to unload. It carried bullets and shells, canned food, and sacks of rice. As each item went over the side, the commander shouted "Hurry, hurry!" again. He wanted to be careful with the important cargo, but it would never do to be caught standing still and offering a target for dive bombers. The other three destroyers were already heading back to their base. He must follow them, quickly.

Finally, about 2:30 a.m., the unloading was complete. Nine hundred men and seventy tons (63.5 metric tons) of supplies had been landed. Hanami wheeled the *Amarigi* about and headed back into Blackett Strait, moving fast. The *Amarigi* was capable of 35 knots (18 m/s), but Hanami, blind in the darkness, thought 30 knots (15 m/s) enough to speed him out of danger. Suddenly his lookout shouted, "Ship ahead!" At almost the same moment, "Ship at two o'clock!" sounded from the foredeck of PT-109. Kennedy, at the wheel, glanced over his shoulder to see a dark silhouette looming ahead. He at first mistakenly took it to be another PT boat, a mistake that cost him a few precious seconds. On the *Amarigi* bridge, Hanami saw the PT-109 and the imminent collision. He decided that his only choice was to ram. Kennedy, idling on a single engine and unable to start the others quickly, had no way to avoid the crash.

On what remained of PT-109, John F. Kennedy feared that the boat's gasoline tanks would explode at any moment. After ordering the crew into the water, he vaulted over the side.

Within seconds, the steel prow of the *Amarigi* sliced through the starboard side of the wooden PT-109, just aft of the cockpit. Two crewmen were apparently crushed by the impact, and their bodies were never found. Kennedy was thrown against the rear wall of the cockpit. His back slammed against a reinforcing bar, aggravating his old injury with results that would plague him until the end of his life. Lying on his back, Kennedy saw the ominous shape pass a few feet from him and cleanly bisect the little boat into fore and aft sections. On the *Amarigi*, Commander Hanami thought a torpedo had hit. *Heavenly Mist* was shuddering from the impact, and its engines were vibrating wildly. Hanami found that by reducing speed, he could halt the vibration. He radioed that he had sunk a PT boat and continued on his homeward route.

On what remained of PT-109, Kennedy feared that the boat's gasoline tanks would explode at any moment. After ordering the crew into the water, he vaulted over the side. Although the sea was aflame, the *Amarigi*'s strong wake had swept much of the fire away from the men in the water. The flames died out, and there

Kennedy, center, and other PT boat commanders gathered in the Solomon Islands in 1943. From left seated are Lts. Jim Reed, Kennedy, and Paul Fay. Lt. Barney Ross, who was on PT 109, is at rear. Fay later served as Undersecretary of the Navy under Kennedy. Photograph in the John F. Kennedy Presidential Library and Museum, Boston.

was no explosion. At a safe distance from the wreckage, the men began to call to each other: "Mr. Kennedy! Mr. Kennedy!" "Over here!" Eleven survivors could be accounted for. Two men were missing and did not respond to calls. Two were badly hurt. Engineer Patrick McMahon, at thirty-seven the oldest crew member, had been in the engine room and been badly burned on the arms and legs. He could stay afloat only with great pain.

Kennedy was not sure what to do. He hoped that the other PTs might recognize their plight and return for them. But could they be seen in the darkness? It was unlikely that U.S. planes would find them, either. And there was the danger the Japanese might spot them first. With daylight coming, that seemed a real risk. Everyone in the South Pacific had heard grisly stories about how brutally the Japanese treated their prisoners.

Swimming was tiring, because the men were fully dressed and wearing shoes. Through the darkness, they could see that PT-109's bow section was still afloat. Kennedy suggested that they swim to it. He knew that the forward lockers contained pistols that might be useful for resistance if they were captured. Several men were poor swimmers, and McMahon was being supported by the others, but they all wore life jackets. Kennedy, the best swimmer, helped McMahon to float on his back. He then took the strap of McMahon's life jacket in his teeth and with McMahon on his back, breaststroked his way to the shattered PT-109. The eleven men clambered onto the boat's deck or clung to the sides. They found a Thompson submachine gun, six .45 pistols, and a .38, and they decided that they would fight unless they were badly outnumbered. "Will we ever get out of this?" a frightened seaman asked Kennedy. "It can be done," Kennedy said. "We'll do it."

ON HIS MAJESTY'S SERVICE

The collision had occurred in Blackett Strait, which is part of a web of waterways feeding into the "Slot." The southern side of the passage was a chain of small islands, roughly in the shape of an anchor. The northern side was the mountainous island of Kolombangara, where the Japanese convoy had been headed. Atop one 2,300-foot (700 m) peak had been constructed what seemed just another native bamboo hut. It housed one resident. Australian Arthur Reginald Evans was equipped with a sub-machine gun, binoculars, a telescope, and most important, radio. He was a member of the Australian coastwatcher service, and from his lofty perch he could look down on the Japanese installation and monitor all shipping into Blackett Strait and the Slot. Evans was to play a key role in the improbable events of the next few days.

Since the crash, the bow section of PT-109 had been gradually filling with water and listing heavily. About 10 a.m. it turned completely over, bottom side up. The men who had been lying on it, sitting on it, or clinging to it scrambled to safety and then repositioned themselves on the upturned hulk. Kennedy recognized that it was only a matter of time until the boat foundered completely and sank to the bottom. If it sank at night, the men would be plunged into the water and perhaps separated again. He concluded that they must head for land.

All of the PT commanders had been given charts and briefed about the islands, but in a war zone no one was sure which were Japanese-held. Landing on Kolombangara with its Japanese garrison was certainly out of the question. They might be swimming right into Japanese arms. Nauru, the largest and closest island, occupied a commanding position on the strait and might be held by Japanese. Other islets seemed too small to conceal eleven men. Plum Pudding Island, named for its Christmas-dessert shape, seemed large enough for them but small enough that the Japanese had probably ignored it.

Kennedy directed the groaning men back into the water. They corralled a 2-by-8-foot (61 cm-by-2.4 m) timber from the floating remnants of the PT boat as a makeshift raft. Four men lined up on each side with Ensign Leonard Thom, the executive officer, at the rear. The nine tied their shoes, lantern, and gun to the timber. Kennedy resumed towing McMahon. The others kicked more or less in unison, holding the plank with one arm while thrashing with the other.

Plum Pudding Island was a disappointing refuge. It had only a few coconut palms, and the nuts were not yet ripe. Kennedy and the other two officers concluded that unless they were rescued soon, they must move to another island and risk capture. First they must redouble efforts to attract rescuers. The PT boats that night might be on patrol. Kennedy swam out to midpassage to try to attract their attention. It was a vain hope. Unknown to Kennedy and his men, the squadron that night was directed to a different area. Kennedy became lost in the cross currents and, exhausted and having seen no one, did not return until daylight. The next night Ensign Ross, another strong swimmer, took his turn, but with the same frustrating result.

EVANS'S EYES AND EARS

From Evans's lofty vantage point, he had been studying wreckage off another island. It could have been a Japanese barge or an abandoned native dugout canoe. He had been informed of the loss of PT-109 and wondered about survivors. Back at the PT base, Commander Thomas Warfield had conducted a cursory search, then called it off. Because air searches had identified no survivors, he could not risk more lives in a seemingly fruitless hunt. Ensign William Battle volunteered to take PT-171 to Blackett Strait, but his offer was denied.

Australian coastwatcher Arthur Reginald Evans played a crucial role in the rescue of the PT-109 survivors.
Associated Press

Evans did not give up so easily. On August 4, almost four days after the crash, he was still asking headquarters about flights over the strait. Then things took a different tack. Biuku Gasa and Eroni Kumana, two young natives with a dugout canoe, served as Evans's eyes and ears. They discovered that the Japanese had landed 300 more soldiers on Gizo Island, off Kolombangara. They climbed to Evans's mountaintop to give him this news. Evans asked if they had seen or heard anything about survivors. The natives said no, and then they went back to their canoe and headed for their home station.

THE HUNGRY HORDE

On Plum Pudding Island, Kennedy's men were becoming ravenous. They had not eaten since dinner four days before. One man tried eating a sand crab. Kennedy decided they must move to a more promising location. Olasana Island was perhaps $1^1/_2$ miles (2.4 km) distant, and it seemed to have a large stand of coconut palms. Back into the water the men went, taking their places along the plank. McMahon returned to Kennedy's back and after an arduous swim through strong current, they reached their new destination. They quickly fell to harvesting coconuts, but after gorging themselves, some fell ill and all soon fell asleep.

Kennedy was restless, though. They seemed to be getting no closer to being saved. Next day, he suggested to Ross that the two of them swim to Nauru and

Here Kennedy was, bearded, gaunt, unshaven, half-naked, blotched with festering coral wounds, cast away on a miserable patch of jungle surrounded by sharks, and he was being addressed as if he were in his father's embassy in London.

"have a look around." It was better than sitting in the shade and waiting, he said. The swim was not too difficult, and they were rewarded when they found in a wrecked Japanese barge a crate of hard candy and a tin of rainwater.

Meanwhile, Evans's native scouts, Biuku and Eroni, had also spotted the wreck, and they landed on the opposite shore of Nauru to investigate. They found two rifles

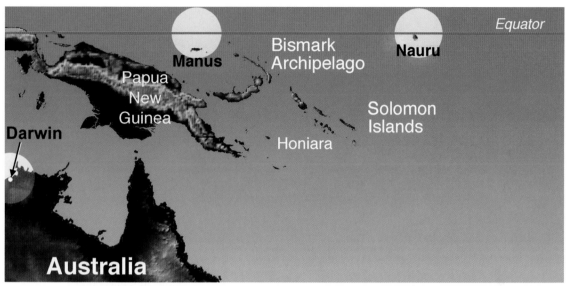

The Solomon Islands in the South Pacific were a hotly contested area during World War II. Honiara, on Guadalcanal Island, is the island's capital and largest city. ARM IMAGES

and were headed back to their canoe when Ross and Kennedy suddenly stumbled out of the trees. Both groups were startled, the Americans alarmed. Suppose these two were in league with the Japanese? Equally frightened, the two natives dashed to their canoe.

The exertions and his fright tired Biuku, and he was thirsty. He persuaded Eroni to turn the canoe and beach at the next island for a coconut and a drink. The island was Olasana, where the rest of the PT-109 crew were waiting for Kennedy and Ross to return.

Three or four of the castaways spotted the approaching canoe and ducked into the brush. The two might be Japanese scouts. But they looked like mere boys. After waiting and watching, Ensign Thom, a husky former Ohio State tackle, took matters into his own hands. He stood up and walked toward the two, beckoning and calling, "Come, come!" Biuku and Enroni scrambled to their canoe and paddled furiously. They had never seen anything quite like this huge, blond-bearded apparition advancing toward them, shouting strange sounds. Thom tried words like "American" and "friend," then had an inspiration. He pointed to the sky and yelled, "White star! White star!"

Evans's coastwatchers had taught scouts to watch for planes marked with the U.S. insignia, a white star set in a white bar, and to treat anyone who came

The Kennedy inaugural parade in 1961 featured a replica of the sunken PT-109. Photograph in the John F. Kennedy Presidential Library and Museum, Boston.

from such planes courteously and bring them to the coastwatcher station. The two youths were convinced to return to shore and, although communication was fragmentary, finally recognized all were on the same side. Pointing to Nauru, Biuku insisted there were Japanese on the island. Thom finally understood that they had seen Kennedy and Ross.

When Kennedy returned to Olasana, he had Biuku fetch a coconut, and he carved a message into the shell: "NAURO ISL NATIVE KNOWS POSIT HE CAN PILOT X11 ALIVE NEED SMALL BOAT KENNEDY." Thom had somehow found a pencil stub and a paper invoice from a South Seas shipping company, and he had written his own message: "Rescue of 11 men lost since

Sunday, August 1st. in enemy action. Native knows our position will bring PT boat back to small island of Nuru [sic]. A small boat (outboard or oars) is needed to take men off as some are seriously burned." Kennedy took Biuku to the shore and pointed to Rendova, indicating both messages should be taken there. Biuku nodded, and he and Eroni climbed back into the canoe.

But instead of Rendova, the natives stopped at a closer U.S. naval base at Roviana Island and showed the shell and paper to an officer. The officer immediately ordered a PT boat to take them to Rendova Harbor. Simultaneously, a dispatch arrived there from Evans, relayed from his headquarters, saying that scouts had told him of the survivors and suggesting a rescue plan. Evans sent seven scouts to Olasana. After an hour's search, they found the castaways in a clearing.

Benjamin Kavu, an English-speaking scout, handed Kennedy a pencil-written letter from Evans addressed to "Senior Officer, Nauru Island," and headed "On His Majesty's Service." Kennedy burst out laughing. As he said to author Robert J. Donovan later, "You've got to hand it to the British." Here Kennedy was, bearded, gaunt, unshaven, half-naked, blotched with festering coral wounds, cast away on a miserable patch of jungle surrounded by sharks, and he was being addressed as if he were in his father's embassy in London.

After the famished crew was fed, the natives took Kennedy by boat to Gomu Island where Evans was waiting. The scouts then moved both men to another island where Lieutenant j.g. William Liebenow and PT-157 met them. At midnight, the PT maneuvered into Olasana, and the survivors of the collision in Blackett Strait were swept to safety and a jubilant reunion with their comrades at Rendova Harbor.

Kennedy remained in the Solomon Islands and returned to duty as skipper of another boat, PT-59. He led a daring rescue of entrapped Marines on Choiseul Island. In January 1944, Kennedy was repatriated for a series of disc operations. He received a medical discharge and was awarded the Navy Medal for his PT-109 exploits. In 1947, he entered politics by successfully campaigning for a seat in the U.S. House of Representatives, then went on to the U.S. Senate and the presidency. The survivors of PT-109 were given a place of honor at Kennedy's presidential inauguration in 1961.

CHAPTER TWENTY-TWO

MIKHAIL GORBACHEV, b. 1931: HOW A BRUSH WITH STALINISM CREATED A BOLD REFORMER

As a child, Mikhail Gorbachev watched in horror as his grandfather was dragged out of the family home in the middle of the night by Stalin's secret police. Decades later, he became a staunch reformer who reshaped a nation.

The day had been an uneventful one. Six-year-old Mikhail Gorbachev was spending the night at his grandparents' home. The boy had developed a strong bond with his grandparents and resided with them for weeks at a time. Mikhail had yet to start school, and he passed his days playing in the fields and accompanying his grandparents as they went about their chores and tended to the land. His grandfather, Pantelei Gopkalo, was often busy meeting with his fellow farmers. It was 1937, and the government policy of *kolkhoz* ("collective economy") was in full force. A communist, Gopkalo was the chairman of the Communist Party of the Soviet Union (CPSU) and responsible for motivating the farmers to organize and increase their productivity. Laughing, Mikhail's grandmother, Vailisa, told him, "Your granddad would spend the whole night organizing, but in the morning everyone's run away."

After dinner that night, Mikhail sat near the stove and listened as his grandfather recited some of his favorite folk tales. As the day grew to a close, Mikhail felt his eyes grow heavy. He retired to his small sleeping pallet and fell asleep. Several hours later, the boy was startled awake by the sounds of pounding on the front door. His grandfather had barely opened the door when a contingent of men barged inside the small house. "There's a traitor in the house!" one of the

As a child, Mikhail Gorbachev watched in horror as Stalin's secret police dragged his grandfather from the family home in the middle of night. New York Public Library

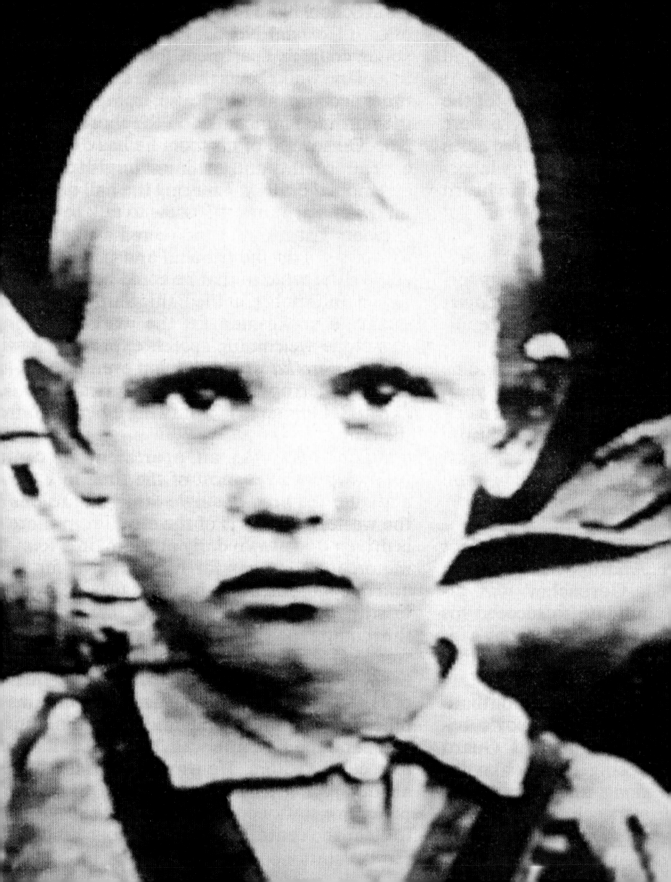

men announced. The men were members of NKVD, Stalin's secret police.

Young Mikhail quietly watched the event unfold. The men's uniforms were dark green with red triangles on the collar, and each had a thin brown leather strap across his chest with a wide belt across the waist. They wore blue hats with a bright red band above the visor. Their voices were harsh and serious. What were these men doing in the house? Were they going to take someone away? Were they here to take the religious pictures his grandmother had hidden behind the other pictures hanging on the wall?

Mikhail couldn't understand everything that was being said because so many people were talking at once. He could tell, though, that the men were in his house because they believed his grandfather had broken the rules of the kolkhoz, the farming collective. The leader began asking questions in an angry voice, and his grandfather kept saying "no, no."

Mikhail heard a name he had heard before—Trotsky—but he wasn't sure he knew who this man was. Every time the leader said it, his grandfather would again say, "No." Mikhail also heard the name Archangel. He knew it was a place, a bad place, but he did not know where it was or how far away. The more his grandparents argued and pleaded, the angrier the man in the green uniform became. After a few more minutes, the men opened the front door and led his grandfather out of the house. Mikhail Gorbachev later learned that his grandfather had been charged with treason and sentenced to nine years in the gulag.

COLLECTIVIZATION EXACTS A HEAVY TOLL

Gopkalo was just one of the many farmers sent to the gulag. By the time he was arrested in 1937, thousands of citizens had been arrested, charged with sedition, and imprisoned. Hundreds were found guilty and executed.

In all of Russia's troubled history, this was one of its darkest times. It was the late 1920s, and the attempts of Joseph Stalin, leader of the Soviet Union, to seize control of the nation's farms were taking their toll. The carcasses of dead livestock were rotting on the fields around Privol'noye, a farming town 200 miles (320 km) from Russia's border with Georgia. The animals lucky enough to be alive were emaciated, roaming the fields hungry and lost. The people of the village didn't fare much better. Virtually every family experienced at least one death from mal-nourishment or disease. Because there was no grain, the cows were barren of

March 2, 1931
Mikhail Sergeyevich Gorbachev is born in Privol'noye, Stavropol, USSR.

September 1950
Enrolls in law school at Moscow University.
September 25, 1953
Marries Raisa Maximovna Titorenko, a philosophy student.
June 1955
Receives his law degree.

1966
Graduates from the Agricultural Institute.
1970
Appointed first secretary for agriculture.
1974
Becomes a representative to the Supreme Soviet and chairman
of the Commission on Youth Affairs.

1979
Elected to the Politburo. Receives the patronage of KGB head Yury Andropov.
March 11, 1985
Becomes general secretary of the Communist Party of the Soviet Union.
July 1985
Appoints Boris Yeltsin the party chief for Moscow.
November 1985
Attends a summit in Geneva and meets with U.S. President Ronald Reagan.

February 1986
Lays out his plans for *perestroika* ("economic restructuring").
November 11, 1987
Fires Boris Yeltsin.
1988
Policy of *glasnost* ("openness") officially adopted.

June, 1991
Boris Yeltsin wins the Russian Federation's first popular presidential election.
December 8, 1991
Gorbachev and Yeltsin agree to dissolve the Soviet Union.
A new Commonwealth of Independent States is declared.
25 December 1991
Gorbachev resigns as president of the USSR. Yeltsin is the new leader of Russia.

May 25, 1989
Appointed chairman of the Supreme Soviet (head of state).
March 15, 1990
Elected president of the Soviet Union by the new parliament.
October 15, 1990
Receives the Nobel Peace Prize.

One of the lucky ones, Gorbachev's grandfather was sent home after being imprisoned for fourteen months. Most citizens accused of sedition were executed. Associated Press

milk. A lack of grain also meant a lack of bread, so that farmers didn't have the strength to plant, tend to, and harvest crops.

The peasants of Privol'noye had no escape from the famine. Food shortages were ravaging the entire country. A days- or even weeks-long journey on foot would reveal the same: starvation, desperation, death. Under the leadership of Stalin, the dream of a classless, industrial society was becoming stark, hideous reality.

Mikhail was too young to understand why any of this was happening. The man who would become the Soviet Union's last head of state, and begin its transition away from Communism, was born in 1931, when Stalin's collectivization plan was already in full swing. Mikhail was blessed with a warm, caring family of farmers who shielded him from a hard and scary world. As the only child for many years, he was cherished and coddled, especially by his grandparents with whom he shared a strong bond. Young Mikhail was the sole male heir and center of attention throughout his childhood. His brother, Aleksandr, wasn't born until Mikhail was sixteen and already taking on adult responsibilities working in the field.

Expressing a powerful curiosity at a young age, Gorbachev learned to read from his parents, and he learned about religion from his mother, who kept her faith secret but did not give it up. Even in this sheltered home, Gorbachev was aware that something was always watching—something bigger than his parents, larger and more powerful than the most important men of his village. He had never seen it, but he knew that it lived far away, in the cities.

Under the leadership of Joseph Stalin, the dream of a classless, industrial society was becoming stark, hideous reality.

When someone's father disappeared from the village, Gorbachev knew that it was because this all-seeing force had willed it. Small groups of men in dark brown jackets and blue hats would be seen on the dirt roads one day, and soon the news would reach his home that so-and-so was taken north to a place called Archangel. Upon hearing the news that a neighbor had been taken away, some people in the house would look scared, while others stared out the window or down at the floor. Then they would ask questions, and Gorbachev, sitting in the corner, could hear anger in their voices.

The anger Gorbachev sensed as a child was more potent than he knew. When Stalin began his first Five-Year Plan to place the nation's agricultural system under state control, he assumed that Russia's peasantry would enthusiastically join in the effort. He was wrong.

After the 1917 October Revolution, in which the Bolshevik Party overthrew the Russian Provisional Government, the vast majority of Russia's population lived in the countryside and worked the fields. Peasants who owned or rented small plots of land constituted as much as 85 percent of the population. In comparison, only about 3 percent of Russians lived in the cities proper. Stalin wanted to rapidly transform the country into a modern industrial power that could repel any attacks from a hostile Western Europe.

To feed the workers who would build and operate the factories and machines that made weapons and materiel, Russian farms needed to become more productive, and the farmers would have to sacrifice the products of their labor for the good of the state. By grouping all farms into large, regional collectives, Stalin believed he could create a supremely efficient system of production and distribution. With the marriage of industry and agriculture, the entire society would become a single, well-oiled machine running for one purpose: the good of the state.

The majority of farms at the time were small, family-operated holdings like that of the Gorbachevs, many of them run strictly on a subsistence basis. Others were owned and run by "middle peasants"—people who grew enough food to feed themselves plus make a small profit on the market. The wealthiest landowners owned larger tracts and were able to grow and sell crops in bulk at market prices. This third group—upper-class peasants known as *kulaks*—were in Stalin's eyes the number-one obstacle to his collectivization plan. Seizing their land would not be a simple matter. To Stalin, kulaks were the bourgeoisie of the farming world. They hoarded their profits, building a disproportionate level of wealth and power for themselves while keeping the poor peasants destitute.

The Communists assumed that the lower-class peasants harbored as much hatred for the kulaks as they themselves did. What Stalin needed was an October Revolution of the countryside where lower and middle peasants would rise up and take the kulaks' land and possessions. "We now have the opportunity to mount a decisive offensive against the kulaks," he said in a speech to the Communist party in 1930, "to break their resistance and destroy them as a class."

Although the poor peasants could be resentful of those better off than themselves, their disdain didn't run as deeply and as viciously as Stalin believed. His efforts toward collectivization were resisted at every turn. In extreme cases, those dead, bloating cows and horses Gorbachev saw in the fields had been killed or starved by their owners, who preferred to oversee the destruction of their own property rather than surrender it to the state.

During the first years of Gorbachev's life, Stalin's collectivization measures became more and more draconian. So hell-bent was he on eradicating the kulaks, more often than not he didn't have them sent to the gulag. It was much easier to simply kill them on their front steps. While in one rural area OGPU (the Unified State Political Administration, a euphemism for Stalin's hit squad, which would later evolve into the dreaded NKVD) operators might surround an entire village and fire machine-guns indiscriminately at peasants, in another village, a kulak or poor peasant might be setting her home on fire as she shouted obscenities at the Communist officials who had come to seize her home for the "greater good."

By the time Gorbachev was five years old, famine had hit Russia, and Stalin had ramped up his persecution of peasants. Only now he focused not just on kulaks; every farmer was now considered an enemy of socialism. To make matters worse, by the mid-1930s, Stalin's purge began focusing on anyone considered to be out of step politically. Suspects were quickly arrested, sometimes accused of being loyal to Stalin's banished rival Trotsky, and sent to the gulag or killed on the spot.

When Stalin enacted his plan to place the nation's agricultural system under state control, he assumed that Russia's peasantry would enthusiastically join in the effort. He was wrong. Getty Images

Until 1937, the Gorbachevs were not directly affected by Stalin's terrorist measures. The family was grateful to Communism in general. Gorbachev's maternal grandfather, Pantelei Gopkalo, fought on the Turkish front in World War I and joined the Communist party in 1928, remaining a dedicated Communist for the rest of his life. As Gorbachev once said, "In the oral history of our family, it was constantly repeated: The revolution gave our family land."

GOPKALO NARROWLY ESCAPES DEATH

Gorbachev later learned that his grandfather had been sentenced to nine years in the gulag because the NKVD believed he had attempted to destroy the kolkhoz by ploughing up the meadows to starve the livestock. They also accused him of "anti-Soviet activities" and of being a Trotsky sympathizer. In an attempt to force a confession, NKVD members broke his arms and covered him in a wet sheepskin coat, and then sat him down on a hot stove. Gopkalo never confessed. "I do not plead guilty. I have never been a member of a counter-revolutionary organization," he told his interrogators. "I deny the accusations categorically."

While his peers remained on the farm, Gorbachev took the rarely trod path to law school, earning his degree from Moscow University. Associated Press

Gopkalo survived fourteen months in the gulag and returned home to tell his tale. Unable to find evidence supporting Gopkalo's guilt, the prosecutor released him. This highly unusual move was prompted in large part by Gopkalo's reputation as a loyal Communist. Remarkably, Gopkalo's ordeal didn't shake his belief in Communism or even Stalin's regime. He excused the injustice by saying that he was sure Stalin himself was unaware of it.

With Gopkalo's arrest came the label of "subversives" for Mikhail Gorbachev's entire family. No one dared visit them during Gopkalo's tenure at Archangel. Gorbachev succeeded in keeping the story from the public during his political career. He didn't reveal it until 1990, in a speech he delivered to Russian intellectuals. Yet, witnessing his grandfather's arrest was one of the most important moments of Gorbachev's life, and it clearly helped shape his political ideals.

Decades later, Gorbachev described the event as his first "real trauma." The terror of seeing his beloved grandfather dragged from his bed in the middle of the night by armed men deeply affected him. "All this was a great shock to me and has remained engraved in my memory ever since," he wrote in his memoirs. When the terror subsided, a young Gorbachev was filled with moral outrage—and later, a desire to reform the Communist system. When Gorbachev was appointed general secretary of the Communist Party, he decried and condemned the "excesses" and "injustice" exacted upon innocent Russian peasants like his grandfather in the 1930s.

While most young collectivization-era Russians tended to remain on the farm the rest of their lives, Gorbachev took the rarely trod path to law school, earning his degree from Moscow University. Afterward, he returned to Stavropol and began climbing the ladder of the local Communist party, eventually becoming his town's party leader, in 1970. His first national post was agriculture secretary, and he joined the politburo in 1980, working closely with Yury Andropov and assuming responsibility for the Soviet Union's economy. When Andropov's successor, Konstantin Chernenko, died in 1985, Gorbachev, the youngest member of the politburo at the time, was named general secretary. In this position, Gorbachev began his historic reform programs.

Gorbachev showed early on that he was not an opportunist willing to embrace Stalinism to quickly climb the ranks of the politburo. While Gorbachev served in his first serious government position as first party secretary of Stavropol in 1970, he enacted reforms on behalf of the peasantry. He gave farmers more say in local planning, as well as more land to farm for private use.

Eventually, Gorbachev grew to embrace Western capitalist ideals and oversaw the complete reconstruction of the Soviet Union through his programs of *perestroika* and *glasnost*. The social, economic, and political restructuring of the country, perestroika "unites socialism with democracy and revives the Leninist concept of socialist construction both in theory and in practice," Gorbachev explained. Glasnost drew back the Iron Curtain, allowing the world an unprecedented look inside. Political and social problems were discussed openly, and restrictions on the dissemination of news and information were lifted.

Gorbachev, like his grandfather, was a dedicated Communist Party member through thick and thin. Although Gorbachev set in motion the process that would eventually topple Communism in the Soviet Union, he did not set out to destroy the party. He just wanted to right the wrongs of Stalinism, which he witnessed from a distance through most of his childhood and up close that one terrifying day.

Gorbachev held one more thing in common with his grandfather: He, too, was arrested by Stalinist-minded *apparatchiks*. On August 19, 1991, members of the State Emergency Committee placed Gorbachev under house arrest to prevent him from signing a treaty that, in essence, provided autonomy to the Soviet republics. The hardliners deemed Gorbachev's actions antithetical to the Soviet Union's cause. Unlike his grandfather, however, Gorbachev was guilty as charged.

Gorbachev's first national post was agriculture secretary. He worked hard to give farmers more rights and relax restrictions on private land use. Associated Press

RESOURCES

CHAPTER 1: HANNIBAL OF CARTHAGE

Bagnall, Nigel. *The Punic Wars: Rome, Carthage and the Struggle for the Mediterranean.* New York: Thomas Dunne Books, 2005.

Baker, George Philip. *Hannibal.* New York: Cooper Square Press, 1999. (Originally published by Dodd, Mead, 1929.)

Cottrell, Leonard. *Hannibal, Enemy of Rome.* New York: Da Capo Press, 1992.

Cummins, Joseph. *The War Chronicles: From Chariots to Flintlocks.* Beverly, MA: Fair Winds Press, 2008.

Goldsworthy, Adrian. *The Punic Wars.* London: Cassell & Co. 2000.

Jacobs, William Jay. *Hannibal, an African Hero.* New York: McGraw Hill, 1973.

Lamb, Harold. *Hannibal: One Man Against Rome.* Garden City, NY: Doubleday & Co., 1958.

CHAPTER 2: JOAN OF ARC

DeVries, Kelly. *Joan of Arc: A Military Leader.* Gloucestershire: Sutton Publishing, 1999.

Fraioli, Deborah. *Joan of Arc: The Early Debate.* London: Boydell Press, 2002.

Gordon, Mary. *Joan of Arc.* New York: Viking Penguin Lives, 2000

Pegg, Mark Gregory. *A Most Holy War.* New York: Oxford University Press, 2008.

Pernoud, Regine, and Marie-Veronique Clin. *Joan of Arc: Her Story.* New York: St. Martin's, 1999.

Pernoud, Regine. *Joan of Arc By Herself and Her Witnesses.* London: Scarborough House, 1994.

Richey, Donald. *Joan of Arc: The Warrior Saint.* Westport, CT: Praeger, 2003.

Sackville-West, Vita. *Saint Joan of Arc.* New York: Grove Press, 2001.

Seward, Desmond. *The Hundred Years War.* New York: Atheneum, 1978.

Spoto, Donald. *Joan: The Mysterious Life of a Heretic Who Became A Saint.* San Francisco: HarperCollins, 2007.

Joan of Arc in Her Own Words. Translated and edited by Willard Trask. New York: B.O.O.K.S. and Co., 1996.

CHAPTER 3: ELIZABETH I

Bassnet, Susan. *Elizabeth I: A Feminist Perspective.* Oxford: Berg Publishers Limited, 1988.

Levin, Carole, Jo Eldridge Carney, and Debra Barrett-Graves. *Elizabeth: Always Her Own Free Woman.* Burlington: Ashgate Publishing, 2003.

MacCaffrey, Wallace. *Elizabeth.* London: Edward Arnold, 1993.

May, Steven W. *Queen Elizabeth I; Selected Works.* New York: Washington Square Press, 2004.

Mumby, Frank A. *The Girlhood of Queen Elizabeth: A narrative in Contemporary Letters.* New York: Houghton Mifflin Company, 1909.

Plowden, Alison. *The Young Elizabeth.* Stroud, UK: Sutton Publishing, 1991.

CHAPTER 4: SAMUEL DE CHAMPLAIN

De Champlain, Samuel. *Narrative of a Voyage to the West Indies and Mexico in the Years 1599–1602.* London: The Hakluyt Society, 1859.

Fischer, David Hackett. *Champlain's Dream: The European Founding of North America.* New York: Simon & Schuster, 2008.

CHAPTER 5: GEORGE WASHINGTON

Alberts, Robert C. *A Charming Field for an Encounter: The Story of Washington's Fort Necessity.* Washington, DC: Division of Publications, National Park Service, 1975, reprinted 2004.

Anderson, Fred. *Crucible of War.* New York: Vintage Press, 2001.

Anderson, Fred. *The War That Made America.* New York: Viking, 2005.

Axelrod, Alan. *Blooding at Great Meadows.* Philadelphia: Running Press, 2007.

Flexner, James Thomas. *George Washington: The Forge of Experience.* Boston: Little, Brown, 1965.

Flexner, James Thomas. *Washington: The Indispensable Man.* Boston: Little, Brown, 1974. Reprinted 1994.

Freeman, Douglas Southall. *Washington.* New York: Scribner's, 1968.

McCullough, David, *1776.* New York: Simon and Schuster, 2005.

Parkman, Francis. *Montcalm and Wolfe.* Introduction by John Keegan. New York: Modern Library, 1990.

Pennsylvania Historical and Museum Commission. *Young Washington in Pennsylvania.* Harrisburg, PA: Pennsylvania Historical and Museum Commission, 1997.

CHAPTER 6: HORATIO NELSON

Adkins, Roy, and Lesley Adkins. *The War for All the Oceans. From Nelson at the Nile to Napoleon at Waterloo.* New York: Viking, 2007.

Coleman, Terry. *The Nelson Touch: The Life and Legend of Horatio Nelson.* New York: Oxford University Press, 2002.

Hattersley, Roy. *Nelson.* New York: Saturday Review Press, 1974.

Hibbert, Christopher. *Nelson: A Personal History.* Menlo Park, CA: Addison-Wesley, 1994.

Howarth, David. *Lord Nelson.* New York: Atheneum, 1969.

Knight, Roger. *The Pursuit of Victory: The Life and Achievements of Horatio Nelson.* New York: Basic Books, 2005.

Pocock, Tom. *Horatio Nelson.* New York: Knopf, 1998.

Southey, Robert. *Life of Nelson.* Annapolis, MD: Naval Institute Press, 1990.

Warner, Oliver. *Nelson.* Chicago: Follett, 1975.

CHAPTER 7: NAPOLEON BONAPARTE

Asprey, Robert B. *The Rise of Napoleon Bonaparte.* New York: Basic Books, 2000.

Dwyer, Philip. *Napoleon: The Path to Power.* New Haven: Yale University Press, 2007.

McLynn, Frank. *Napoleon: A Biography* New York: Arcade Publishers, 1997.

Schama, Simon. *Citizens: A Chronicle of the French Revolution.* New York: Alfred A. Knopf, 1989.

CHAPTER 8: SIMÓN BOLÍVAR

Lynch, John. *Simón Bolívar: A Life.* New Haven: Yale University Press, 2006.

CHAPTER 9: GIUSEPPE GARIBALDI

Hales, E.E.Y. *Mazzini and the Secret Societies: The Making of a Myth.* New York: P.J. Kenedy & Sons, 1956.

Hibbert, Christopher. *Garibaldi and His Enemies: The Clash of Arms and Personalities in the Making of Italy.* Boston: Little, Brown, 1965.

Parris, John. *The Lion of Caprera: A Biography of Giuseppe Garibaldi.* New York: David McKay Company, 1962.

Sart, Roland. *Mazzini: A Life for the Religion of Politics.* Praeger, 1997.

Smith, Denis Mack. *Garibaldi: A Great Life in Brief.* New York: Alfred A. Knopf, 1956.

CHAPTER 10: ABRAHAM LINCOLN

Burchard, Peter. *Lincoln and Slavery.* New York: Atheneum, 1999.

Donald, David Herbert. *Lincoln.* New York: Simon and Schuster, 1995.

Harrison, Lowell H. *Lincoln of Kentucky.* Lexington, KY: University Press of Kentucky, 2000.

Herndon, William, and Jesse Weik. *Herndon's Lincoln.* Edited by Douglas L. Wilson and Rodney G. Davis. Urbana, IL: University of Illinois Press, 2006.

Sandburg, Carl. *Abraham Lincoln, the Prairie Years.* Pleasantville, NY: The Reader's Digest Association, 1970.

Tarbell, Ida M. *Life of Lincoln.* New York: Macmillan, 1928.

Thomas, Benjamin P. *Abraham Lincoln, A Biography.* New York: Alfred Knopf, 1957.

CHAPTER 11: ULYSSES S. GRANT

Bunting, Josiah III. *Ulysses S. Grant.* New York: Times Books, 2004.

Grant, Ulysses S. *Personal Memoirs of U.S. Grant.* St. Petersburg, FL: Red and Black Press, 2008.

Lewis, Lloyd. *Captain Sam Grant.* Boston: Little, Brown, 1950.

Longacre, Edward G. *General U.S. Grant, the Soldier and the Man.* Cambridge, MA: DaCapo Press, 2006.

McFeely, William S. *Ulysses S. Grant: An Album.* New York: Norton, 2004.

Mosier, John. *Grant.* New York: Palgrave Macmillan, 2006.

Simpson, Brooks D. *Ulysses S. Grant: Triumph Over Adversity, 1822–1865.* Boston: Houghton Mifflin, 2000.

Smith, Jean Edward. *Grant.* New York: Simon & Schuster, 2001.

CHAPTER 12: THEODORE ROOSEVELT

Auchincloss, Louis. *Theodore Roosevelt.* New York: Times Books, 2002.

Braun, Matt. *Dakota.* New York: St. Martin's Press, 2005.

Donald, Aida D. *Lion in the White House: A Life of Theodore Roosevelt.* New York: Basic Books, 2007.

McCullough, David. *Mornings on Horseback.* New York: Simon & Schuster, 2001.

Morris, Edmund. *The Rise of Theodore Roosevelt.* New York: Coward, McCann and Geoghegan, 1979.

Morris, Edmund. *Theodore Rex.* New York: Random House, 2001.

Roosevelt, Teddy. *My Tour of Europe, by Teddy Roosevelt, aged 10.* Edited by Ellen Jackson. Brookfield, CT: Millbrook Press, 2003.

Roosevelt, Theodore. *The Autobiography of Theodore Roosevelt.* New York: Scribner's, 1958.

Roosevelt, Theodore. *Hunting Trips of a Ranchman.* New York: Modern Library, 2004.

Roosevelt, Theodore. *The Rough Riders: An Autobiography.* Edited by Louis Auchincloss. New York: Library of America, 2004.

Roosevelt, Theodore. *The Strenuous Life.* New York: Review of Reviews Company, 1900.

CHAPTER 13: EDITH COWAN

Cowan, Peter. *A Unique Position: A Biography of Edith Dircksey Cowan 1861-1932.* Nedlands W.A.: University of Western Australia Press, 1978.

CHAPTER 14: MOHANDAS GANDHI

Brown, Judith. *Prisoner of Hope.* New Haven: Yale University Press, 1989.

Erikson, Erik H. *Gandhi's Truth.* New York: W.W. Norton & Company. 1969.

Gandhi, Karamchand (Mahatma). *Collected Works of Mahatma Gandhi,* 1st edition. Austin: Greenleaf Books, 1983.

Gandhi, Karamchand (Mahatma). *Gandhi An Autobiography: The Story of My Experiments With Truth.* Boston: Beacon Press, 1993.

Sheean, Vincent. *Lead Kindly Light.* Random House, 1949.

Yap, Melanie, and Dianne Leong Man. *Colour, Confusion and Concessions.* Hong Kong University Press, 1996.

CHAPTER 15: WINSTON CHURCHILL

Churchill, Winston S. *My Early Life: A Roving Commission.* New York: Charles Scribner's Sons, 1930.

D'Este, Carlo. *Warlord. A Life of Winston Churchill at War, 1874–1945.* New York: HarperCollins, 2008.

Gilbert, Martin. *Churchill: A Life.* New York: Holt, 1991.

Jenkins, Roy. *Churchill, A Biography.* New York: Farrar, Straus and Giroux, 2001.

Keegan, John. *Winston Churchill.* New York: Lipper/Penguin, 2002.

Morgan, Ted. *Churchill, Young Man in a Hurry—1874–1915.* New York: Simon and Schuster, 1982.

Woods, Frederick, ed. *Young Winston's Wars. The Original Dispatches of Winston S. Churchill, War Correspondent, 1897–1900.* New York: Viking, 1973.

Ziegler, Philip. *Omdurman.* New York: Alfred A. Knopf, 1974.

CHAPTER 16: ALBERT EINSTEIN

Brian, Denis. *Einstein: A Life.* New York: John Wiley & Sons, 1996.

Einstein, Albert. *Relativity: The Special and General Theory.* Translated by Robert W. Lawson. New York: Henry Holt and Company, 1920

Goldberg, Jake. *Albert Einstein: The Rebel behind Relativity.* Danbury: Franklin Watts, 1996.

Hoffmann, Banesh. *Albert Einstein: Creator and Rebel.* New York: Viking Press, 1972.

Isaacson, Walter. *Einstein: His Life and Universe.* New York: Simon & Schuster, 2008.

Schilpp, Paul. *Albert Einstein: Philosopher-Scientist.* La Salle (IL): Open Court, 1970.

CHAPTER 17: KEMAL ATATÜRK

Aksan, Virginia H. *Ottoman Wars 1700–1870.* Harlow, England: Longman/Pearson, 2007.

Armstrong, H.C. *Grey Wolf: The Life of Kemal Ataturk.* New York: Capricorn, 1961.

Brennan, Kristine. *The First World War and the End of Ottoman Order.* Philadelphia: Mason Crest Publishers, 2007.

Chua, Amy. *Day of Empire.* New York: Doubleday, 2007.

Kiester, Edwin Jr. *An Incomplete History of World War I.* Sydney, Australia: Murdoch Books, 2006.

Kinross, Patrick Balfour, Baron. *Ataturk: A Biography of Mustafa Kemal, Father of Modern Turkey.* New York: Morrow, 1992.

Mango, Andrew. *Ataturk, The Biography of the Founder of Modern Turkey.* Woodstock, NY: Overlook Press, 2000.

Milton, Giles. *Paradise Lost: Smyrna 1922.* New York: Basic Books, 2008.

Moorehead, Alan. *Gallipoli.* New York: Ballantine Books, 1982.

Tachau, Frank. *Kemal Ataturk.* New York: Chelsea House, 1987.

CHAPTER 18: HO CHI MINH

Duiker, William J. *Ho Chi Minh, A Life.* New York: Hyperion, 2000.

Fall, Bernard. *Hell in a Very Small Place.* Philadelphia: Lippincott, 1967.

Fall, Bernard. *Last Reflections on a War.* Foreword by Don Oberdorfer. Mechanicsburg, PA: Stackpole Books, 2000.

Fall, Bernard. *Street Without Joy.* Harrisburg, PA: Stackpole Press, 1967.

Karnow, Stanley. *Vietnam, A History.* New York: Viking Press, 1983.

Lacouture, Jean. *Ho Chi Minh, A Political Biography.* Translated from the French by Peter Wiles. New York: Random House, 1968.

Sheehan, Neil. *A Bright Shining Lie.* New York: Vintage Books, 1989.

CHAPTER 19: CHARLES DE GAULLE

Cook, Don. *Charles DeGaulle, A Biography.* New York: G.P. Putnam's Sons, 1983.

FirstWorldWar.com. "Battles: The Battle of Verdun, 1916." http: www.firstworldwar.com/battles/verdun.htm.

Kiester, Edwin Jr. *An Incomplete History of World War I.* Sydney, Australia, Murdoch Books, 2006.

Lacouture, Jean. *DeGaulle,* 2 vol. Translated from the French by Peter Wiles. New York: Norton, 1990–92.

Ledwidge, Bernard. *DeGaulle.* New York: St. Martin's Press, 1982.

Williams, Charles. *The Last Great Frenchman.* New York: John Wiley & Sons, 1993.

CHAPTER 20: ROSA PARKS

Branch, Taylor. *Parting The Waters.* New York: Simon & Schuster, 1989.

Burns, Stewart. *Daybreak of Freedom: The Montgomery Bus Boycott.* Chapel Hill: University of North Carolina Press, 1997.

Cott, Nancy F. *No Small Courage: A History of Women in the United States.* New York: Oxford University Press, 2000.

Dove, Rita. "Heroes and Icons: Rosa Parks." *Time,* June 14, 1999.

Parks, Rosa, and James Haskins. *Rosa Parks: My Story.* New York: Dial Books, 1992.

"Parks Recalls Bus Boycott, Excerpts from an interview with Lynn Neary." National Public Radio, 1992.

Williams, Donnie, and Wayne Greenhaw. *The Thunder of Angels: The Montgomery Bus Boycott and the People who Broke the Back of Jim Crow.* Chicago: Chicago Review Press, 2005.

CHAPTER 21: JOHN F. KENNEDY

Blair, Joan, and Clay Blair Jr. *The Search for JFK.* New York: Putnam, 1974.

Burns, James McGregor. *John Kennedy.* New York: Harcourt, Brace, 1959.

Dallek, Robert. *An Unfinished Life. John F. Kennedy 1917–1963.* Boston: Little, Brown & Co. 2003.

Donovan, Robert J. *PT-109: John F. Kennedy in World War II.* New York: McGraw-Hill, 1961.

Goodwin, Doris Kearns. *The Fitzgeralds and the Kennedys.* New York: Simon & Schuster, 1987.

Kennedy, John F. *Why England Slept.* New York: Wilfred Funk, 1940.

Perret, Geoffrey. *Jack: A Life Like No Other.* New York: Random House, 2001.

Sorensen, Theodore C. *Kennedy.* New York: Perennial Library, 1988. (Originally published by Harper & Row, 1965.)

White, W.L. *They Were Expendable.* New York: Harcourt, Brace, 1942.

CHAPTER 22: MIKHAIL GORBACHEV

Brown, Archie. *The Gorbachev Factor.* New York: Oxford University Press, 1997.

Evans, David. *Stalin's Russia.* Chicago: Contemporary Books, 2005.

Encyclopedia of European Social History. "Collectivization." New York: Charles Scribners Sons, 2001.

Gorbachev, Mikhail. *Memoirs.* New York: Doubleday, 1996.

Medveded, Zhores A. *Gorbachev.* New York: W.W. Norton, 1986.

ACKNOWLEDGMENTS

First, my thanks to William Edwin Kiester, Fair Winds Press's creative publisher, who conceived the intriguing idea for this book and then invited me to write it. Also my appreciation to Cara Connors, who as developmental editor shepherded it through birth and delivery, and to Larry Shapiro for editorial guidance and smoothing out the sometimes gnarled prose. Sheila Hart, Peter Long, and Daria Perreault deserve thanks for the elegant design.

As always, the research librarians at the Carnegie Library of Pittsburgh and C.C. Mellor Library in Edgewood, Pennsylvania, provided valuable assistance, and were both patient and helpful.

I must also thank Juré Fiorillo and Tom Craughwell for the excellent chapters they contributed.

This is the first book I have ever written without the assistance and advice of my multi-talented collaborator, researcher, adviser, and sharp-eyed critic, my late wife Sally Valente Kiester, Ed.D., but her memory is reflected on every page.

ABOUT THE AUTHOR

Edwin Kiester has written over 2,000 magazine articles and twelve books on subjects ranging from science to history. His most recent books are *An Incomplete History of World War I* and *An Incomplete History of World War II* (both B&N 2007). He is a staff writer for *Smithsonian* magazine.

INDEX

Note: Page numbers in italics indicate figures.

A

abolition, 123
Acadia, 51
Afghanistan, 174, *178–179*, 183
African-Americans, 104–105, 120–129,
  238–247
Africans, 17
the *Agamemnon*, 75, 80
Agincourt, France, 26
Agricultural Institute, 265
Aguirre, José Bolívar, 103
Ajaccio, Corisa, 90
Alabama, 238, 241, 242–243
Albania, 207
Albigensian Crusade, 24
Alexander I, Tsar, 89
Alexandria, Egypt, 82, 89
Algeria, 229
Algonquin tribe, 51, 55
Ali, Haidar, 78
Allegheny Mountains, 65
Allegheny River, 64
Allene, Guillaume, 53–54, 57
Allies. *See also* Anzacs
  in World War I, 208–212, 236
  in World War II, 217, 229
All-India Home Rule League, 167
All Saints' Day, 30
the Alps, 11, 17, 18, *19*
the *Amarigi*, 253–256
American colonies, 98, 105
American Revolutionary War, 60, 63, 78,
  79, 92–93, 94, 98, 105, 114
American Transportation Association, 247
the Americas, 54. *See also specific countries and
  regions*
Amigoni, Jacopo, *9*
the *Amiral Latouche-Trevellis*, 217, 220
Anatolia, Turkey, 203
Andropov, Yury, 265, 270
Andujar, Father, 107
Angostura, Venezuela, 101
Ankara, Turkey, 203, 212
Annam, Vietnam, 216, 220
Anne of Cleves, 39
Antietam, Maryland, 123
anti-Semitism, 195, 197
Anzac Cove, 203, 210
Anzacs, 177, 203, 210
Appalachian Mountains, 62, 64
apparatchiks, 271
Appomattox Court House, 123, 133, 141

Archangel, 267, 270
the Arctic, 75, 78
Ari Burnu, 203, 210
Arkansas, 123
the Armagnacs, 27, 28
Army of the Potomac, 123, 133
Ashley, Kat, 36, 38, 40–41, 42, 43, 44
Asiatic Ordinance, 171, 172–173
Atatürk, (Mustafa) Kemal, 7, 200–213, *201,
  202, 212*
Attlee, Clement, 177
Austerlitz, 89
Australia, 154, 156, 157, 158–163, 210
Australian Parliament, 162–163
Austria, 89, 113, 114, 119. *See also* Austria-
  Hungary
Austria-Hungary, 114, 204, 206, 207,
  208–212. *See also* Austria
Austro-Hungarian Empire. *See* Austria-
  Hungary
Ave Maria, 26
Aventine Hill, 98, 100, 102

B

Baal, 10
the *Badger*, 75, 79
the "Bad Lands", 142
Balearic Islands, 17
the Balkans, 204, 208. *See also specific countries*
Bao Dai, Emperor, 224
Barca, Hamilcar, 8, 10, 11, 12, 13, *20*
Barca, Hannibal, 6, 8–21, *9, 19, 21*
Barca, Hasdrubal, 11, 13–14
Barca clan, 8
Barker, Thomas Jones, *76–77*
the Bastard of Orléans, 30. *See also* Dunois,
  Comte de
Bastien-Lepage, Jules, *23*
Battle, Ensign William, 257
Baudricourt, Robert de, 29
Bay of Fundy, 51
Beale, Joseph Boggs, *121, 126*
Beauharnais, Josephine de, 89
Bedford, Duke of, 27
Belgium, 229, 230
Bello, Andrés, 107
Belloc, Hilaire, 176
Benedict XV, Pope, 25
Benton, Thomas Hart, 151
Bernetti, Cardinal Tommaso, 116
Berry, Captain Edward, 82
Big Berthas, 231
Big Four Powers, 214
Big Horn Mountains, Wyoming, 150
Bilbao, Spain, 107, 109

Billings County, 151
Bishop Hale's School, 158
Biuku Gasa, 258–259, 260, 261
Blackett Strait, 250, 251, 256, 261
Black Hawk War, 123
the Black Sea, 209, 235
Blake, James, 244
Blavet, France, 51, 53
Blenheim Palace, Oxfordshire, England,
  177, 180
Blood, Sir Bindon, 181, *182*, 183
Blum, Léon, 222
Boers, 185–189
Boer War, 167, 171, 177, 185–189
Boggs, Herny, 139
Boleyn, Anne, 38, 39
Bolívar, Simón, 98–109, *99, 105, 108*
Bolívar, Simón de, 102–103
Bolívar family, 102–104
Bolivia, 57, 98, 100, 101, 108
Bolsheviks, 210, 267
Bombay, India, 167
Bonaparte, Jerome, 89
Bonaparte, Joseph, 89, 91
Bonaparte, Louis, 89
Bonaparte, Lucien, 88, 91
Bonaparte, Maria Letizia, 88, 90–91
Bonaparte, Napoleon, 6, 72, 80, 85, 86–97,
  90, 96, 101, 109, 114
Booth, John Wilkes, 123
Bordeaux, France, 91
Borodin, Mikhail, 217, 223
Bosnia-Herzogovina, 204, 207
the "Boston Massacre", 63
the "Boston Tea Party", 63
Boullé, Hélène, 51
Boyacá, Battle of, 101
Braddock, Edward, 63, *70*, 71
Brantingham, Henry, 248, 250
Brazil, 113, 119
Brest, France, 72
Bridges, Richard, *73*
Brienne, 89
the *Bristol*, 75
Britain, Battle of, 177
British Parliament, 174, 177, 180, 185, 189
Brockie, Sergeant Major A., 188
Brookline, Massachusetts, 251
Brouage, France, 51
Brown, Blanche, 154
Brown, Edith. *See* Cowan, Edith
Brown, Kenneth, 154, 156, 157, 158
Brown, Maitland, 154, 156
Brown, Mrs., 154
the Browns, 154

Buchanan, Colonel Robert, 135–136
Buchanan, James, 140
the Buffs, 176
Bulgaria, 203, 208, 209
Bulkeley, John D., 252, 253
Bull Run, First Battle of, 123
Bull Run, Second Battle of, 123
Burgoyne, John, 63
the Burgundians, 25, 27, 28, 33
Burnham Thorpe, Great Britain, 74, 75, 79, 80

C

Cádiz, Spain, 51, 75, 85
Cady, Anne C., *59*
Cairo, Egypt, 89, 96
California, 132, 134–135, 136–137
Calixtus III, Pope, 25
Calvi, Corsica, 75
Calvi, Siege of, 75
Cambodia, 216
Campania, 20
Canada, 48, 51, 52, 63, 64
Canary Islands, 104
Cannae, 11, 20
Canosa, 20
Canton, China, 223
Cape Cod, Massachusetts, 252
Cape Colony, 169, 185, 186
Cape Horn, 78
Cape Saint Vincent, Battle of, 72, *73*, 75, 80
Cape Trafalgar. *See* Trafalgar, Battle of
Caprera, Italy, 113
the *Captain*, 72–85
Carabobo, Venezuela, 101
Caracas, Venezuela, 101, 104, 105–106, 107
the Carbonari, 114
the Caribbean, 51, 78, 104. *See also specific countries*
Carlton Hotel, 221
Carow, Edith, 145
Carow, Edith Kermit, 147–148, 151, 152
Carraciolo, Francesco, 75, 83–84
Carteaux, Jean François, 86, 88, 91, 93–94
Cartegena, Colombia, 101
Carthage, 8–21
Cartier, Jacques, 53
Cathedral of Reims, 25, 32
Catherine, Saint, 24
Catherine of Aragon, 38
Catherine of Valois, 26
the Catholic Church. *See* Catholicism
Catholicism, 25, 38, 50, 51, 52, 58, 98, 102, 104, 107, 114, 116–117. *See also* Christianity
Caucasus, 203, 210
Cauchon, Pierre, Bishop of Beauvais, 33
Celtiberians, 13, 17
Celts, 12
Central America, 55. *See also specific countries*
Central Power, 208–212

"Certificate of Whiteness", 104
Chamberlain, Neville, 177
Champaubert, 89
Champlain, Samuel de, *52*
Chancellorsville, Virginia, 123
Chapultepec, Mexico, 132
Chargeurs-Reunis steamship company, 219–220
Charles, Napolean Francis, 89
Charles, South Carolina, 123
Charles "Le Dauphin", 25, 28–30, 32–33. *See also* Charles VII, King
Charleston, South Carolina, 140–141
Charles V, King, 27
Charles VI, King, 26, 27
Charles VII, King, 25, 29, *31*, 32–33
Chernenko, Konstantin, 270
Chestnut Hill, Massachusetts, 148–149
Chiang Kai-shek, 217, 223
Children's Court, 157
Children's Protection Society, 157, 160
children's rights, 157, 162
China, 216, 217, 223, 224
Chinese immigrants, 136–137
Chinon palace, 25, 28, 29
Choate School, 251
Choiseul Island, 261
Christianity, 105, 114, 116–117. *See also* Catholicism; Protestantism
Churchill, Clementine. *See* Hozier, Clementine
Churchill, Jennie Jerome, 177, 180, 181
Churchill, John, 180
Churchill, Sir Randolph, 177, 180
Churchill, Winston, 6, 174–189, *175*, 209
The River War, 185
The Story of the Malakand Field Force, 183, 184
the Churchills, 177, 180–181, *186*
civil rights, 157, 160–163, 164–173, 238–247
Civil Rights Movement, 238–247
Clinton, Bill, 241
La Clorinda, 110
Clovis, King, 32
Cochin China, 216, 219
cochineal, 55–56, 57
collectivization, 264–269, *269*
Coloma, Don Francisco, 54
Colombey-les-Deux-Eglises, 229
Colombia, 98, 100, 101, 108, 109
Columbia River, 134
Columbia Valley, 134
the Comintern, 217
Commission of Youth Affairs, 265
Committee for Unity and Progress (CUP), 203, 204, 207
Committee of Public Safety, 86, 92, 93, 94
Commonwealth of Independent States, 265
Communism, 217, 221–223, 224, 262–271
Communist Party of the Soviet Union (CPSU), 262, 265, 271

Compiègne, France, 25, 33
Concord, Massachusetts, 63
the Confederacy, 123, 128, 133, 140–141
Confucian learning system, 218
Congressional Gold Medal, 241, 247
Conkling, Roscoe, 147
Conservative Party, 177, 180, 185
Constantinople, 203, 204, 205, 209, 210, 212. *See also* Istanbul
the Constitutional Convention, 63
Conyers, John, 241
coolies, 166, 168
Copenhagen, Battle of, 75
Cornwallis, Lord Charles, 63, 92–93
Coro, Venezuela, 104–105
Corsica, 10, 11, 12, 75, 80, 88, 89, 91
Cowan, Agnes, 158
Cowan, Blanche, 157
Cowan, Dircksey, 157
Cowan, Edith, 154, *154*, 154–163, *158*
Cowan, James, 157, *158*, 158–159
Crécy, France, 27
Creoles, 104, 105–106, 109
Cuba, 145, 153
Cumberland, Earl of, 54
Cumberland, Maryland. *See* Wills Creek, Maryland
Cumberland River, 141
Custis, Martha Dandridge, 63
Cyrenaica (Libya), 203, 208

D

the *Daily Graphic*, 181
the *Daily Telegraph*, 183
Dakota Territory, 142, 145, 149, 150
Damascus, Syria, 210
d'Anjou, Marie, 28
the *Dannebrog*, 85
Danube River, 226, 235
d'Arc, Jacques, 24, 25, 26
d'Arc, Jeanne. *See* Joan of Arc
the Dardanelles, 209, 210
da Silva, Ana Ribeiro da, 113
Davis, Jefferson, 141
D-Day, 229
de Champlain, Samuel, 48–59, *49*, *55*, *59*
A Brief Discourse of the Most Remarkable Things that Samuel de Champlain of Brouge Reconnoitered in the West Indies, 57
the Declaration of Independence, 63, 225
de Gaulle, Charles, 226–237, *227*, *234*
de Gaulle, Henri, 228, 229
de Gaulle, Xavier, 228
Delaware River, 63
Delaware tribe, 60
Democratic Party, 149
Denmark, 75, 84–85
Dent, Colonel Frederick, 132, 136–137, 139
Dent, Julia Boggs, 132, 133, 135, 137, 139, *139*, *141*

Dervishes, 184–185. *See also* Mahdists
de Sainte-Pierre, Jacques Lepardeur, 64–65
Desaix, Louis, 94
Detroit, Michigan, 241
de Vauban, Sébastien Le Prestre, 92
diamond mines, 185
Dickinson, Dakota Territory, 152
Dien Bien Phu, Vietnam, 217, 225
Dinant Bridge, Battle of, 229, 230
Dinwiddie, Governor Robert, 62, 64, 65, 66–67, 71
Dommartin, Captain Elzeár, 86
Domrémy, France, 22–35
Donovan, Robert J., 261
Doppet, François-Amédée, 94
Douaumont, France, 233–234
double-envelopment strategy, 20
Douglas, Stephen A., 123, 140
Dow, Wilmot, 150, 152
Draper, T.P., 162, *163*
Dresden, Germany, 75
Duchesne, Madam, 125–126
the Duchy of Lucca, 112
the Duchy of Modena, 112, 114
the Duchy of Parma, 112, 114
Ducret, Captain, 226, 228
Dugommier, Jacques, 94, 95, 96, 97
Dundas, David, 92, 93
Dunois, Comte de, 30–31
Duroc, Géraud Christophe Michel, 94
Dutch East Indies, 223, 252

E

East Indies, 75, 78
Ebro River, 15
Ecole Militaire, St. Cyr, 228, 229
Ecuador, 98, 100, 101, 108, 109
Eden, Anthony, 177
Edwards, Leona, 241
Edwards, Sylvester, 240, 243
Edward VI, King, 36, 39, 41, 43, 45, 46
Edward VII, King, 183, 206
Egypt, 74, 82, 89, 96, 184, 185, 202
Einstein, Albert, 190–199, *191*, *192*, *199*
  Relativity, 196
Einstein, Elsa. *See* Löwenthal, Elsa
Einstein, Hermann, 190, 192
Einstein, Maja (Marie), 192, *192*
Einstein, Margot, *197*
Einstein, Mileva. *See* Maric, Mileva
Einstein, Pauline, 190, 192
Elba, 89
Elizabeth I, Queen, 36–47, *37*, *44*, *46*
Elkhorn Ranch, 142, 150, 151
Emancipation Proclamation, 128
Empire Theatre, 171
Eroni Kumana, 260, 261
Escoffier, Auguste, 221
España, José María, 105

Estcourt, South Africa, 186
Evans, Arthur Reginald, 256, *257*, 257–258, 259–260
Everest, Elizabeth, 180

F

Fabius Maximus, 15–16
Fairfax, Lord Thomas, 60, 63, 64
the Falkland Islands, 78
the "Father of the Waters", 62
Fay, Paul, *255*
Federal Institute of Technology, 193, 194–195
Ferdinand II, King, 82, 83
Ferris, Sylvane, 153
Financial Panic of 1857, 137–138, *138*, 139
Finnegan, Red, 152
First Balkan War, 203
First Continental Congress, 63
First Punic War, 8, 12
Five-Year Plan, 267
flatboats, *126*, 126–127
Fontainebleau, France, 217
Forbes, John, 63, 71
Forks of the Ohio, 62, 64, 65, 71
Fort Donelson, 133, 141
Fort Douaumont, 229
Fort Duquesne, 65, 66, 71
Fort Henry, 141
Fort Humboldt, 135
Fort IX, 226, 228, 235, 237
Fort LeBoeuf, Pennsylvania, 63, 64, 68–69
Fort L'Eguillette, 94, 96
Fort Machault, Pennsylvania, 64
Fort Mulgrave, 94
Fort Necessity, 63, 70, 71
Fort Pitt, 71
Fort Presque Isle, 64
Fort San Juan, 79
Fort Sumter, 123, 133, 140–141
Fort Vancouver, 134
Fouché, Joseph, 97
the Fourteen Points, 214
France, 22–35, 51, 98, 104, 119, 177, 207
  England and, 26–27
  in the Franco-Prussian War, 113, 231
  Indochina and, 216–225
  Napolean and, 86–97
  in North America, 55–58, 62–69
  Spain and, 53, 72–85
  in World War I, 208–212, 226, 228, 230–237
  in World War II, 217, 223–225, 229, 237
Franco-Prussian War, 113, 231
Fredericksburg, Virginia, 123
Free French, 229, 237
Free South Africa Movement, 247
Frémont, John C., 140
French and Indian War, 66
French Communist Party, 217, 222
French Creek, 64

French Indochina, 214–225
French Revolution, 72–85, 88, 98, 104, 114, 221
French Socialist Party (FSP), 217, 221
Fresch, Joseph, 91
Frobisher, Martin, 53
Fry, Major Joshua, 65

G

Gades (Cádiz, Spain), 12, 13, 14
Galena, Illinois, 140
Gallic tribes, 20
Gallipoli, Turkey, 177, 203, 209, 210
Gandhi, Gopalkrishna, 173
Gandhi, Mohandas, 6, 7, 164–173, *165*, *166*, *170*
Garabaldi, Angelo, 112
Garibaldi, Domenico, 112, 113, 118
Garibaldi, Giuseppe, 110–119, *111*, *117*, *118–119*
Garibaldi, Rosa Raimondi, 112, 113, 118
Gascony, France, 27
Gaul, 18, *19*
Geneva, Switzerland, 217, 225, 265
Genoa, Italy, 113, 117, 118
Gentry, Allen, 123
Gentry, James, 124, 125, *126*, 126, 127
George, David Lloyd, 177, 212
George II, King, 62
Georgia (country), 264
Geraldton, Australia, 156
Germany, 177, 206, 208, 229
  in World War I, 208–212, 226, 228, 230–237
  in World War II, 217, 223, 251
Gettysburg, Pennsylvania, 123
Gettysburg Address, 123
La giovine Italia, 114
Girondins, 88
Gist, Christopher, 64
Gizo Island, 258
glasnost, 265, 271
Glengarry, Australia, 156, 157, 158
"goddams", 27
gold mines, 136–137, 185
the Gold Rush, 132, 134–135
Gomu Island, 261
Gopkalo, Pantelei, 262, 264, 269–271
Gopkalo, Vailisa, 262
Gorbachev, Aleksandr, 267
Gorbachev, Mikhail, 262–271, *263*, *270*, *271*
Gorbachev, Raisa. *See* Titorenko, Raisa Maximovna
Gordon, Charles, 183–184
the Grand Duchy of Tuscany, 112
Grand National Assembly, 203
Grant, Buck. *See* Grant, Ulysses Jr.
Grant, Frederick, 132, *141*
Grant, Jesse, 140
Grant, Julia Dent. *See* Dent, Julia Boggs
Grant, Orvil, 141

Grant, Ulysses Jr., 132
Grant, Ulysses S., 123, 130–141, *131*, *141*
Great Britain, 12, 36–47, 89, 92–93, 98, 160, 177
  in Afghanistan, *178–179*, 183
  in Africa, 167, 169, 172, 177, 183–189
  in the Boer War, 167, 177, 185–189
  Bolívar and, 101
  France and, 26–31
  in the Hundred Years' War, 26–31, 33
  in India, 181, 183
  in North America, 62–69
  Ottoman Empire and, 202, 204, 206
  in the Siege of Toulon, 95–97
  in South Africa, 167, 169, 172
  Spain and, 72–85
  in Sudan, 183–185
  in World War I, 208–212
  in World War II, 177
the Great Meadows, 66–67
the Great Powers, 206–207
the Great War. *See* World War I
Greco-Turkish War, 206
Greece, 202, 203, 206, 207, 210, 212
Greeks, 13, 210
Greeley, Horace, 128
Greenwich, England, 39
Gregory XVI, Pope, 116
Guadalcanal Island, 248
Guadeloupe, 54
Gual, Manuel, 105
Guam, 252
Gujarat, India, 167
the gulag, 264, *266*, 268, 270

H

Hafiz, Kaymak, 200
Haiti. *See* Saint-Domingue
the Haitian Revolution, 104, 114
Haldane, Captain Aylmer, 186, 188
the "Half-King", 62, 66, 67
Hamburg, Germany, 75, 85
Hamilton, Horatia, 83
Hamilton, Lady Emma, 74, 75, *83*, 83, 84
Hamilton, Sir William, 75
Hamilton, William, 83
Hanami, Commander Kohei, 253, 254
Hanks, John, 127, 128
Hannibal of Carthage. *See* Barca, Hannibal
Hanno clan, 8
Hanoi, Vietnam, 216, 217, 219, 225
Hapsburg, Marie-Louise von, 89
Hapsburg Empire. *See* Austro-Hungarian Empire
Hardin County, Kentucky, 122
Hardscrabble, 137, 139
Harrison, Benjamin, 152–153
Harrow School, 177, 181
Harvard College, 145, 149, 251, 252
Hatfield, England, 36
Havana, Cuba, 145

Hayes, Rutherford B., 147
the *Heavenly Mist. See* the *Amarigi*
Henry IV, King, 51, 55, *56*, 57–58
Henry V, King, 26
Henry VI, King, 27
Henry VIII, King, 38, 39, 40, 41
Herndon, William, 127, *128*–129
Hessian troops, 63
Hillingford, Robert Alexander, *45*
the *Hinchinbrook*, 75, 79
Hiroshima, Japan, 225
Hitler, Adolf, 197
Hoang Tru, Vietnam, 216, 217
Ho Chi Minh, 214–225, *219*, *222–223*
Ho Chi Minh City, Vietnam, 225. *See also* Saigon, Vietnam
Hodgenville, Kentucky, 123
Hodges, Henry, 135
Holland. *See* the Netherlands
the Homestead Act, 123
Hong Kong, China, 217, 223
Hood, Samuel, 92, 96
House, Edward, 216
House of Burgesses, 63
House of Commons, 84, 184
Howard, Catherine, 39, 40
Howard, John, 189
howitzers, 132
Hozier, Clementine, 177
Hughes, Victor, 176
Hull, Cordell, 224
Humanitarian Award, 247
Humboldt, Alexander von, 106
Hundred Years' War, 26–27, 28, 33
Huron tribe, 51, 55
Hussar Regiment, 177, 181, 183

I

the Iberian Peninsula, 13–14, 72. *See also* Spain
Illinois, 123
the Illinois militia, 133
immigrants' rights, 157
India, 78, 82, 166, 173, 174, 177, 181, 183
Indian Ambulance Corps, 167
Indian Franchise Bill, 168–169
Indians, 48–59, *49*, 78, *103*, 104–105, 136. *See also specific tribes*
Indochina, 214–225
Indochinese Communist Party, 217
Ingolstadt, Germany, 226, 228, 235, 237
the Inquisition, 25, 50, *52*
Institute for Advanced Studies, 193, 197
International Conference for Women, 163
Iraq, 212
Ireland, 81–82
Iron Curtain, 271
Iroquois Confederacy, 60
Iroquois tribe, 51, 55, 60, 62, 66
Isabeau of Bavaria, Prince, 27

Istanbul, 208–209, 212. *See also* Constantinople
Isthmus of Panama, 57, 134
Italian peninsula, 10, 11, 18, *19*, 110–119
Italo-Turkish War, 203
Italy, 82, 89, 92, 93, 94
  Ottoman Empire and, 203, 210
  reunification of, 110–119
  in World War II, 217, 251
Izmir, 210. *See also* Smyrna

J

Jacobins, 88, 90, 91, 92, 97
Jamaica, 101
Jamaica Letter, 106
James I, King, 39, 46
Jameson raid, 186
Japan, 177
  in Indochina, 217, 223–225
  in World War II, 217, 223, 224–225, 248, 251–256
Jefferson, Thomas, 108
Jena, Germany, 89
Jervis, Sir John, 72–73, 80–81
Jesuits, 53. *See also* missionaries
Jim Crow laws, 244, 245
Joan of Arc, 6, 22–35, *23*, *34*
Johannesburg, South Africa, 167, 171
John, King, 27
Johnson, Andrew, 123
Johnston, Sarah bush, 123
Jordan, 212
Jumonville, Joseph Coulon de, 66, 69
Junot, Jean-Andoche, 94

K

Kaiser Wilhelm Institute, 196
Karrakatta Club, 157, 159, 160, *161*, 162
Kavu, Benjamin, 261
Keith, Lord, 84
Kennedy, John F., 7, 248–261, *249*, *255*
  Why England Slept, 251, 252
Kennedy, Joseph Patrick, 251, 252
Kennedy, Rose Fitzgerald, 251
the Kennedy family, 252
Kentucky, 122, 128
KGB, 265
King, Martin Luther Jr., 243, 246
the Kingdom of the Two Sicilies, 112, *118–119. See also* Sicily
King Edward Memorial Hospital for Women, 157
Kings Park, 163
Kipling, Rudyard, 176
Kitchener, Horatio Herbert, 184, 185
kolkhoz, 262, 264, *269*
Kolombangara Island, 253, 256
Kosovo, Albania, 207
Kruger, "Oom Paul", 185–186
Ku Klux Klan, 238, 240, *242*, 242–243
kulaks, 268, 269
Kumana, Eroni, 258–259

Kuomintang nationalist party, 223–225
Kuwait, 212

L

Lachine Rapids, 51
Ladysmith, South Africa, 186
Lake Erie, 64
Lake Huron, 51
Lake Ontario, 51
Lake Trasimeno, 11, 20
Lancers, 177, 184–185
Laos, 216
Lapoype, Jean François Cornu de, 92, 94, 96
Lasinio, Carlo, *92*
Lassois, Durand, 28–30
the "last great cavalry charge", 177, 183–185
La Valette, France, 90–91
League of Nations, 212
Lebanon, 212
Lee, Alice Hathaway, 145, *148*, 148, *148*, 148–149, 153
Lee, George Cabot, 148
Lee, Robert E., 123, 132, 133
Lefevre, Robert, *96*
Leigh, Vivien, 83
Leipzig, 89
Lenin, Vladimir, 222
Leninism, 271
the Levant, 82
Lexington, Massachusetts, 63
L'Humanité, 216, 221
Liberal Party, 177
Libya, 13, 17
Liebenow, William, 261
Liguria, Italy, 113
Ligurians, 13
Lille, France, 228, 229
Liman von Sanders, Otto, 209, 210
Lincoln, Abraham, 6, 119, 120–129, *121*, *126*, 133, 140
Lincoln, Mary Todd. *See* Todd, Mary
Lincoln, Nancy Hanks, 123, 124
Lincoln, Thomas, 123, 124
Lithuania, 235
Little Missouri, 151
Little Missouri River, 151–152
Little Mount Baptist Church, 124
Little Pigeon Creek, 124
Loan, 218
Locke, John, 107
Lodge, Henry Cabot Jr., 251
Loire Valley, 25, 28
Lombardy-Venetia, 112, 114
London, Great Britain, 74
Long, C.J., 186
Long, John D., 153
Longstreet, James, 132
Louisiana, 120, 121, 125, 127, 128
Louis XV, King, 65
Louis XVI, King, 80, 88, 92

Löwenthal, Elsa, 193, 196, *197*
the *Lowestoffe*, 75, 79
Lubeck, port of, 85
Lucca, Italy, 112
Lunacharsky, A.V., 198
lynchings, 243, 244
Lyon, France, 91

M

MacArthur, Douglas, 252
Macedonia, 200–213
Madhists, 184–185
Madrid, Spain, 89, 105–106
the *Maine*, 145, 153
Mainz, Germany, 235
Maisen, Louis Edouard, 220
Makhanji, Kastruba, 167
Malakand Field Force, 174, 177, *178–179*, 183
Malta, 82, 89
Maltese Cross, 150
Manastir, Macedonia, 203, 205
Mandan, 152
Mango, Andrew, 210
Manhattan, New York, 149–150
Manila, Phillipines, 252
Manund Valley, 183
Margaret, Saint, 24
Maria Carolina, Queen, 83
Maric, Mileva, 193
Marie Antoinette, 80, 83
Marlowe, Christopher, 46
Marmont, Auguste de, 94
the Marne, Battle of, 230
Marques, Domngo, *16–17*
Marseille, France, 91, 92, 117, 217, 220. *See also* Massilotes (Marseille, France)
Marxism, 222. *See also* Communism
Mary, Queen of Scots, 39, 41, 45, 46
Massiolotes (Marseille, France), 14–15, 18
Mazzini, Giuseppe, 113, *114*, 114, 115, 116–117, 119
McCauley, Edward, 241
McCauley, Rosa. *See* Parks, Rosa
McCauley family, 238, 240, 241
McClellan, George, 123
McKinley, William, 145, 153
McMahon, Patrick, 255, 256, 257, 258
Meade, George, 123
Mediterranean Sea, 10, 11, 12, 14–15, 74, 80, 82, 209
Mekong Delta, 216, 219
Melbourne, Australia, 156
Meliart shrine, 10
Mendela, Nelson, 173
Messina, Italy, 17
Meuse River, 230
Meuse River Valley, 22, 25, 27
Mexican-American War, 123, 132, 133, 136, 139, 140

Mexico, 48, 50, 51, 52, 53–54, 55, 136. *See also* Mexican-American War; New Spain
Mexico City, Mexico, 132
Michael the Archangel, Saint, 24
Million Man March, 241
Mingusville, 142
Minorca, 84
missionaries, 104. *See also* Jesuits
Mississippi River, 62, 124, 125, *126*, 127
Missouri, 136
the *Missouri*, 177, 251
Modena, Italy, 112, 114
Monongahela River, 64, 65–66
Montagnais tribe, 51
Montagnards, 88
Montana territory, 142
Montauban hill, 86, 93
Montereau, France, 89
Monte Sacro, 98
Montgomery, Alabama, 241, 243–247
Montgomery bus boycott, 241, 245–246, *247*
Montgomery Bus Company, 244–246
Montgomery Improvement Association (MIA), 246
Montmirail, France, 89
Montreal, Canada, 51
the *Morning Post*, 177, 184, 186, 189
Moscow, Russia, 89, 217, 222–223, 265
Moscow University, 265, 270
Mount Byrsa, 10
Mount Faron, 92, 94–97
Mount Magnet, 156
Mount McGregor, New York, 133
Mount Rushmore, 144, 153
Mount Vernon, Virginia, 63
Muhammad V, Sultan, 204, 205
Muhammad VI, Sultan, 212
Murat, Joachim, 89
Murchison River, 156
Mysore, 78

N

Nagasaki, Japan, 225
Naples, Italy, 75, 82–83, 84, 85, 89, 92, 119
Napoleonic Wars, 185
Nashville, Tennessee, 141
Natal, South Africa, 167, 168–169, 172, 185
Natal Congress, 168–169
Natal Indian Congress, 167, 169, *170*
Natal Supreme Court, 169
National Assembly, 229
National Association for the Advancement of Colored People (NAACP), 241, 243, 245–246
the Nations, Battle of, 89
Nauru Island, 256–261
Navy and Marine Corps Medal, 251
Navy Medal, 261
Nazi Party, 197
Neisse, Germany, 235
Nelson, Lord Horatio, 72–85, *76–77*, 89

"Nelson Touch", 74, 82
the Netherlands, 78, 89, 169, 229
Nevis, 75, 79
New Amsterdam, 144
New Carthage, 11, 14
New France, 50, 52–53, 57–58, 64, 65
New Georgia Sound, 248
New Granada, 101
New Jersey, 63
New Orleans, Louisiana, 120, *121*, 124, 127, 128
New South Wales, Australia, 162
New Spain, 53–54, 55–56, 57. *See also* Mexico
Newton, Isaac, 194
New York, 63, 149–150, 152–153
New York City, 149–150, 152–153
New York Tribune, 128
New Zealand, 210
Ney, Marchal Michel, 89
Ngo Dinh Diem, 217, 225
Nguyen Sinh Cung, 217. *See also* Ho Chi Minh
Nguyen Sinh Sac, 216
Nguyen Tat Tranh, 214, 216. *See also* Ho Chi Minh
Nicaragua, 79
Nice, France, 112, 118
Nicholas II, Tsar, 206
the Nile, 183, 184. *See also* the Nile, Battle of
the Nile, Battle of, 74, 82–83, 84, 89
Nisbet, Frances, 75, 79
Nisbet, Josiah, 81
Nixon, Richard, 225, 251
NKVD, 264, 269
nonviolence. *See* passive resistance
Norfolk, Great Britain, 74, 75
the Norman conquest, 26
Normandy, France, 177, 229
North Africa, 10, 207, 208. *See also specific countries*
North America, 48–59, 60–71. *See also specific countries*
North Carolina, 123
North Fremantle Board of Education, 160
North Vietnam, 217, 225
Northwestern University, 252, 253
North-West Frontier Agency, 181
Northwest Passage, 53
Numidian cavalry, 13, 17, 20
Nuremberg, Germany, 237
"Nyugen Ai Quoc". *See* Ho Chi Minh
Nyugen Sinh Cung, 218
Nyugen Sinh Sac, 216, 218

O
October Revolution, 267
OGPU (Unified State Political Administration), 268–269
O'Hara, Charles, 92–93, 94–95
Ohio, 133, 134
Ohio Country, 62, 63, 64, 65, 69, 71

Ohio River, 62, 64, 123, 124, 128
Olasana Island, 258, 259, 260, 261
Oldham, Great Britain, 185
Olivier, Laurence, 83
Omdurman, Sudan, 177, 185
Onslow, Lady Madeline, 159–160
Orange Free State, 169, 185
Oregon Territory, 134
L'Orient, 82
Orléans, Battles at, 25, 30–31, *32*, 33
Orléans, France, 25, 30–31, *32*, 33
Ostwald, Wilhelm, 195
Ottawa River, 51
Ottoman Empire, 200–213
Oyster Bay, New York, 152, 153

P
pacificism, 199
Pakistan, 174
Palacios, Carlos, 106–107
Palacios, Esteban, 106
Palestine, 203, 212
Palestrina, Italy, 113
Panama, 51, 57, 98, 100, 101, 108, 109, 134
Panama Canal, 145
the Papacy, 116–117
the Papal States, 112, 113, 114, 115, 119
pardos, 104–105
Paris, France, 86, 92, 223
Paris, Martial de (aka Auvergne), *32*
Parker, Hyde, 84
Parker, Peter, 79
Parks, Raymond, 241, 243, 245
Parks, Rosa, 238–247, *245*, *247*
    Rosa Parks: My Story, 241
Parma, Italy, 112, 114
Parr, Catherine, 39, 40–41
Parry, Tom, 36, 38, 41, 42, 43, 44
Pasha, Enver, 207, 208, 208–209, *209*, 210
passive resistance, 169, 171–173
Patented Bridge for Boarding First-Rates, 74, 80
Paternoster, 26
Pathans, 176, *178–179*, 183
Patrois, Isidore, *34*
le paturage, 22
Paul, Tsar, 84–85
Paul III, Pope, 54–55
Peale, Charles Wilson, *67*
Pearl Harbor, 177, 217, 251, 252
Pennsylvania, 60–71
perestroika, 265, 271
Perth, Australia, 154, 156, 157, 158–159, 162
Peru, 57, 98, 100, 101, 108, 109
Petain, Henri-Philippe, 228, 232
Peter the Great, Tsar, 110
Phan Van Truong, 216
Philip IV, King, 27
Philip of Valois, Count, 27
Phillipines, 252
Phoenicia, 10, 12

Phoenicians, 12
Pietermaritzburg Station, 164, 167
Pigeon Creek settlement, Illinois, 123, 124
Pine Level, Alabama, 238, 243
Pius X, Pope, 25, 35
plantations, 122, 125, 136–137
Plum Pudding Island, 256–257, 258
Poeni, 12
Point Pleasant, Ohio, 133
Poitiers, France, 27
Poland, 217, 229, 251
Politburo, 265, 270, 271
Pope, John, 123
Popular Front, 222
Po River, 20
Portobello, Panama, 57
Port Royal, 51
Portugal, 78, 89
Pourbus, Frans II, *56*
Prague, Czechoslovakia, 75
Presidential Medal of Freedom, 247
Pretoria, Transvaal, 164, 166, 168–169, 172, 188
Princeton, New Jersey, 197–198
Privol'noye, Stavropol, USSR, 264, 266, 270–271
the Privy Council, 39, 41, 43, 46
Protestantism, 50, 58. *See also* Christianity
Prussia, 89, 231
PT boats, 248, 250, 251, 252–253, 254–261
Publius Cornelius Scipio, 18
La Pucelle, 32
Puerto Rico, 54
the Pyramids, Battle of, 89
Pyrenees Mountains, 11, 15

Q
Quebec, Canada, 51
Quebec City, Canada, 51
the *Queen Elizabeth*, 51, 209–210
Quintus Fabius Maximus, 20

R
racism, 104–105, 166, 167, 168, 171, 238–247. *See also* segregation
the *Raisonnable*, 74, 75
Reagan, Ronald, 265
redcoats, 63
the Red River Delta, 216
Redstone Creek, Pennsylvania, 65–66
Reed, Jim, *255*
the Reformation, 50
Regulus, 12
the Reign of Terror, 80, 91, 104
Reims, France, 32–33
Rendova, 261
Republican Party, 123, 147, 149
Revel (Tallinn, Estonia), 206
Revere, Paul, 63
revolution, 116
Rheims, 89

the Rhone River, 18, 20
Richmond, Virginia, 141
Ripanda, Jacopo, *21*
the Risorgimento, 119
Robespierre, Maximilien, 91, 92, 97
Rock of Gibraltar, 12
Rodríguez, Simón, 98, 100, 101, 107, 109
Rodríguez del Toro y Alayza, Maria Teresa, 101, 107, 109
Roman Empire, 8–21, 10–11, 102
Roman Senate, 102
Rome, Italy, 75, 89, 98, 100, 102, 112, 113, 114, 115, 119. *See also* Roman Empire
Romée, Isabelle, 24, 25, 26
Roosevelt, Alice Hathaway. *See* Lee, Alice Hathaway
Roosevelt, Alice Lee, 145, 150
Roosevelt, Anna, 144
Roosevelt, Bamie, 150
Roosevelt, Corrine, 144
Roosevelt, Edith. *See* Carow, Edith
Roosevelt, Eleanor, 144
Roosevelt, Elliott, 144, 146, 147, 149, 150
Roosevelt, Franklin D., 224
Roosevelt, Franklin Delano, 144
Roosevelt, Martha "Mittie" Bulloch, 145, 147–148, 150
Roosevelt, Theodore, 142–153, *143*, *151*
Hunting Trips of a Ranchman, 151
The Naval War of 1812. See Carow, Edith
Roosevelt, Theodore Jr., 145
Roosevelt, Theodore Sr., 145, 147
the "Roosevelt Bill", 149, 150
the Roosevelts, 144
Rosa and Raymond Parks Institute for Self Development, 241, 247
Rosa Parks Day, 247
Rosenberg, Franconia, 237
Ross, Ensign George, 250, 258, 259, 260
Rouen, France, 25, 35
Rough Riders, *143*, 145, 153
Rousseau, Jean-Jacques, 105, 107, 108
Roviana Island, 261
royalists, 80, 83–84, 86–97
Royal Military Academy at Sandhurst, 177, 181
Royal Privy Council, 36
Royal Scots Fusiliers, 177
Royal Western Australian Historical Society, 157
Ruffo, Cardinal Fabrizio, 83
Rumsfeld, Donald, 68
Russia, 84–85, 89, 210
Ottoman Empire and, 203, 206
under Stalinism, 262–271
in World War I, 208–212, 231, 236, 269
Russian Provisional Government, 267
Russo-Japanese War, 145
Ryder, Dr. Emily, 159

S
Sagamore Hill, New York, 145, 152, 153
Saguenay River, 51
Saguntum, Battle of, 14–17, *16–17*
Saguntum (Sagunto), 11, 15
Saigon, Vietnam, 216, 219–220, 225
Saigon River, 219
Saint-Domingue, 104, 114
the *Saint-Julien*, 53, 54
Saint Lawrence River, 51
Saint-Maximin, France, 91
Saint Vincent, Lord, 80–81, 84. *See also* Jervis, Sir John
Sakarya, Battle of, 203
Saliceti, Antonio Cristofor, 91, *92*, 97
Salonika, Macedonia, 200, 203, 204, 205
Saltonstall, Dick, 148
Saltonstall family, 148
San Cosme Church, 132
San Cosme *garita*, 132
San Francisco, California, 134, 135
Sangamon River, 123, 124, 125
the *San Jose*, 74
the *San Josef*, *76–77*
San Juan Hill, Cuba, 145, 153
San Mateo, Venezuela, 103
the *San Nicolas*, 74
Santa Cruz de Tenerife, Canary Islands, 75, 81
Santa Marta, Venezuela, 101
the *Santissima Trinidad*, 72
Sarah, Countess of Essex, *40*
Saratoga, New York, 63
Sardinia, 10, 11, 12, 112, 119
satyagraha, 169, 171–173
satyagrahi. See satyagraha
Schaffhausen, Germany, 228, 235, 237
Schlieffen Plan, 20
Scipio Africanus, 11, 21
Scottsboro Boys, 243
Sea of Azov, 110
secession, 123, 133, 140
Secessio plebes, 98, 102
Second Balkan War, 203, 208
Second Continental Congress, 63
Second Punic War, 11
segregation, 167–172, 244–247
Sepoy Mutiny, 174
Serbia, 203, 207, 208
Seven Days Campaign, 123
Seven Years' War, 66
Sewall, Bill, 150, 152
Seymour, Edward, 41, 43
Seymour, Jane, 39, 40
Seymour, Lord Thomas, 36, *40*, 40–41, 42, 43, 44–45
the Seymour Affair, 36–47
Shakespeare, William, 46
Shaw, George Bernard, *Saint Joan*, 33
Shawnee tribe, 60
Shenandoah Valley, Virginia, 63

Sherman, William Tecumseh, 123
Sicily, 11, 12, 75, 82, 112, *118–119*
Sikhs, 174, 176
Six-Fours hill, 93
Six Nations, 60
slavery, *121*, 127, *129*
in the United States, 120–129, 132, 136–137, 240
in Venezuela, 104–105, *108*
the Slot, 256
Smuts, Jan, 172
Smyrna, 210, 212
Socialism, 216, 217, 221, 271
Social Questions Committee, 160
Sofia, Bulgaria, 203, 208, 209
Solomon Islands, 253, 254–261, *255*, *259*
the South, 140–141, 238–247. *See also* the Confederacy; *specific states*
South Africa, 164–173, 185–189
South America, 53, 57, 98–109, 113, 119, 171. *See also specific countries*
South Australia, 162
South Carolina, 68–69, 123, 133, 140–141
South Carolina militia, 68–69
the South Pacific, 248–261, *259. See also specific islands*
South Vietnam, 217, 225
the Southwest Passage, 53, 55, 57
the Soviet Union. *See* Russia
Spain, 11, 13, 21, 89, 180. *See also* the Iberian peninsula
in the Americas, 48, 51, 53–55, 57, 98–109, *103*, *143*, 145, 153
France and, 72, 74–75, 78–79, 81, 85
Spanish-American War, *143*, 145, 153
Spanish-American War, *143*, 145, 153
the Spanish Armada, 39
Speed, Joshua, 128
Springfield, Illinois, 123
Staff College, 203, 205
Stalin, Joseph, 262, 264, 266, 267, 268, 270
Stalinism, 262–271
State Emergency Committee, 271
State Model School, 188
Stavropol, USSR, 264, 266, 270–271
St. George's Reading Circle, 159
St. Helena, 89
St. Louis, Missouri, 137, 139
Stockmens' Association, 151
Subic Bay, 252
Suchet, Louis-Gabriel, 94
Suckling, Sir Maurice, 74, 78, 79
Suckling family, 74
Sudan, 177, 183–185
"Sugar Coast", 125
Sully, Duc de, 58
Supreme Soviet, 265
Surrey, Great Britain, 75
Suvla Bay, 203
Sweden, 84–85, 89

Sweeting, Reverend, 158
Syria, 11, 203, 204, 207, 210, 212

T
Taft, William Howard, 145
Taganrog, Russia, 110, 112, 113
Taguanes, Battle of, 101
Tanacharison, 62
Tardiu, Colonel, 235
Tartossa (Barcelona), 15
Taylor, Zachary, 132
Tennesee, 123
Tennesee River, 141
Tet Offensive, 217
That Hamilton Woman, 83
theory of relativity, 194, 196
Thom, Leonard, 257, 259, 260–261
Thrace, 210, 212
Till, Emmett, 244
Titorenko, Raisa Maximovna, 265
Tobruk, 207, 208
Todd, Mary, 123, 128
the "Tokyo Express", 248, 253
Tonkin, Vietnam, 216
Toulon, France, 80, 81, 84, 86, *90*, 91,
   92–95, *95. See also* Toulon, Siege of
Toulon, Siege of, 86–97, *88*, *95*
Tours Congress, 217, 221–222, *222–223*
the Tower Green, 44
the Tower of London, 36, 39, 40
Trafalgar, Battle of, 75, 85, 89
Trafalgar Square, 74
Transvaal, 164, 166, 167, 171, 172–173,
   185–186
Transvaal British India Association, 167
Treaty of Lausanne, 203, 212
Treaty of Paris, 63, 145
Treaty of Sevrès, 203, 210, 212
Treaty of Tilsit, 89
Treaty of Troyes, 27
Treaty of Versailles, 214, *215*
Trenton, New Jersey, 63
tribunes, 102
Trieste, Italy, 75
Trotsky, Leon, 222, 269
Tudor, Edward. *See* Edward VI, King
Tudor, Elizabeth. *See* Elizabeth I, Queen
Tukhachevesky, Mikhayl, 236
Tunis, 10
Turkey, 82, 177, 200–213
Turkish National Movement, 212
Turko-Grecian War, 203
Turks, 200–213
Twain, Mark, *Huckleberry Finn*, 125
Tyrwhit, Sir Robert, 36, 42, 43, 44–45

U
uitlanders, 185–186
Ulm, Germany, 89, 193, 194
unified field theory, 193

the Union, 123, 140–141
the Union Jack, 65, 71, 74
the United Nations, 216, 224
the United States, 60–71, 130–141,
   220–221. *See also specific branches of
   government; specific states and regions*
   Indochina and, 217, 224–225
   in the Spanish-American War, 153
   in the Vietnam War, 217
   in World War I, 236
   in World War II, 177, 217, 224–225,
      248–261
"untouchables", 167
Uruguay, 113
U.S. Civil War, 122, 123, 133, 140–141
U.S. Congress. *See* U.S. Senate
U.S. House of Representatives, 123, 251, 261
U.S. Naval Reserve, 248–261
U.S. Senate, 123, 251, 261
USSR. *See* Russia
U.S. Supreme Court, 246
Uztariz, Marquis de, 107

V
Valley Forge, Pennsylvania, 63
van Braam, Jacob, 68–69, 70
the Vatican, 119
V-E Day, 251
Velletri, Italy, 113
Venezuela, 98–109
Venice, Italy, 113
Venice, Siege of, 113
Verdun, Battle of, 229, 231–232, *232–233*
Verdun, France. *See* Verdun, Battle of
Versailles Palace, 214, *215*, 216, 217, 221
Vicksburg, Mississippi, 123, 133
Victoria Women's Suffrage Society, 160–161
Victor-Perrin, Claude, 94
the *Victory*, 72
Vienna, Austria, 75
the Viet Cong, 217
the Viet Minh, 217, 224, 225
Vietnam, 214–225
Vietnam New Year (Tet) Offensive, 217
Vietnam War, 217
Vila, 253
Villars, Fanny Dervieu de, 109
Villeneuve, Pierre-Charles de, 85
Villiers, Louis Coulon de, 69
Virginia, 60, 62, 63, 123, 141
Virginia militia, 63, 66–69
V-J Day, 251
Voltaire, 107
von Falkenhayn, Erich, 231, 232
Vo Nguyen Giap, 224, *224*
voting rights, 157, 159, 160–163, 168–169

W
Wallen, Henry, 134, 135
Wallingford, Connecticut, 251

Walpole, Horace, 66
Walpole, Sir Robert, 74
War College, 203, 205
War Democrats, 123
Warfield, Thomas, 257
War of Spanish Succession, 180
Washington, Augustine, 63
Washington, DC, 123, 241, *242*, 247
Washington, George, 60–71, *61*, *67*, 92
Washington, Lawrence, 60, 63
Washington, Martha. *See* Custis, Martha
   Dandridge
Washington, Mary Ball, 63
Waterford, Pennsylvania. *See* Fort LeBoeuf,
   Pennsylvania
Waterloo, Battle of, 89
Weber, Heinrich, 195
Wellington, Duke of, 89
Western Australia, 156, 157, 158, 159, 160,
   162, 163
Western Australian Parliament, 157, 162
West Indies, 74, 75, 78, 79
Westmoreland County, Virginia, 63
Westphalia, Germany, 89
West Point, 132, 133
Whig Party, 123
White, William L., *They Were Expendable*, 252
White Haven, 132, 136, 137, 139
whites, 104. *See also* segregation
Wilhelm II, Kaiser, 231
Williamsburg, Virginia, 64
Wills Creek, Maryland, 65, 67
Wilson, Woodrow, 145, 214, *215*, 216, 217,
   221
Wittenoom, Mary Eliza Dircksey, 156
Women's Political Council, 246
women's rights, 157, 159, 160–163
Women's Service Guild, 157
the *Worcester*, 75, 79
World War I, 177, 203, 208–212, 214, 226,
   228, 229, 230–237, 269
World War II, 177, 189, 217, 229, 237,
   248–261

Y
Yates, Richard, 141
Yeltsin, Boris, 265
Yorktown, Virginia, 63
Young Italy, 114–115, 117
Young Turk movement, 203, 204, 205, *206*,
   206–207, 208

Z
Zuma, Battle of, 11